NUTRITION SUPPORT in HOME HEALTH

Edited by

Mindy Hermann-Zaidins, M.B.A., R.D.

Memorial Sloan-Kettering Cancer Research Center
New York, New York
The Hermann Group
Mt. Kisco, New York

Riva Touger-Decker, M.A., R.D.

Bronx Veterans Administration Medical Center
Bronx, New York
New York University
New York, New York

AN ASPEN PUBLICATION®
Aspen Publishers, Inc.
Rockville, Maryland
1989

Library of Congress Cataloging-in-Publication Data

Nutrition support in home health.

"An Aspen publication."
Includes bibliographies and index.
1. Diet therapy--Handbooks, manuals, etc.
2. Home care services--Handbooks, manuals, etc.
3. Diet in disease--Handbooks, manuals, etc.
I. Hermann-Zaidins, Mindy. II. Touger-Decker, Riva.
[DNLM: 1. Diet Therapy. 2. Home Care Services.
3. Nutrition. WB 400 N97653]
RM217.N77   1989   615.8′54   89-6701
ISBN: 0-8342-0059-7

Aspen Publishers, Inc., is not affiliated with the
American Society of Parenteral and Enteral Nutrition.

The authors have made every effort to ensure the accuracy of the information herein,
particularly with regard to drug selection and dose. However, appropriate information
sources should be consulted, especially for new or unfamiliar procedures. It is the
responsibility of every practitioner to evaluate the appropriateness of a particular
opinion in the context of actual clinical situations and with due consideration to new
developments. Authors, editors, and the publisher cannot be held responsible for any
typographical or other errors found in this book.

Editorial Services: Susan Bedford

Library of Congress Catalog Card Number: 89-6701
ISBN: 0-8342-0059-7

Printed in the United States of America

1 2 3 4 5

Table of Contents

Contributors

Kathleen S. Babich, M.A., R.D.
President, Nutrition Innovations
Edison, New Jersey

Abby S. Bloch, M.S., R.D.
Director, Clinical Nutrition Support Kitchen
Memorial Sloan Kettering Cancer Center
New York, New York

Karen Mueller Buzby, R.D., C.N.S.D.
Nutrition Consultant
Bala Cynwyd, Pennsylvania

Susan W. Cooning, R.N., M.S.
College of Nursing
University of Arizona
Tucson, Arizona

Jo Ann Davey-McCrae, M.S., R.D., C.N.S.D.
Nutrition Consultant
Philadelphia, Pennsylvania

Judith A. Gilbride, Ph.D., R.D.
Associate Professor
Department of Home Economics and Nutrition
New York University
New York, New York

Mindy Hermann-Zaidins, M.B.A., R.D.
Clinical Diet/Nutrition Specialist
Memorial Sloan Kettering Cancer Center
New York, New York
President, The Hermann Group
Nutrition and Health Care Consultants
Mt. Kisco, New York

Dorothy King, Ph.D., R.D.
Clinical Nutritionist
New York, New York

Maureen E. Laflam, R.D.
Gastroenterology Dietitian Specialist
New England Deaconess Hospital
Boston, Massachusetts

Carol E. Lang, M.S., R.D.
Director, Department of Dietetics
New England Deaconess Hospital
Boston, Massachusetts

Karen Londa, A.C.S.W., C.S.W.
Department of Social Work
Memorial Sloan Kettering Cancer Center
New York, New York

Lucinda K. Lysen, R.N., R.D., B.S.N.
Consultant in Nutritional Support
Stuart, Florida

Karen Masino, R.D.
Clinical Dietitian
Ingalls Memorial Hospital
Harvey, Illinois

Jennifer Nelson, M.S., R.D.
Coordinator, Clinical Dietetics
Mayo Clinic
Rochester, Minnesota

Julie O'Sullivan-Maillet, M.A., R.D.
Dietetic Internship Director
University of Medicine and Dentistry of New Jersey
Newark, New Jersey

Alan Parver, Esq.
Attorney at Law
Powell, Goldstein, Frazer, and Murphy
Washington, D.C.

Patricia Queen, M.M.Sc., R.D.
Assistant Director of Clinical Nutrition
Children's Hospital
Boston, Massachusetts

Maurice E. Shils, M.D., Sc.D.
Consultant in Clinical Nutrition
Memorial Sloan Kettering Cancer Center
Professor Emeritus of Medicine
Cornell University Medical College
New York, New York

Margaret D. Simko, Ph.D., R.D.
Professor Emeritus
New York University
New York, New York

Annalynn Skipper, M.S., R.D., C.N.S.D.
Nutritional Support Coordinator
Department of Food and Nutrition Services
Pennsylvania Hospital
Philadelphia, Pennsylvania

Riva Touger-Decker, M.A., R.D.
Director, Dietetic Internship
Bronx Veterans Administration Medical Center
Bronx, New York
Adjunct Instructor
New York University
New York, New York

Thomas VonderBrink
National Sales Manager
Sandoz Nutrition Clinical Slimming Division
Minneapolis, Minnesota

Ann Winborn, M.A., M.S., R.D.
Nutrition Support Dietitian Specialist
Saint Joseph Hospital
Chicago, Illinois

Karen Yowell-Warman, M.S., R.D.
Clinical Dietitian
Children's Hospital
Boston, Massachusetts

Preface

The registered dietitian plays the most unique role in the home care system. Within the hospital and in formal outpatient settings, such as nursing homes, the dietitian assesses nutritional status and plans, delivers, and monitors feedings accordingly. Nutrition support protocols are coordinated with physicians, nurses, pharmacists, and other members of the health care team, enabling the dietitian to provide necessary and optimal services. After the patient is discharged, the dietitian's responsibilities may be shared with nurses, home health aides, physicians, and pharmacists, all of whom are able to provide and be reimbursed for home feeding services. For these reasons, the dietitian is and must remain closely involved with home care.

This book is an important addition to the library of any dietitian or other health care provider who is marginally or integrally involved with the planning of home nutrition support programs. The chapters are organized to provide detailed information on the clinical management of home oral, enteral, and parenteral nutrition and include such topics as patient identification and selection, setting up monitoring systems for patients, management of complications, education, and psychosocial issues. The majority of the book refers to nutrition care of the adult; however, an extensive chapter on pediatric home nutrition support is included. Administrative and managerial chapters focus on regulatory and reimbursement issues surrounding home nutrition support, setting up supply and management structures, determination of cost benefit and cost effectiveness of services, setting up the actual "team," and determining standards of practice for home nutrition support. Ethics of withholding and withdrawing feeding are reviewed to apprise the reader of cases, issues for consideration, and terminology. Appendix A gives sample forms and additional resource documents for the dietitian in home nutrition support.

The purpose of this book is to provide a comprehensive guide to home nutrition support that defines the complex and essential role of the dietitian in addition to emphasizing the importance of synchronizing all home care services for the optimal nourishment of the patient. The goals are threefold:

1. to introduce the reader to concept and practice of home nutrition support and factors affecting it;
2. to serve as a user-friendly resource manual that provides methods, materials, and tools for patient management to the dietitian practicing home nutrition support; and
3. to apprise health care providers of the broad range of technological, medical, nutritional, ethical, psychosocial, and economic components of nutrition care at home.

The authors have prepared this book with the hope of assisting professionals in nutrition to provide appropriate, safe, and effective nutrition support to the patient at home.

Methods of home nutrition management and strategies for care stated in this book reflect those of the individual authors and the current state of the art. Practices differ from facility to facility. The reader is encouraged to tailor methods selected to the capabilities of the facility or agency and the needs of the patient population.

Acknowledgment

The editors and publisher wish to extend their thanks to Sherwood Medical for supplying the enteral formulas chart that is enclosed with *Nutrition Support in Home Health*.

Introduction—The Evolution of Home Nutrition Support and the Role of the Dietitian

Maurice E. Shils

The phrase "home nutrition support" is here discussed in the context of specialized formulas for medical purposes fed either by enteral (tube) or by intravenous routes. The more usual type of nutrition support in the form of oral feeding has, of course, been prescribed since shaman or witch doctors and their physician successors recommended their versions of special diets. Gastrostomy feedings—until recently through surgically prepared stomas—were undoubtedly used decades ago on some occasions at home in the form of blenderized or liquid formulas for the support of patients who either refused or were unable, because of paralysis of the swallowing mechanism, coma, or mental disorders, to ingest sufficient food orally.

Among the earliest special formulas for home use, one would have to list Nutramigen, introduced in 1942, and the phenylketonuric (PKU) diet Lofenalac, both pioneered by Mead Johnson. These were not usually given as tube formulas, although undoubtedly they were fed by tube when there was resistance to voluntary intake.

With the increasing recognition of the negative impact on nutritional status of various gastrointestinal diseases and/or bowel resection, which induced malabsorption in long-term patients, the need arose for a home nutrition program on the part of physicians interested and knowledgeable in nutrition. The initial approach involved working with research dietitians to purchase discrete nutrients, such as hydrolyzed casein, required for a complete formula and teaching the patient or family member to mix the formula and administer it, usually through a prepared gastrostomy. In the 1950s and 1960s, with the availability of small bore silastic tubing, some physicians adapted such tubing into nasogastric tubes. This in turn led to commercially available weighted, soft, narrow bore silastic tubes. Next came commercial interest in and development of stable and nutritionally complete formulas as a result of the recognition that genetic or disease-induced malabsorption and lactose intolerance were fairly common. The availability of such formulas, of well-tolerated feeding tubes, and of practical infusion pumps beginning in the 1960s led to a revolution in home feeding by tube.

Special formulas were produced, e.g., with their amino acid sources in the forms of intact and relatively purified proteins, hydrolyzed protein, or crystalline free amino acids; fats in the form of long chain, long chain-medium chain mixtures and combinations including so-called structured fat; and carbohydrates in poly-, oligo-, di-, and monosaccharide forms. Vitamins in stable liquid form have been available since the 1950s. Recent information on the human requirements for selenium, chromium, and ultra-trace elements has led to their inclusion in many formulations together with the better known trace elements.

Despite these advances, there remains a relative lack of information about the usefulness of a number of these formulations in various disease states and associated nutritional and metabolic problems; these have been reviewed periodically.[1-3]

The term "defined formula diet" as a general descriptor of purified formulas with a reasonably definite chemical composition was initially suggested in 1975 and has now been widely adopted.[4] Subdivision of formulas based on their amino acid and carbohydrate sources (for example, polymeric and monomeric formulations) has tended to replace designations such as "elemental," "chemical," and "purified." Enteral feeding for patients with normal digestion and absorption who cannot or will not eat and for patients with varying degrees and types of malabsorption has proven to be very effective and, in a number of instances, lifesaving. What is needed in the future is (a) more information on the optimum diet for specific types of illness in preventive and therapeutic approaches to allow a more informed decision on the use of the best and the least expensive formulas, (b) a progressive reduction in the cost of such formulas and equipment to the patient, and (c) a more professional and understanding attitude of HCFA and insurance carriers in meeting the costs of enteral nutrition support as prescribed by physicians.

With the discharge of the first patient on home total parenteral nutrition in December, 1969, there began a progressive and rapidly expanding activity in this field which was documented in the Registry of home TPN patients at the New York Academy of Medicine.[5] Advances in this field have been characterized by (a) commercial availability of improved amino acid sources, well-tolerated intravenous lipid emulsions, more adequate multivitamin preparations, and more trace elements; (b) improved catheters for central venous access and their subcutaneous placement decreasing the chance of infection; (c) gradual improvement in the knowledge and experience of physicians, who had not been previously trained in clinical nutrition; (d) development of home care companies expert in preparation, provision, and supervision of patients on home parenteral nutrition; and (e) availability of a wide spectrum of antibiotics to combat infection, together with an understanding of the need to initiate adequate antibiotic therapy early in infection.

There are still some unresolved problems occurring in some patients on very long term parenteral feeding (e.g., development of osteopenia for unknown reasons[6] or development of cirrhosis of the liver in those with massive small bowel resection[7]). Nevertheless, it is quite clear that patients may be supported entirely or almost entirely by this technique for very long periods. Some individuals have now passed their 17th year on home total parenteral nutrition (HTPN). It is likely that with proper management, based on our current knowledge, a normal life span is possible in a large number of these patients free of systemic illness. Women have been carried through pregnancy, giving birth to normal healthy children, and young children have been raised on TPN.[8] This is a great tribute to the activities of those in basic and applied research and in clinical care who have brought their knowledge, technology, and experience to this stage.

Future research in this area undoubtedly will relate to (a) the factors causing the osteopenia and cirrhosis mentioned above, (b) the development of formulations of amino acids to meet the needs of specific illnesses (both preventive and therapeutic), (c) better knowledge of quantitative vitamin and trace element needs, (d) the availability of more appropriate vitamin preparations and their use in the premature underweight infant, (e) more data on the possible requirements of ultra trace elements, and (f) the usefulness and safety of new calorie sources, particularly those with modified lipids and carbohydrates.

The role of the dietitian in the management of patients on home parenteral nutrition is less direct than it is with enteral home feeding. Nevertheless, the dietitian, particularly one who is a member of an active clinical nutrition team, has various roles to play; these include involvement in the assessment of patients during the transition period when they are being weaned from parenteral feeding to enteral or oral feedings, and educating physicians, house staff, and nurses in issues related to the nutrition needs of enterally-fed patients prior to and following discharge. In my opinion, a very valuable contribution toward improving the nutrition education of medical students and physicians at all levels is the appointment of highly trained research-oriented dietitians to faculty positions in medical schools and affiliated teaching hospitals. Together with physicians who are knowledgeable in nutrition, such faculty dietitians can have a major impact in education and research.

NOTES

1. Maurice E. Shils, ed., *Defined Formula Diets for Medical Purposes. (Proceedings of the 1975 Symposium)* Chicago: American Medical Association, 1977.

2. Henry T. Randall, "Tube Feeding in Acute and Chronic Illness," *Journal of Parenteral and Enteral Nutrition* 8 (March-April 1984): 113–36.

3. John L. Rombeau and Michael D. Caldwell, eds., *Enteral and Tube Feeding.* (Philadelphia: W.B. Saunders Company, 1984).

4. Maurice E. Shils, "Introduction to the Proceedings," in *Defined Formula Diets for Medical Purposes. (Proceedings of the 1975 Symposium)*, ed. Maurice E. Shils (Chicago: American Medical Association, 1977).

5. Lyn Howard and A.V. Michalek, "Home Parenteral Nutrition (HPN)," *Annual Review of Nutrition* 4 (1984): 69–99.

6. Moshe Shike, Maurice E. Shils, Arthur Heller, Nancy Alcock, Vincent Vigorita, Roberta Brockman, Michael F. Holick, Joseph Lane, and Carlos Flombaum, "Bone Disease in Prolonged Parenteral Nutrition: Osteopenia without Mineralization Defect," *American Journal of Clinical Nutrition* 44 (July 1986): 89–98.

7. Ronald T. Stanko, Girija Nathan, Harvey Mendelow, and Siamak A. Adibi, "Development of Hepatic Cholestases and Fibrosis in Patients with Massive Loss of Intestine Supported by Prolonged Parenteral Nutrition," *Gastroenterology* 92 (1987): 197–202.

8. Harry L. Greene, K. Michael Hambridge, Richard Schanler, and Reginald C. Tsang, "Guidelines for the Use of Vitamins, Trace Elements, Calcium, Magnesium, and Phosphorus in Infants and Children Receiving Total Parenteral Nutrition: Report of the Subcommittee on Pediatric Parenteral Nutrient Requirements from the Committee on Clinical Practice Issues of The American Society for Clinical Nutrition," *American Journal of Clinical Nutrition* 48 (November 1988): 1324–42.

Chapter 1

Introduction to Home Nutrition Support

Mindy Hermann-Zaidins and Riva Touger-Decker

The practice of feeding patients outside the hospital setting has existed for many years. Convalescent homes were established as an interim measure to bridge the gap between acute treatment of a patient's disease and his or her return to normal daily living. The development over the past two decades of sophisticated nutrient infusion methodologies, namely, enteral and parenteral nutrition, has expanded permanently the scope of home care into arenas of both short- and long-term outpatient feeding.

In 1983 approximately 2,700 patients were receiving home parenteral nutrition support; expectations for 1987 were 5,700.[1] Home nutrition support has grown from a trend to a standard of practice. Multiple factors have contributed to the growth of both the home care industry and home nutrition support. They are depicted in Exhibits 1-1 and 1-2, respectively.

Consumer demands are a major force driving the home care industry. As medical needs become more diverse and people live longer, health care extends beyond the hospital or the physician's office. The proportion of elderly persons in the United States has increased. Consequently, so will their use of acute and chronic care services. Medicare expenditures show a projected 137% increase from $1.2 billion in 1982 to $2.8 billion in 1988.[1] As a result, the number of home care companies has doubled since 1980.[1] Hospital-owned durable medical equipment suppliers and home care agencies also have developed.

The prospective payment system has increased the incentive for hospitals to discharge patients early. The advent of diagnosis-related groups and other cost-containment measures likewise has magnified the popularity of home feeding. Diagnosis-related groups are resulting in shorter hospitalizations and prolonged home recovery time.

Hospitals have tapped the home care market so they can offer an umbrella of patient services, from inpatient care to ambulatory care to home. By diversifying care options, hospitals appear more attractive to the community. Their appeal in this sense may be based on cost, as well as on

1

Exhibit 1-1 Factors Causing Changes in the Home Care Industry

Increased utilization of services
Increased competition among providers
Increased government regulations
Incentives for hospital-home care company arrangements
Health planning, marketing, and financial incentives for hospitals

convenience and familiarity. Hospital corporations may offer member prices that include discounted services for package deals (e.g., hospital, preventive, therapeutic, and home care). Familiarity with not only the setting but a team of caregivers may be a priority for some.

The growth of home nutrition support is tied to a number of technological, physiologic, and psychologic factors. Advances in medical technology have led to longer life spans. Equipment for enteral and parenteral nutrition has become more readily available and consumer-friendly with lightweight, easy-to-operate pumps. Outpatient nutrition care has been shown to decrease patient admissions, length of stay, and cost of long-term care, attractive outcomes to the cost-conscious hospital.

The patient is the ultimate recipient of benefits derived from enhanced home care. A well-synchronized system can reduce acute care costs and, optimally, morbidity and mortality. Quality of life improves from increased independence and an improved feeling of well-being. Advances in home nutrition support allow patients to live out the old adage, "home is where the heart is," and recuperate in the warmth and comfort of home. The terminally ill patient may desire to spend the final days with his or her loved ones.

The home care industry has grown and diversified even more rapidly than hospital-based programs. Many traditional inpatient procedures, such as antibiotic infusions, respiratory support, and minor surgeries, have moved into the home or the out-of-hospital arena. Nursing homes, hos-

Exhibit 1-2 Factors Influencing the Growth of Home Nutrition Support

Advances in medical technology
Psychosocial elements
Consumer desire for care at home
Improvements in quality and quantity of equipment and services
Diagnosis-related groups
Extended life span

pices, geriatric day hospitals, and senior centers provide interim or long-term care for patients requiring management not feasible in the home. Furthermore, the emergence of joint ventures and fee-for-service arrangements between hospitals and for-profit home care providers strengthens working relationships among the numerous participants along the patient care continuum.

NOTE

1. P.I. Halter, "Trends in Home Nutrition Support." *Biomedical Business International* 9 (1986): 37.

Chapter 2

Reimbursement and Regulatory Processes

Alan Parver, Thomas VonderBrink, and
Jennifer Nelson

OVERVIEW OF ISSUES*

Because of the nature of today's health care market, it is imperative for health care professionals to understand precisely whether and to what extent a clinical procedure is covered and reimbursed under third-party payment programs, both public and private. Recognition of the procedure by such programs, coupled with fair and reasonable reimbursement, is essential for providers to be able to initiate and sustain the provision of such procedures.

This chapter summarizes the Medicare principles of coverage and reimbursement for parenteral and enteral nutrition therapy and provides a brief history of the events leading to federal legislation mandating the use of a particular reimbursement approach for home parenteral and enteral nutrition. In addition, Medicaid and private third-party payers' approaches to this therapy are discussed.

The emphasis on Medicare reflects the commonly held belief that the Medicare program is the single most important payer of health services and equipment. State Medicaid programs and private payers often are guided by (or at least consider) Medicare coverage and reimbursement criteria for a particular item of equipment or procedure. Medicare remains the single largest purchaser of health services and equipment on behalf of its beneficiaries. In 1988 the Medicare program spent more than $87 billion for health and related services. No other payer's expenditures come close to that figure.

Besides Medicare, the state Medicaid programs collectively comprise a significant portion of the nation's total spending for health care services and equipment. In 1988 just the federal share of Medicaid expenditures

---

*This section was written by Alan Parver, Esq., and Thomas VonderBrink.

amounted to more than $30 billion; the states' contribution will near that amount. Unlike Medicare, however, the Medicaid program is actually an amalgam of 53 Medicaid programs that must comply with general federal guidelines. As such, Medicaid does not lend easily to broad generalizations about policies, because the programs differ in approach on many of the coverage and reimbursement issues that are relevant to this discussion. Likewise, private insurers differ significantly in their handling of parenteral and enteral nutrition therapy claims—differences occur even (or especially) among local Blue Cross plans.

Medicare

Congress enacted Title XVIII of the Social Security Act in 1965, commonly known as the Medicare program. This legislation established a health insurance system for eligible elderly and disabled persons under which hospitals, physicians, and other providers would be reimbursed directly through the health insurance programs for covered services provided to Medicare beneficiaries.[1]

There are significant distinctions between Medicare coverage and reimbursement policies for inpatient hospital care and those for alternative care settings (i.e., nursing homes, patient homes, clinics, and the like). The development and implementation of the prospective payment system for inpatient hospital care has not been duplicated for nonhospital services, supplies, and equipment (other than the capitated payments for the still limited number of Medicare-certified health maintenance organizations [HMOs]). Reimbursement for these services and equipment is governed either by cost or by charge-based criteria, depending on the particular service or item.

The Medicare program is an exclusively federal program that is divided into two parts. Part A concerns the coverage and payment for inpatient hospital care, skilled nursing care, home health care, hospice care, and care provided through an HMO. Part B provides coverage for the provision of "medical and other services," which are primarily physician services but also include provision of durable medical equipment, prosthetic devices, clinic services, and therapy and rehabilitation services. Part A is the larger of the two, but Part B represents a steadily growing component of the health care system due in large part to the recent incentives to move patients out of the nation's hospitals "quicker and sicker" into alternative care settings (where much of the care is covered under Part B).

Medicare is administered at the federal level by the Health Care Financing Administration (HCFA) of the Department of Health and Human Services. HCFA contracts with private entities—usually insurance carriers—to implement the Medicare coverage and payment policies on a claim-by-claim basis. The entities responsible for Part A claims are termed *intermediaries*; those for Part B claims are referred to as *carriers*. It was decided initially to use such entities because such private sector organizations are experienced both in administrating complex systems of health benefits and in processing numerous claims for such services and supplies.

Medicare Part A Coverage of Hospital Care

Beginning with the cost-reporting periods commencing on or after October 1, 1983, Medicare payments for inpatient hospital services changed from a cost-based, retrospective reimbursement system to a prospective payment system (PPS), wherein payment is made at a predetermined, specific rate for each patient discharge. Every discharge is classified according to a particular diagnosis-related group (DRG).

Under the PPS, a hospital is paid a specific amount for each patient on the basis of primary diagnosis. Generally, a hospital is paid that particular amount regardless of the number or types of services provided. Clearly, the purpose of a PPS is to reward hospitals for reducing costs of treatment during the course of hospital stays. A PPS encourages the hospitals and the treating physicians to consider the benefits of additional services against their added costs. Hospitals that incur costs that exceed the particular reimbursement for a patient's diagnosis normally will have to absorb the loss. Payment under the PPS is considered to be payment in full; the hospital may not look to the patient to make up the difference.

The impact of the PPS on the provision of nutrition support is multifaceted. There are no specific DRGs assigned to nutrition support. Reimbursement for parenteral and enteral nutrition is incorporated in the fixed payment associated with those DRGs for which nutrition support is a necessary part of patient care.

Regardless of whether a hospital chooses to maintain nutrition support teams or to provide nutrition support to its patients, the basic, unequivocable incentives of the PPS' fixed rates serve to motivate hospitals to discharge nutrition support patients as soon as such discharges are clinically appropriate. The reimbursement benefits of discharging a patient and thus limiting hospital costs for the patient remain clear and compelling. An obvious result is that Medicare nutrition support patients are receiving nutrition therapy at home or in a nursing home for longer lengths of time. Because the implementation of the PPS coincided roughly with the initiation of Part B coverage of the provision of home nutrition support, there was a convergence of events that contributed to the rapid expansion of Medicare expenditures for home nutrition support.

Medicare Part B Coverage of Home Nutrition Support

Parenteral and enteral nutrition were provided in hospitals long before their value in alternative care settings was recognized in the Medicare program. Only recently have technological advances permitted these therapies to be provided safely in the home. Once the technological basis for home parenteral and enteral nutrition was established, an important justification for the proliferation of home nutrition support has been its cost effectiveness, in comparison with the costs of providing that support in the hospital. This is not to say, however, that the Medicare program has welcomed and encouraged the expansion of home nutrition support since it was first acknowledged by the program in 1981 in an amendment to the *Medicare Carriers Manual.* The growth in the provision (and in the cost) of home nutrition support has been of concern to HCFA officials, who have subjected the therapies to a virtually unprecedented level of scrutiny during the past five years.

Home parenteral and enteral nutrition (i.e., equipment, supplies, and nutrients) are covered under Medicare Part B under the prosthetic device benefit.[2] The selection of this particular vehicle for coverage was an artful choice by HCFA. The other available benefits in which parenteral and enteral nutrition could have been pigeonholed—that is, the home health benefit and the durable medical equipment benefit—would have provided significantly less coverage than that provided under the prosthetic device benefit. HCFA identified the feeding or intravenous (IV) tube as the prosthetic device that is replacing all or part of a body organ or function. HCFA then decided if the Medicare program was going to pay for the tube, the benefit would be worthwhile only if the program also paid for the nutrients and solutions that flowed through it. Services associated with the provision of parenteral and enteral nutrition are not covered. Only home care suppliers, nursing homes, and home health agencies can bill for the provision of parenteral and enteral nutrition supplies and equipment under Medicare Part B.

The Medicare program does not provide a precise definition of either parenteral or enteral nutrition. Rather, the therapies are described as follows:

> Daily parenteral nutrition is considered reasonable and necessary for a patient with severe pathology of the alimentary tract which does not allow absorption of sufficient nutrients to maintain weight and strength commensurate with patient's general condition. Since the alimentary tract of such a patient does not function adequately, an in-dwelling catheter is placed percutaneously in the subclavian vein and then advanced into the superior vena cava

where intravenous infusion of nutrients is given for part of the day. The catheter is then plugged by the patient until the next infusion. Following a period of hospitalization, which is required to initiate parenteral nutrition and to train the patient in catheter care, solution preparation, and infusion technique, the parenteral nutrition can be provided safely and effectively in the patient's home by non-professional persons who have undergone special training.[3]

Enteral nutrition is described as

reasonable and necessary for a patient with a functional gastrointestinal tract, who, due to pathology to or non-function of the structures that normally permit food to reach the digestive tract, cannot maintain weight and strength commensurate with his or her general condition. Enteral therapy may be given by nasogastric, jejunostomy, or gastronomy tubes, and can be provided safely and effectively in the home by non-professional persons who have undergone special training.[4]

Medicare will cover and pay for the provision of home parenteral and enteral nutrition supplies and equipment if the attending physician documents adequately the medical necessity for the therapy. In addition to a "physician's written order or prescription," there must be "sufficient medical documentation to permit an independent conclusion that the requirements of the prosthetic device benefit are met and parenteral or enteral nutrition is medically necessary."[5]

The necessary documentation includes the following:

- certification of medical necessity (this must be completed at the time the patient begins home nutrition therapy)
- recertification (The first recertification must be completed no more than 90 days after the initial certification; subsequent recertifications may be performed at intervals of 180 days for up to two years)
- a prescription provided on an annual basis (Any changes in the prescription must be documented)

Parenteral and enteral nutrition therapy will be reimbursed under the prosthetic device benefit if, in addition to the general medical necessity criteria being met, the patient has a "permanently inoperative internal body organ or function thereof."[6] The test of permanence will be met if the medical record (which includes the judgment of the attending physician) indicates that the impairment will be of a "long and indefinite duration."[7]

In practice, this provision is interpreted by HCFA and the carriers as requiring an impairment of at least 90 days. Thus temporary impairments, that is, those with an anticipated duration of less than 90 days, will not be covered, regardless of the otherwise indisputable need for the therapy.

In 1983 and 1984, HCFA studied the coverage and payment practices for parenteral and enteral nutrition of the 43 carriers implementing the program. Concluding that such practices were inconsistent and confusing, HCFA decided to designate two carriers to process all home parenteral and enteral nutrition claims as of December 1, 1984. Since that date, all claims have been handled by Blue Cross and Blue Shield of South Carolina for claims east of the Mississippi River and by Transamerica Occidental of Los Angeles, California for claims west of the river.

Medicare Part B Payment of Home Parenteral and
Enteral Nutrition

Medicare Part B generally pays physicians and suppliers for furnishing covered items and services on the basis of reasonable charges, unless otherwise provided by statute. Carriers administering the Part B program must consider the following charge factors and apply whichever is lowest to determine the reasonable charge:

1. the actual charge
2. the customary charge for similar services generally made by the physician or supplier furnishing the service
3. the prevailing charge in the locality for similar services (calculated to be at the 75th percentile of the array of customary charges within the locality)
4. the carrier's usual amount of reimbursement for comparable services to its own policyholders under comparable circumstances
5. in the case of medical services, supplies, and equipment that do not generally vary in quality from one supplier to another, the charges may not exceed the lowest charge levels at which these services, supplies, and equipment are available in a locality
6. for nonphysician services, supplies, and equipment, an inflation-indexed charge limit (i.e., increases in charges may not exceed the Consumer Price Index Urban Index inflation rate)
7. the charge limit for outpatient services
8. other factors that may be appropriate in judging whether the charge is inherently reasonable

These are the general criteria. HCFA or the particular carrier (or both), however, determine which and to what extent these criteria are applicable to each covered procedure or item. For the first several years of coverage by Medicare, items and equipment for parenteral and enteral nutrition were reimbursed on the basis of the lower of the actual, customary, and prevailing charges. HCFA determined after its 1983 study, however, that numerous carriers were simply paying the actual submitted charges for therapy, without making the necessary customary charge and prevailing charge calculations. HCFA also noted that there was little or no consistency in the payment levels for similar products or equipment items. For example, the price of a can of an enteral nutrient was shown to vary as much as 400% among various regions of the country.

As a result of these disturbing findings, HCFA decided to develop national prevailing charges for parenteral and enteral nutrition, with the assistance of the two specialty carriers. To achieve such a result, HCFA deemed the entire country to be one locality for the purpose of calculating the prevailing levels, a decision which was welcomed by many of the regional and national suppliers.

HCFA determined that the charges for parenteral and enteral nutrition supplies and equipment were uniformly excessive, rather than basing their decision on the prevailing allowances on charges, as would be expected for items covered under Part B. Citing its authority to examine other factors to ensure that payment levels are inherently reasonable, otherwise known as its "inherent reasonableness" authority, HCFA and the specialty carriers considered evaluating retail and wholesale prices and other noncharge data in the determination of the prevailing allowances. Had they used noncharge data, reimbursement levels would have been significantly lower than the payment amounts calculated by the normal workings of the reasonable charge criteria.

This was the first time that HCFA sought to use the inherent reasonableness authority to craft a national reimbursement method; previously, its use had been sporadic, limited to situations involving individual providers and individual localities. The efforts to apply inherent reasonableness to parenteral and enteral nutrition attracted widespread attention from the industry and the trade press, as well as from other Part B-related providers who feared that similar efforts would be directed at their activities.

In 1986 Congress directed HCFA to apply the lowest charge level reimbursement method to parenteral and enteral nutrition. This method was created initially by statute in 1977 and provides that reasonable charges for Medicare services, supplies, and equipment that, in the judgment of the secretary (of HCFA) do not vary significantly in quality from one supplier to another, may not exceed the lowest charge levels at which such services, supplies, and equipment are widely and consistently available. Thus when items are comparable in function and quality, HCFA may choose to pay no more than the lowest charge level at which such items are available. Federal regulations implementing this provision have established the lowest charge levels at the 25th percentile of the charges submitted for the items or services in question.

Previously, the lowest charge level method had been used for only three items: standard hospital beds, wheelchairs, and, for a short time, certain laboratory services. Thus the level of expertise and comfort with the lowest charge level method as applicable to parenteral and enteral nutrition was not high. Further, it was not clear whether and to what extent parenteral and enteral nutrition supplies could be determined to be of like function and quality, or whether such supplies were available nationally.

The conference report issued by Congress is important in the understanding of the current reimbursement structure for parenteral and enteral nutrition and is set forth as follows:

> In establishing the "lowest charge level" for parenteral and enteral supplies, the Secretary would be required to base payments at the 25th percentile as currently set forth in regulations (42 CFR 405.511(c)). The conferees expect that all available charge data submitted by suppliers of such services would be used in calculating the lowest charge levels. The Secretary and carriers would therefore be prohibited from using "inherent reasonableness" in establishing the lowest charge levels. In addition, the conferees are concerned that some items (e.g., supply and administration kits) are billed on a partial monthly basis which may distort the charge data. The conferees expect the Secretary to ensure that the data used in establishing the lowest charge level for these items are accurate. In comparing charges submitted for various items, the conferees expect the Secretary to compare like products which are of comparable quality and nutritional content rather than looking solely at the volume of nutrients or calorie content. In addition, the conferees expect that the Secretary would not group together products of dissimilar quality or function. The conferees are concerned that current categories for reimbursing premixed parenteral solutions may be inappropriate. The conferees therefore expect the Secretary to establish new categories for premixed parenteral solutions based on the amount of proteins prescribed per day. The Secretary would be expected to calculate payment levels at the 25th percentile based on the charge data available for the new categories. To provide sufficient time to collect the data, the effective date for parenteral products would be October 1, 1987.
>
> Between January 1, 1987, and October 1, 1987 the Secretary is to apply existing charge screens to the parenteral nutrients. However, rather than applying many different screens to the var-

ious states, the Secretary should apply uniform screens throughout the nation, or uniform screens throughout each of the two carrier areas.

It is the conferees' understanding that certain parenteral nutrition patients require special parenteral solutions such as renal failure solutions, hepatic failure solutions, or acute metabolic stress formulas. The Secretary would be expected to provide for separate categorization or appropriate exceptions to accommodate these patients and for other special circumstances.

The provision would be effective for parenteral nutrients October 1, 1987, and for all other services and supplies on January 1, 1987.[8]

The important points of the conference report may be summarized briefly. The secretary was required to use all available charge data in calculating the lowest charge levels. The secretary also was explicitly prohibited from using inherent reasonableness in establishing the lowest charge levels. This is in response to the criticisms of the national prevailing charge levels under development by HCFA that substantial percentages of charges were discarded and ignored in the establishment of payment rates.

Further, Congress, in directing the secretary to "ensure that the data used in establishing the lowest charge level for [supply kits and administration kits] are accurate," acknowledged that such items have been handled inaccurately from a reimbursement viewpoint. Supply kits and administration kits often are provided on a partial monthly basis, but payments historically have been calculated on a monthly basis. The carriers responded to this point by providing for claims mechanisms so that partial monthly billings would not be included in the calculation of lowest charge levels for such kits.

As an integral part of the application of the lowest charge level, the secretary was required to compare only like products in terms of quality, content, and function. The conference report reflected the expectation that the existing HCFA common procedure codes (HCPCs) would be used to satisfy this requirement.[9]

Congress also noted that the HCPCs in effect at that time regarding premixed parenteral nutrients did not reflect comparisons of products of like quality. Congress agreed with the assertions of parenteral and enteral nutrition professionals that the amount of amino acids is the single best measure of comparing parenteral solutions. The secretary was directed to establish new categories for premixed parenteral solutions on the basis of the amount of amino acids prescribed per day. Reimbursement for these new categories would be based on the 25th percentile of the charge data gathered from each new category. The need to gather such new data was the reason Congress postponed the effective date of the lowest charge level provision for premixed parenteral nutrients until October 1, 1987. Besides the premixed parenteral nutrients, all other parenteral and enteral nutrition supplies and equipment were subject to the lowest charge level approach as of January 1, 1987.

Current Medicare Reimbursement Issues Affecting Parenteral and Enteral Nutrition

Resolution of the national coverage and reimbursement issues has resulted in the shifting of emphasis of HCFA and carrier concern to technical claims administration issues. Such issues are extremely important to the workings of the parenteral and enteral nutrition benefit. Poor decisions or policies on claims processing will have a direct and immediate impact on the Medicare beneficiaries who require parenteral and enteral nutrition therapy.

Technical claims administration issues center around proper documentation of the medical necessity of parenteral and enteral nutrition therapy for individual patients and the special documentation requirements for enteral pumps, blenderized nutrients, calories in excess of 2,000 per day, and lipids in excess of 12 500 mL bottles per month. This has produced a degree of tension in communications between suppliers and carriers, with carriers insisting on "adequate" documentation in support of claims and suppliers quarreling with what they perceive to be a varying standard of adequacy. In addition, suppliers claim that the best documentation of the medical necessity for a particular application of parenteral and enteral nutrition therapy is in the hospital records, which often are difficult to obtain from the hospitals.

Medicaid

Medicaid is a federal-state program designed to provide medical care for the indigent. It varies significantly from state to state and thus does not embody a single approach to parenteral and enteral nutrition. From the federal perspective, there are no particular criteria or procedures concerning the development of standards relating to the provision of parenteral and enteral nutrition. The states have considerable discretion in judging the cost effectiveness of and the need for medical services. Further, states have substantial freedom to implement safeguards against unnecessary utilization of care and services. For example, numerous states require preauthorization from the state Medicaid program as a condition of coverage of a particular item or service. This often is true with respect to parenteral and enteral nutrition. The preauthorization procedure usually includes

- medical data establishing the nature and severity of the condition,
- recommendation of medical necessity by the treating physician, and
- individual review of each case by a state Medicaid team, which may include a medical consultant, nurses, and analysts.

Generally, for care provided in hospitals and skilled nursing facilities, the coverage of parenteral and enteral nutrition therapy is guided by general medical necessity criteria, and payment for the therapy is folded into the per diem rates. In nonfacility situations, the extent of coverage for the therapy often depends on the pigeonhole in which the state Medicaid program has selected to place parenteral and enteral nutrition; that is, whether the therapy is considered to be durable medical equipment, a prosthetic device, a part of home health care, or within any other designation. Reimbursement may be based on a variety of factors, not necessarily charge data, and from a legal viewpoint is bound only by liberal interpretations of what is reasonable. Such factors may include the cost of an item or service, the cost plus a pre-established markup, or flat rates based on groupings, averages, or percentages of the array of charges or costs. The state can fashion the reimbursement components of its program in any reasonable way to enable it to respond to the needs of its Medicaid population and to its budgetary considerations.

Private Insurers

There is no single standard by which the commercial carriers deal with parenteral and enteral nutrition. It appears, however, that many of the large carriers have similar policies with respect to these therapies. These carriers can be grouped into three categories:

1. carriers that follow closely the Medicare principles of reimbursement;
2. carriers that are aggressively pursuing cost-containment measures, sometimes far beyond the Medicare program's efforts; and
3. carriers that do not treat parenteral and enteral nutrition differently from any basic or core benefit and thus handle parenteral and enteral nutrition claims routinely and with little noticeable attention.

The last category is rapidly diminishing in numbers, because recognition of the cost of parenteral and enteral nutrition therapy is prompting increased levels of scrutiny. A common coverage requirement is that the use of parenteral and enteral nutrition be approved by the carrier before such therapy actually is administered to a patient. Also, preapproval often is necessary for significant deviations from the initial regimen of care. Home parenteral and enteral nutrition can be covered under a home care rider or a major medical policy (or both). Unlike Part B of Medicare, the medically necessary services that normally accompany the provision of home parenteral and enteral nutrition often are covered. Equally often, however, the carriers apply a per diem, lifetime, or other limitation on the payment amount.

ISSUES FOR DIETITIANS—A COMMMENTARY*

The preceding discussion demonstrates the significant impact of regulatory and reimbursement issues on nutrition support. Prospective payment has resulted in a greater degree of cost-conscious medicine. The settings for nutrition support are shifting. Patients who can be treated successfully in less costly settings are increasingly being treated outside the hospital. It is estimated that at any given time there are more than 1 million people receiving parenteral and enteral nutrition. According to a 1986 report 2,000 to 5,000 patients are on home parenteral support, and 15,000 to 20,000 are on home enteral support.[10] The number of persons receiving parenteral and enteral nutrition support in extended care facilities is not known, but 34,000 is an estimated figure.[11]

The effect of regulatory and reimbursement issues on the role of dietitians in nutrition support, as well as the impact on their patients in various settings, is of vital concern to professionals in nutrition. The question of what actions can be taken to ensure continued participation in care of the nutrition support patient by the dietitian has yet to be answered.

Impact of Regulatory and Reimbursement Issues on Dietitians

Hospitals

Inpatient hospital care has fixed reimbursement based on DRGs. Only three DRGs address nutrition specifically, but nutrition care is not a limited phenomenon and may be required for the treatment of any number of diagnoses. Reimbursement for nutrition care in other diagnoses must be incorporated as an overhead cost. This has led to efforts to identify efficiently only those patients in need of nutrition support and to ensure its cost-effective application.[12]

---

*This section was written by Jennifer Nelson.

Nutrition support dietitians are in a particularly strong position to meet these challenges. As the recognized expert in nutrition care, the dietitian can quickly and accurately identify the patient needing nutrition support. Ongoing nutritional monitoring by the dietitian ensures timely transition from the more expensive nutrition support system to an oral diet with further cost savings.

Skilled Nursing Facilities

Nursing homes are now receiving patients who are sicker and require more acute care.[13] From 1968 to 1985 the average length of hospital stay for persons older than 65 years dropped from 13.4 days to 8.8 days. Not surprisingly, nutrition support in the nursing home setting is increasing.[14]

Home Health Agencies

The use of nutrition support for patients who return home is well established.[15,16] This is in part due to third-party assistance with the costs of equipment and supplies and home care industry's willingness to provide services and supplies. A survey of local and national home care agencies revealed that 75 percent of national agencies and 25 percent of local agencies provide enteral or parenteral support.[17]

The dietitian is becoming an integral part of home health care. Although only 50 percent of agencies nationwide have registered dietitians on staff, the remainder contract for dietitian services on a consulting basis. Frequently, the dietitian from the discharge facility is used as the resource.[18] The reluctance to employ dietitians may be due in part to the limitations of Medicare, Medicaid, and other third-party payers for dietitian services. Agencies that use dietitian services typically absorb expenses for these services as administrative costs.[19]

Actions to Consider

Reimbursement for Dietitian Services

Given decreasing lengths of stay and shrinking inpatient numbers, more hospitals are seeking alternative ways to generate revenue. Offering hospital-based nutrition support services for home patients is becoming an attractive alternative. In a recent survey of hospitals, more than 25 percent are offering home health care services and 75 percent of the institutions plan to add or expand such services.[20]

In providing home health care services, hospitals have several choices. They can refer patients to outside vendors, establish joint ventures, or establish independent programs. Such programs are usually established as a unit and provided separately from the other functions of the acute care hospital to avoid conflict of interest. Advantages of the programs are improvement and continuity in patient care and revenue generation. The patient is already known to the home care team, usually composed of members of the hospital nutrition support team. Close follow-up is maintained, and patient management is enhanced. Also, services provided to the patient qualify for reimbursement. Some institutions receive reimbursement from vendors for training the patient before discharge. Others extend collaborative agreements to vendors who offer profit-sharing incentives. Still others establish an independent and comprehensive home nutrition program and rely on current third-party reimbursement levels for products and supplies to cover the costs of clinical expertise needed to maintain the home patient, because clinical management is not reimbursable.

As a member of the health care team, the dietitian is key to continued involvement in the care of the nutrition support patient within the hospital, outpatient clinic, or extended care facility. The dietitian has been identified as the health care professional most involved in monitoring and training of patients (particularly those receiving enteral support).[21] Return appointments for follow-up monitoring can qualify for reimbursement as "incident to," that is, in physician services.[22] This revenue further supports dietitians' involvement in home care.

Education of Health Administrators and Third-Party Payers

The services and unique skills provided by dietitians are recognized as a vitally important and established part of the nutrition support team within the hospital setting. Their role in the care of home patients, however, is only beginning to be recognized. Nutrition support dietitians must take the initiative to promote their role to health administrators and third-party payers. Key to this is the differentiation of the dietitian's role from that of other members of the nutrition support team. Administrators and third-party payers must recognize that provision of nutrition support without the participation of the registered dietitian is not quality care. The Dietitians in Nutrition Support—Dietetic Practice Group (previously Dietitians in Critical Care) Legislative Committee has published a legislative and public policy statement.[23] This statement addresses the need for a registered dietitian in managing home nutrition support patients, as well as provision of reimbursement for these services.[24]

Another important way to assist administrators and third-party payers in recognizing the contribution of the nutrition support dietitian is to establish a fee-for-service system. Placing a fee on nutrition services provides specific cost-per-case services and, more importantly, establishes a value for the dietitian's contribution to patient care. These data also allow dietitians to compete for the limited funds currently reimbursed under prospective payment. Services that do not generate their own revenue may suffer without this mechanism.

Guidelines for implementing a nutrition services payment system have been published by the American Dietetic Association.[25] Topics include establishing a rationale for implementing a payment system, description of services provided, fee-setting guidelines, billing procedures, monitoring systems for reimbursement received, and suggested documentation for services rendered, as well as education of the health care community.[26]

Impact of Regulatory and Reimbursement Issues on Nutrition Support Patients

Nutrition support patients in hospitals, in skilled nursing facilities, at home, or in any other setting are affected by regulatory and reimbursement issues. Costs for nutrition support are high, and many patients need financial assistance to meet them. It has been estimated that more than half the patients in the United States who receive enteral nutrition are older than 65 years.[27] As such, Medicare provides an estimated 40 percent of reimbursement for enteral nutrition.[28] Concerned that the ever-increasing home health care bill is reaching the limits of Medicare's ability to pay for it, legislators have implemented multiple schemes to control coverage. Other third-party payers frequently follow Medicare's lead and implement similar regulations for coverage. A sample of the Medicare payment screens for enteral nutrition can be found in Appendix A (see Exhibit A-8B).

Medicare guidelines for coverage of specialized nutrition support are discussed in other chapters of this book. (The complete guideline handbook is available on written request.[29]) Nutrition support dietitians who are aware of the Medicare model can lend their expertise in establishing enteral care plans and facilitate eligibility for third-party coverage. In Table 2-1 selected Medicare guidelines for enteral nutrition are highlighted, and in the following discussion some strategies dietitians might consider are outlined.

Patients are eligible for Medicare coverage if there is "a nonfunction of the structures that normally permit food to reach the digestive tract."[30] Patients with head and neck cancer or neurological deficits that interfere with ingestion of nutrients are typical of those who meet this criterion. Also, patients with conditions that affect digestion and absorption, metabolism, and excretion or who demand specialized formulations along with controlled infusion require and qualify for enteral nutrition. On the other hand, nonstructural impairments, such as anorexia, periodic nausea and vomiting, or weight loss, do not warrant reimbursement by Medicare unless they are associated with a reimbursable diagnosis.

Table 2-1 Medicare Guidelines for Enteral Nutrition

Requirements	Criteria
Diagnosis	Nonfunction of the structures that normally permit food to reach the digestive tract
Permanence	Condition is not temporary (at least 90 consecutive days' duration)
Total nourishment	Tube feeding is sole source of nourishment
Calories	Not to exceed 2,000 per day
Blenderized nutrients	Demonstrated intolerance to semisynthetic formulas
Enteral pump	Documentation of physiologic reaction to gravity feeding
Completeness and timeliness	Certification for Parenteral and Enteral Nutrition form complete and submitted

All claims for coverage for enteral nutrition are approved on a case-by-case basis. To facilitate coverage, the dietitian can prepare a concise rationale explaining the medical necessity of enteral nutrition for the patient. A clear and direct connection must be made between the patient's medical condition and the inability to be maintained on oral feeding.

The medical condition must be of long and indefinite duration (at least 90 consecutive days). The test for permanence is important because reimbursement for parenteral and enteral nutrition is administered under Medicare's prosthetic device provision, which requires that the patient have a "permanently inoperative internal body organ or function thereof."[31] Documentation that the medical condition is lifelong for patients with a life expectancy of less than 90 days is important.

Tube feeding must be the patient's sole source of nutrition to qualify for Medicare reimbursement. If not, an explanation must be given. The dietitian should document that intake is limited to "sips," that nutrient intake checks medicate the oral diet does not contribute significantly to total needs, or that it is anticipated that the patient's condition will change rapidly, making adequate oral intake impossible.

Medicare officials will review all initial claims when enteral support is less than 750 calories or greater than 2,000 calories per day. Medical progress notes, hospital records, or supporting documentation explaining the necessity for reduced or additional calories is needed at the time the claim is filed to ensure acceptance.

Likewise, the need for a blenderized formula must be established by documenting the patient's physiological intolerance to semisynthetic formulas. If the formula selection rationale is unsatisfactory, Medicare will reimburse at the lesser category I (semisynthetic formula) rate, a difference of more than $7 per 1,000 calories. The dietitian should be responsible for providing such documentation.

In documenting the need for pump-assisted feeding it must be clearly stated that an adverse physiological reaction occurred after a trial of gravity feeding. A fair trial of gravity feeding must be closely monitored to meet this criterion. Intolerances such as distention, nausea, vomiting, or diarrhea should be carefully noted. It also is helpful to document failure to meet nutritional goals because of intolerances when gravity techniques are used.

The Certification for Parenteral and Enteral Nutrition form (Exhibit 2-1) must be completed. Accuracy and thoroughness are imperative. Certification forms cannot be altered once completed. The initial certification must be submitted at the time therapy is initiated. Thereafter, recertification is required after 90 days, 180 days after the first recertification, and every 180 days thereafter. The fifth and subsequent recertifications are requested at the discretion of Medicare on a case-by-case basis. The certification form must document that the physician saw the patient during the period before the dates of service on the claim. The only exception is for home patients, and exceptions for these patients are made on a case-by-case review. Exceptions include home visits by a certified home health nurse on a regular basis or visits on an irregular basis if the geographic location is such that it would be difficult for the physician to see the patient. Documentation must include information from the home health nurse about the patient's condition and a description of the reason why the physician cannot see the patient regularly. Any change in the nutrition support program (e.g., nutrients, volume involving one or more liters, infusion technique), requires another certification, usually within 30 days of the change.

If a claim for Medicare coverage is denied, it should be resubmitted. The most frequent reason for denial is errors in completing the certification form. Errors should be identified and corrected. If not resolved, a formal review and hearing can be requested.

When a patient does not meet the eligibility requirements for Medicare coverage (or coverage by other third-party payers), enteral nutrition support should not be denied. The nutrition support dietitian should continue to make every effort to lower the costs of nutrition support and achieve a low-cost, high-quality enteral support system. With a thorough knowledge of generically equivalent enteral formulas and tube feeding equipment, the dietitian can help the patient find appropriate supplies. Comparison shopping on behalf of the patient can be beneficial to identify low-cost products from reliable sources. Such sources can include nutrition support vendors, local hospitals, durable medical equipment suppliers, pharmacies, and discount department stores. Although not routinely recommended for enteral

Exhibit 2-1 Certification for Parenteral and Enteral Nutrition

This is: ☐ Initial Certification for the period of _____ to _____

☐ Recertification for the period of   _____ to _____

☐ Change in Prescription effective   _____

I BENEFICIARY IDENTIFICATION	Beneficiary: _____ First Name Last Name HIC Number Street Address City State Zip Telephone Number Beneficiary is in: Home ☐ SNF ☐ ICF ☐ Non-Skilled Facility ☐

II BENEFICIARY'S GENERAL CONDITION	A. Date of initial home or NH therapy _____
	    Est. duration of therapy _____ _____ _____
	                Mos Yrs Life Time
	B. Age _____ Height (ins) _____ Weight (lbs) _____
	C. Ambulatory ☐ Non-Ambulatory ☐
	    Is Consciousness impaired? Yes ☐ No ☐
	D. Other therapy/treatment that may affect patient's nutritional needs _____

III CLINICAL ASSESSMENT	A. All Diagnoses (use standard medical nomenclature with modifiers and include applicable ICD-9 codes) _____
	B. Description of patient's functional impairment of the alimentary tract _____
	_____
	C. Is this type feeding the only form of nutritional intake for this patient?
	    Yes ☐ No ☐
	    If no, explain _____
	D. Date patient last seen by physician during this certification/recertification period
	_____
	    If not seen by physician, explain: _____
	    Physician nonvisit medical evaluation is based on: Visiting Nurse ☐
	    Lab/Clinical Reports ☐ Other _____

IV PARENTERAL NUTRITION	A. Self-Mixed _____ Pre-Mixed _____
	    Reason for Pre-Mixed _____
	B. Frequency Fed _____ p/week
	C. Formula Component:
	    Amino
	    Acid _____ (÷ 100 = _____ · _____ ×) _____ = _____
	        (ml/day) (Concentration) (gms/day)
	    Dextros _____ = _____ %
	        (ml/day) (Concentration)
	    Lipids _____ ml/ _____ per/week _____ %
	            Frequency (Concentration)

continues

Exhibit 2-1 continued

V ENTERAL NUTRITION	A. Product Name _____ B. Calories p/day _____ C. Frequency Fed _____ D. Method of Administration: Syringe ☐ Gravity ☐ Pump ☐ E. If pump fed, what is patient's physical condition that necessitates use of pump _____ F. Administration Technique: Nasogastric Tube ☐ Gastrostomy ☐ Jejunostomy ☐

VI SUPPLIER/ PHYSICIAN INFO	AUTHORIZED PHYSICIAN	CERTIFIED SUPPLIER Supplier ID Number
	Physician's Name Phone ( )	Supplier's Name Phone ( )
	Street Address	Street Address
	City State Zip	City State Zip

VII CERTI- FICATION	I certify that the use of the indicated equipment/supplies is medically necessary and I will be supervising this patient's treatment. _____ _____ Physician's Signature Date Signed

Abbreviations: HIC, health insurance carrier; ICD-9, *International Code of Diseases*, 9th ed.; ICF, intermediate care facility; NH, nursing home; SNF, skilled nursing facility.

Source: Reprinted from *Parenteral and Enteral Nutrition Therapy Provider Manual*, Blue Cross and Blue Shield of South Carolina, April 1987.

patients, do-it-yourself home-blenderized foods could be considered for persons who are not at nutritional risk and whose feeding tube can accommodate this form of feeding.

Conclusions

Regulatory and reimbursement issues have impacted significantly on the practice of nutrition support. In turn, the role of the nutrition support dietitian in hospitals, nursing homes, and home health agencies has been challenged and is changing. In the hospital the role of the dietitian seems more secure, whereas in skilled nursing facilities access to dietitians has always been limited and is now proposed to be deregulated. Home health agencies are increasingly employing dietitians as more patients return home on specialized nutrition support.

Creativity and resourcefulness are required for the dietitian to remain an active team member in the nutrition care of hospitalized and home patients. This includes establishing alternative systems for caring for patients such as hospital-based nutrition services. Diligent education of health care administrators and third-party payers regarding the essentialness of the nutrition support dietitian also is necessary. This can be accomplished through high-quality patient care that is cost-effective. Also, establishment of fee-for-service can help to value and strengthen the role of the nutrition support dietitian.

The nutrition support dietitian should stay abreast of regulatory and reimbursement issues and how they affect home patients' eligibility for third-party reimbursement. A dietitian who is aware of these regulations and who has a strong knowledge of the application of enteral nutrition can help to ensure appropriate and cost-effective nutrition support.

NOTES

1. 42 U.S.C. 1395 *et seq.*

2. Nutrition supplementation, described as the provision of "medicine between meals to boost protein-caloric intake or the mainstay of a daily nutritional plan," is not covered under Medicare Part B. "Appendix Coverage of Issues," Sec. 65-10.3, in *Medicare Carriers Manual.*

3. *Medicare Carriers Manual*, ibid., Sec. 65-10.1.

4. Ibid., Sec. 65-10.2.

5. Ibid.

6. Ibid., Sec. 65-10.

7. Ibid.

8. *Congressional Record*, October 17, 1986, p. H 11414.

9. HCPCs are categories of products and equipment in which the items are grouped according to ingredients, function, or other special properties. The lowest charge levels were calculated by arraying in ascending order the charges for all of the products in a particular HCPC and identifying the 25th percentile of those charges. That charge associated with the 25th percentile becomes the allowable charge for every product in that category.

10. Lyn Howard, Lenore Heaphey, and Maryann Timchalk, "A Review of the Current National Status of Home Parenteral and Enteral Nutrition from the Provider and Consumer Perspective," *Journal of Parenteral and Enteral Nutrition* 10 (1986): 416-24.

11. "Washington Review—New Congressional Report on Life-Sustaining Technologies and the Elderly Covers Nutrition Support," *Nutrition in Clinical Practice* 2 (1987): 179-80.

12. Dee Dee O'Brien et al., "Recommendations of Nutrition Support Team Promote Cost Containment," *Journal of Parenteral and Enteral Nutrition* 10 (1986): 300-302.

13. P.L. Grimaldi, "DRG's and Long-Term Care," *American Health Care Association Journal* 11 (1985): 6.

14. Dennis Sullivan, Ronni Chernoff, and David Lipschitz, "Nutritional Support in Long-Term Care Facilities," *Nutrition in Clinical Practice* 2 (1987): 6-13.

15. Jennifer K. Nelson, Pasquale J. Palumbo, and Peter C. O'Brien, "Home Enteral Nutrition: Observations of a Newly Established Program," *Nutrition in Clinical Practice* 1 (1986): 179-92.

16. Cathleen Marien et al., "Home Parenteral Nutrition," *Nutrition in Clinical Practice* 1 (1986): 179-92.

17. Beth Cavanaugh, "Dietitians in Home Health Care: Outlook and Opportunities," *Dietetic Currents* 13 (1986): 21-24.

18. Ibid.

19. Alan K. Parver, *Coverage and Reimbursement Policies for Nutrition Care Services. A Report Prepared for the American Dietetic Association* (Chicago, Ill.: American Dietetic Association, 1986).

20. David A. Zilz, "Current Trends in Home Health Care," *American Journal of Hospital Pharmacy* 42 (1985): 2520-25.

21. Martha V. Reitz, Mildred Mattfeldt-Beman, Charlotte M. Ridley, "Current Practices in Home Nutrition Support," *Nutritional Support Services* 8 (1988): 8-11.

22. Parver, *Coverage and Reimbursement Policies for Nutrition Care Services*.

23. Dietitians in Critical Care Practice Group, "Board Approves Timely Statement—Nutrition Support Services in Home Health Care," *Journal of the American Dietetic Association* 85 (1985): 982.

24. Ibid.

25. American Dietetic Association, *Nutrition Services Payment System—Guidelines for Implementation* (Chicago, Ill.: American Dietetic Association, 1985).

26. Janice N. Neville and Carol J. Gillmore, "President's Page: A Report on Nutrition Services Payment System Activities," *Journal of the American Dietetic Association* 88 (1988): 953-55.

27. "Washington Review."

28. Neville and Gillmore, "President's Page."

29. *Parenteral and Enteral Nutrition Therapy Provider Manual* (Camden, South Carolina: Blue Cross and Blue Shield of South Carolina, April 1987).

30. Ibid.

31. Ibid.

Chapter 3

Supply and Management Structures

Mindy Hermann-Zaidins and Riva Touger-Decker

INTRODUCTION

Given the growth and advances in home nutrition support that have occurred in the past ten years, we thought it would be of value to examine hospital-supplier structures and relationships on a national scale. A brief survey was developed to look at trends in home nutrition support supply and management structures. An informal survey was conducted using a geographic sample of 30 hospital-based nutrition support teams. The findings provide a perspective on home nutrition support structures used by hospitals in 1988.

Hospitals today tend to rely primarily on home care companies for equipment, supplies, and formulas. Less than 10 percent of the facilities surveyed provide these services independently. The majority of institutions limit the number of home care companies with which they affiliate. The most common types of structures include contracts, joint ventures, and hospital-based corporations. Services contracted for most frequently include hardware, monitoring, nursing follow-up, and training and education materials. Provider reports to the hospital team or physician focus on home setting evaluation, clinical and laboratory data, medical progress, and supply and delivery usage.

Most institutions have informal criteria for selection of a home care company including

- cost
- available services
- type and number of personnel
- willingness to cover partial/no pays
- ability to monitor patients

In some cases, hospital-supplier contracts for other services (e.g., ostomy care, respiratory support) will dictate agreement for nutrition services as well. Providers are selected by the hospital administration or nutrition support team (or both); a registered dietitian is usually involved in the selection process.

Referrals for home nutrition support are most frequently (greater than 75 percent of the time) initiated by the nutrition support team nurse and to a lesser degree by the nutrition support team dietitian or physician. After the referral, the predischarge care also is coordinated by the nutrition support team nurse; the dietitian works with nursing in training the patient and with the physician in determining the home feeding regimen. Part of the hospital-provider agreement may include reimbursement of hospital personnel for predischarge training and education and coordination of services.

Coordination of postdischarge services varies with the management structure chosen. When the hospital nutrition support team provides patient monitoring and follow-up, its registered nurse and dietitian undertake these responsibilities. In such instances, the home care company may reimburse the hospital. When arrangements do not include postdischarge visits, the provider's nurse or visiting nurse service provides care. Supply pickup and delivery is usually coordinated by the home care company. The patient's primary physician is ultimately responsible for formula changes and monitoring.

In the institutions surveyed, the dietitian's role in postdischarge care is limited. This may be due in part to difficulty in obtaining third-party reimbursement for services. Nursing and physician care may be billed per visit and are reimbursed by insurance companies.

Establishing the hospital-supplier relationship is a multistep process. Some of the issues to consider are shown in Exhibit 3-1 and outlined in the following discussion. Steps progress from a broad to a narrow focus, with an intended outcome of defining a workable supply and management structure. Outcomes of each of these processes (e.g., needs assessment, analysis of strengths and weaknesses, and a survey of population requirements) will determine many of the criteria for provider selection.

TRENDS IN HOME NUTRITION SUPPORT

A survey of trends in the field of home nutrition support is the first step in evaluating a supply and management structure for this service in a hospital. Conducting a full survey is unrealistic for hospitals. Networking with colleagues, attending related meetings and seminars, calling select established home care programs, and setting up meetings with companies

Exhibit 3-1 Issues in Setting Up A Supply/Management Structure

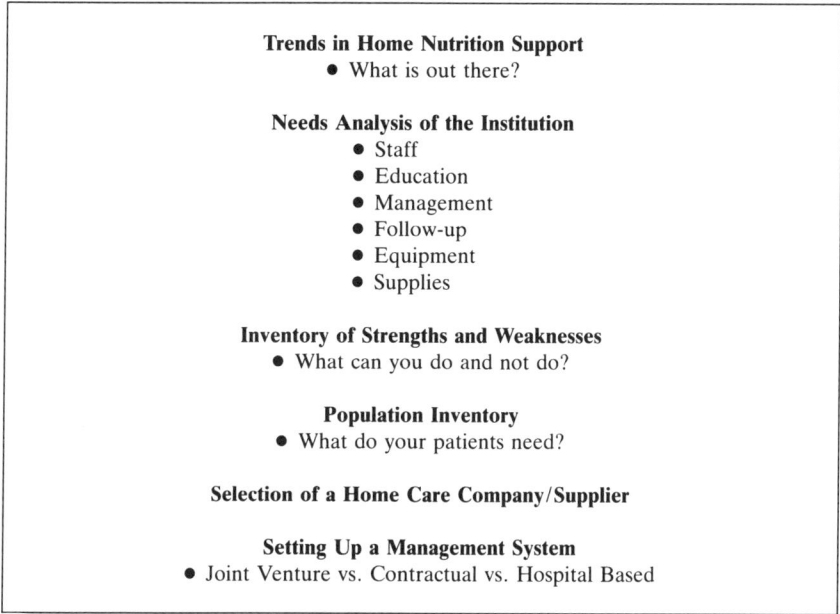

Trends in Home Nutrition Support
- What is out there?

Needs Analysis of the Institution
- Staff
- Education
- Management
- Follow-up
- Equipment
- Supplies

Inventory of Strengths and Weaknesses
- What can you do and not do?

Population Inventory
- What do your patients need?

Selection of a Home Care Company/Supplier

Setting Up a Management System
- Joint Venture vs. Contractual vs. Hospital Based

---

are feasible alternatives and provide valuable preliminary information in establishing a home program.

NEEDS ASSESSMENT AND IDENTIFICATION OF STRENGTHS AND WEAKNESSES

Needs assessment is a process by which the health care team can analyze what resources it has available for home care management. In identifying its specific strengths and weaknesses, a team is better able to solicit for and select vendors whose services complement those already available or that are being provided through the hospital (Exhibit 3-2). The benefits of this process include cost control, maximum utilization of existing personnel, and coordinated patient management.

Staff

Hospital-based home care teams[1] often are composed of professionals as well as full-time paraprofessionals whose activities include but are not limited to outpatient management. The availability and specialization areas

Exhibit 3-2 Decision Tree—Conducting a Needs Assessment

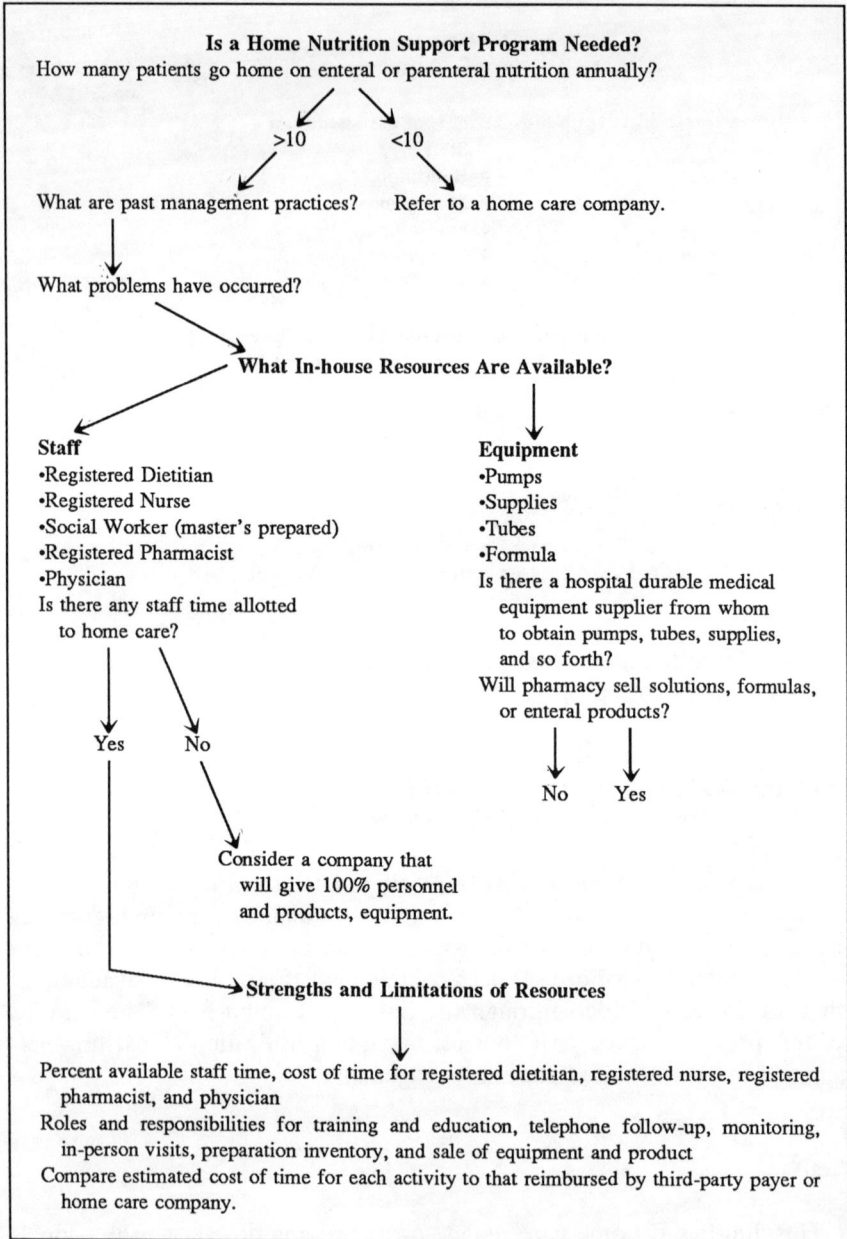

Is a Home Nutrition Support Program Needed?

How many patients go home on enteral or parenteral nutrition annually?

>10   <10

What are past management practices?   Refer to a home care company.

What problems have occurred?

What In-house Resources Are Available?

Staff
•Registered Dietitian
•Registered Nurse
•Social Worker (master's prepared)
•Registered Pharmacist
•Physician
Is there any staff time allotted
    to home care?

Yes   No

Equipment
•Pumps
•Supplies
•Tubes
•Formula
Is there a hospital durable medical
    equipment supplier from whom
    to obtain pumps, tubes, supplies,
    and so forth?
Will pharmacy sell solutions, formulas,
    or enteral products?

No   Yes

Consider a company that
    will give 100% personnel
    and products, equipment.

Strengths and Limitations of Resources

Percent available staff time, cost of time for registered dietitian, registered nurse, registered
    pharmacist, and physician
Roles and responsibilities for training and education, telephone follow-up, monitoring,
    in-person visits, preparation inventory, and sale of equipment and product
Compare estimated cost of time for each activity to that reimbursed by third-party payer or
    home care company.

of these staff members determine in part the amount of patient training and management that the team will be able to undertake. Limited access to key personnel, such as physicians, nurses, or pharmacists, may necessitate that they be provided by the supplier (Table 3-1). A nutrition support or outpatient dietitian responsible for patient management may serve as a link among patient, supplier, and team.

One or more services may be responsible for home care referrals. If the discharge planning or social work department coordinates outpatient services, staff members who manage the patient's nutrition regimen must establish in-house lines of communication and encourage interdepartmental participation in the vendor selection process.

Education

Patient and family education, a key to the success of home feeding programs, may be performed by the nutrition support staff or home care company (or both). A team with well-established patient care procedures may prefer to retain all training functions. When a hospital-based education system is in place and completely staffed, it makes little sense to turn all training over to a supplier, whose protocols may differ greatly from those of the team. Hospital-based training fosters bonds between the team and the patient and builds the foundation for a long-term relationship.

Most suppliers can provide home nutrition training and work with the patient during hospitalization or at the time the patient is discharged to home. By utilizing vendors in this capacity, the team can ensure quality training without having to undertake the actual education process. Comprehensive education materials may be available to teams who work directly with the patient but lack the time and resources to develop printed materials.

Table 3-1 Hospital- and Supplier-Based Staff

Hospital Based	*Supplier Based*
Physician	Physician
Nurse	Nurse
Pharmacist	Pharmacist
Pharmacy Technician	Pharmacy Technician
Dietitian	Dietitian
Social Worker	Insurance Specialist
Physical Therapist	

Management and Follow-Up

Continuity of care ensures consistent patient management during hospitalization, throughout training and adjustment periods, and while the patient is using home services. Teams vary in their ability and desire to follow up on patients after discharge, and, as such, must select the supplier best able to augment their services.

Many suppliers retain physician consultants to assist in the medical care of home patients. In this capacity they review laboratory data, prescribe or evaluate formula changes, and communicate with hospital-based physicians. This feature offers the assurance to hospitals and physicians with limited nutrition management expertise or capabilities that quality of care will be maintained outside the hospital.

Nursing staffs perform a wide range of functions. Many suppliers offer nursing services for training, home visitation, hands-on care, and patient follow-up. The referring team, physician, nurse, or social worker may be able to select from a menu of patient care options, identifying those components that best supplement existing activities.

Hospital pharmacies have become increasingly more involved with home nutrition services. Many centers have established for-profit home care subsidiaries in which the pharmacy compounds all parenteral solutions, including total parenteral nutrition, antibiotics, and chemotherapy. In other settings, pharmacists are responsible for reviewing formula prescriptions and interfacing with suppliers. The team with a strong and active pharmacist and support staff may not need a supplier who focuses on pharmacy support.

Dietitians, in comparison with other staff, are less commonly employed by home care providers. As such, the registered dietitian responsible for in-house nutrition support often maintains patient contact after discharge, communicating relevant information and observations to the supplier and serving as a liaison between supplier and team. In settings in which the dietitian can devote only limited time to outpatient management, he or she should play an important role in the establishment of patient care criteria, identification of qualified vendors, and communication of patient needs to the home provider.

Equipment

Home equipment needs may be met by the hospital or the vendor or through a combination of sources. Centers with established durable medical equipment subsidiaries can supply all the equipment needed by their out-patient populations. Other hospitals can provide only smaller items, such as syringes, formulas, and feeding sets. Teams that train patients in the use of particular equipment must ensure that the vendor can provide adequate supplies for the preferred models and styles.

Other Services

Vendor selection and coordination of home services can be time-consuming processes. Exhibit 3-3 lists some of the forms required for each new home enteral patient. Hospitals that do not have adequate staffing to gather the referral information should consider vendors who are willing to assume those functions. Comprehensive discharge planning usually requires input from the team or staff physician (or both), nurse, social worker, pharmacist, and dietitian.

As documentation requirements for the justification of home feeding intensify, the dietitian's role will become even more critical. Assessment information gathered by the registered dietitian is required for the supplier's completion of reimbursement applications. In this manner, he or she can serve as a key member of the discharge planning team.

Exhibit 3-3 Documentation for Home Enteral Program

Before Contract
Insurance Information Form
Home Enteral Form and Telephone Log
Quality Assurance Check Sheet

Under Contract
Insurance Information Form
Home Enteral Form and Care Plan (revised and expanded)
Home Enteral Follow-Up Form (revised and expanded)
Home Enteral Training and Quality Control Summaries
Home Patient Agreement
Physician Statement of Medical Authorization
Recertification of Medical Necessity

Source: Courtesy of Memorial Sloan-Kettering Cancer Center, Nutrition Support Service, New York, New York.

SELECTION OF A SUPPLIER

Features To Consider

Completion of a needs assessment provides the team with guidelines for vendor selection. Weak areas of team staffing can be filled in, and services can be sought to complement those provided by the hospital. After identifying potential suppliers, the team must examine each one further to evaluate its operating features and policies, patient service philosophy, and ability to respond to the needs of the patient and team. Exhibit 3-4 lists some of the factors to consider in selecting a supplier. Through a comprehensive process, only the most appropriate vendors will be chosen.

Ultimately, the team must decide how much control they desire and can assume over home care. In a comprehensive care setting in which close patient contact is maintained, such as in cancer treatment centers, vendors may be asked to assume strictly a supplier role. An acute care hospital with little patient contact after discharge requires a more intense level of service.

Scope of Inventory

Suppliers vary in their ability to provide equipment, formulas, and ancillary items. Some maintain large, comprehensive inventories that include most major product lines. This type of vendor should be sought by centers that discharge large numbers of patients or those that need specific brands of supplies. Other vendors limit themselves to fewer lines and can be utilized if the team is less particular about brand name or if it discharges a small number of patients. A diverse patient population that requires a

Exhibit 3-4 Factors To Consider in Selecting a Home Care Company

Limitations defined in Exhibits 3-1 and 3-2
Reimbursement to hospital for personnel time
Types and quality of equipment
Home setting evaluation
System of follow-up: frequency, by whom, how
Geographical scope of services
Personnel on staff
24-hour services

wide variety of ancillary supplies will be best serviced by a vendor who is willing to order special items as needed.

Patient Services

Vendor response time is an important consideration in home care management. The nature of discharge planning, often on short notice, has created the need for suppliers to fill and deliver initial orders within 24 hours. In settings in which discharge dates are usually known well in advance, immediate service is less critical.

The amount of time the vendor requires to replace malfunctioning equipment and respond to prescription changes is a consideration. Access to a 24-hour on-call telephone number and contact person within the vendor's organization usually is essential.

Vendors may be selected for their ability to provide or arrange services not handled by the referring team. A supplier may send a staff member, usually a registered nurse, to the hospital to assess comprehensively the patient's clinical and psychosocial status. Teams that are able to undertake specific responsibilities such as inpatient evaluation can seek out those vendors able to fill in the gaps in information gathering. Patient education, especially when initiated in house by the team and continued in the home by the supplier, is extremely successful when the team-supplier working relationship is well-defined to prevent role overlap and fighting over turf.

Ancillary Personnel

Many patients require home assistance for their medical and nutrition care. Suppliers certified as home health agencies can provide skilled personnel trained in feeding procedures. This feature ensures comprehensive home care, coordinates multiple services, and minimizes confusion. When comprehensive care cannot be provided by only one agency, a team member—registered nurse, registered dietitian, or social worker—should coordinate communication among agencies or provide names and telephone numbers to enable vendors to contact each other.

Billing, Insurance, and Reimbursement

Home care charges vary greatly with the products, personnel, and supplier. For this reason, the vendor should be available to discuss service features and costs with the patient and family before initiation of service.

The hospital-based team must ensure that the patient recognizes his or her option to choose from a number of appropriate and approved suppliers. It may be helpful to develop performance criteria for potential suppliers.

Usually vendors either work directly with third-party payers or bill the patient for services and supplies. Billing procedures and approximate cost of services and supplies should be explained to the patient by the supplier. At some point in the discharge planning process, the team or vendor (or both) must apprise the patient and family of their financial obligation beyond what is reimbursed by insurance. This will prevent surprises when the first bill is received. Communication between patient and supplier regarding bill payment schedules should be encouraged.

The emergence of HMOs, preferred provider organizations (PPOs), managed care, and other health care cost-containment measures has impacted on home supply options. Many organizations have identified reimbursable products and services, and incorporated them into their policies. Many may have developed a vendor network. The hospital team should establish a dialogue with the provider and confirm the patient's insurance coverage before selecting potential suppliers. This communication may result in a mutually acceptable and maximally reimbursed home feeding system for the patient.

Supplier-Hospital Communications

Vendor services range from supply delivery to comprehensive case management. As discussed earlier, the team must inventory its resources and identify those activities that need to be referred to an outside source. A vendor may require that team members collect preliminary data on patient assessment, clinical status, and insurance coverage to facilitate transfer of patient care. If a team is unable to perform this function, it must ensure that suppliers can gain access to relevant information by establishing relationships with appropriate hospital-based clinicians and administrators and gaining access to inpatient chart information.

The team should identify suppliers best able to meet its needs for patient monitoring at home. Essential information that the vendor should provide includes documentation of deliveries and records of telephone conversations with the patient. Reports on blood sample analyses, follow-up nursing visits, and patient education should be generated in a timely manner as services are rendered. It may be helpful to set up regular conferences or telephone conversations to maintain continuity of care and to strengthen the hospital-supplier relationship.

Quality Control

Quality control procedures help ensure continuity of patient care after discharge. Verification by the supplier of all new and refill orders prevents delivery errors and reduces patient confusion resulting from receipt of incorrect items. The patient who has learned basic inventory checking procedures from either a team or a vendor staff member will be able to spot mistakes and notify a designated party. The vendor should identify a staff member, often a patient representative, with whom the patient can communicate regarding supplies and inventory.

Setting Up Selection Criteria

Defining vendor selection criteria serves several purposes. Team members can identify those services and performance standards most important to their particular patient population. The criteria provide potential vendors with information on service needs. Standards can be utilized to evaluate vendor performance and provide feedback on service deficiencies.

Suppliers should be invited individually to deliver formal presentations to all members of the patient home care team. This process allows group input into the vendor selection process, efficiently disseminates information to hospital staff members, and prevents fragmentation of patient referrals.

Special Features

Geographical Coverage

Patient population characteristics impact on vendor selection. A center that attracts patients nationwide and worldwide should identify at least one domestic and one international supplier. Community hospitals may be better serviced by a local or a regional vendor. In Table 3-2 the characteristics of regional and local vendors are compared.

Vacation Delivery

Many vendors offer service, including delivery of total parenteral nutrition solutions, to ambulatory outpatients vacationing in the United States or overseas. A team member may have to contact an overseas satellite service center to arrange this and provide the center with the patient's prescription, supply needs, and travel itinerary. The patient's supplies and equipment may differ slightly if domestic brands are unavailable abroad.

Table 3-2 Regional versus Local Vendors

Regional	Local
Large inventory	Small inventory
Weak community ties	Strong community ties
Broad geographic range	Limited geographic range
Less personal service	More personal service

Other Services

Many vendors have developed comprehensive services, including home antibiotic, chemotherapy, and pain medication infusions. Selection of this type of supplier coordinates home care under one umbrella, minimizes time spent on patient referrals, and reduces potential confusion about patients' orders.

SETTING UP THE MANAGEMENT SYSTEM

The hospital-supplier relationship can remain loosely structured or be established in a formal contract. The degree to which the hospital commits financial and human resources to the home care venture depends on its desire for program control and revenue sharing and its willingness to undertake the risk of operating its own business.

Alternative Structures

Joint Ventures

In a hospital-supplier joint venture, a new corporation is created with resources contributed by each party. This structure provides the hospital and its team with more control over service, management, and decision making. The legal implications of a joint venture are greater and include risk of Medicare fraud and abuse charges from the steering of patients into the hospital's program and away from independent operations.

Contractual Agreements

Home care contracts define the respective functions and obligations of the hospital team and the supplier. Each party contributes its expertise and resources independently and a new corporation is not created. This type of relationship allows each party to maintain its autonomy.

Hospital-Owned Agency

A hospital may decide to create its own supply company or to purchase an existing operation. In doing so, it retains total control over home care and has the greatest potential for financial gain. Outpatient team members are employed directly by the home care subsidiary.

Policies and Procedures

Operating Policies

Establishment of formal policies and procedures clarifies the roles of hospital and supplier teams. A joint development effort between the two teams builds a strong working relationship, establishes lines of communication, and reduces task redundancy. The vendor must understand the hospital team's mission, philosophy, and operation style to tailor and coordinate its services.

A policy manual should cover all aspects of the home care operation. A sample of one hospital's procedure manual is outlined in Appendix A-6. The vendor's manual covers similar issues plus procedures for delivery of supplies, follow-up servicing, and clinical and administrative communication with the referring team.

Fee Structures

Under certain agreements, hospitals may be reimbursed by the vendor for home care services rendered. These services must be well-defined in the contract and procedure manuals. Meticulous records and documentation maintained by the team and vendor substantiate that the appropriate activities were performed and that the service fee was justifiable.

HMOs and PPOs

Many HMOs have established relationships with particular vendors whereby services are rendered at a discount or according to a prearranged fee schedule. A supplier operating under a PPO arrangement provides services at defined or discounted prices, and the subscriber is offered cost incentives to use the preferred provider, in this case, a specified vendor. It behooves the hospital-based team to work closely with local HMO administrators to ensure that appropriate home care vendors and services are selected for HMO contracts.

LEGAL IMPLICATIONS

Hospital-supplier relationships are under increasing legal scrutiny for several categories of impropriety. Hallmark cases point out the need for the hospital and the vendor to work closely with their respective attorneys before entering into a formal home care agreement.

Medicare Fraud and Abuse

Medicare fraud and abuse can be charged if it appears that the hospital or physician is receiving remuneration in return for referring a patient or steering them to the vendor. All remuneration must be linked to specific services rendered and documented as performed.

Antitrust

Antitrust charges imply that the hospital has restrained unfairly the access of other agencies and suppliers to its patient population. Several questions can be asked to address this issue.

- Does an existing hospital-supplier agreement preclude other vendors?
- Has the hospital entered into an exclusive dealing arrangement?
- Does a joint venture have monopoly over all home health referrals?
- Is the hospital reselling products at an unfairly low price?
- Are patients made aware of their supply options?

An answer of *yes* to any of these questions necessitates that the team and vendor reexamine closely their relationship with the assistance of legal counsel.

CONCLUSION

The ultimate goal in establishing the hospital-supplier relationship is to ensure comprehensive, cost-effective, safe, and ethical patient care. Any combination of services from any number of suppliers can be acceptable, as long as patient needs are met in the most appropriate manner.

NOTE

1. Throughout this chapter the term *team* is used broadly to designate staff members working with home nutrition patients, regardless of whether a formal support team exists.

BIBLIOGRAPHY

Halter, P.I. "Trends in Home Nutrition Support." *Biomedical Business International* 9 (1986): 37.
Lifshitz, Jere Ziffers. "Home Parenteral Nutrition." *Clinical Nutrition* 6 (1987): 7–16.

Chapter 4

Oral Nutrition Management

Lucinda K. Lysen and Karen Masino

Often, patients and their significant others do not assign the same importance to oral nutrition support as that given to other modes of support such as tube feedings and parenteral nutrition. These patients, however, are at significant risk for developing problems with poor appetite; nausea and vomiting, which compromise intake and lead to weight loss; and the sequelae of compromised nutrition status and malnutrition. Patients on home oral nutrition support may seem easy to manage but, in practice, are challenging to follow. Maintaining contact with these patients and enlisting their continuing interest are two of the unique challenges the dietitian faces. Establishing a system for follow-up, diet and weight record keeping, telephone contact, and clinic or office visits before discharge is essential.

EVALUATION OF THE PATIENT

A number of factors affect whether a patient will have an adequate oral intake after discharge from the hospital, including his or her disease, prognosis, current nutrient requirements, nutrition status at the time of discharge, access to food, and support systems to aid in food shopping and preparation and in encouragement of intake.

Before discharge, the registered dietitian should be involved in planning and implementing the program for home oral nutrition support. Adequate time should be provided for the patient to adjust to the diet and supplement routine that he or she will follow at home. The nutrition care program should be initiated in the hospital, and patient tolerance should be exhibited before discharge. Optimal management of the patient going home requires coordinated efforts among all health care team members, including physician, registered nurse, registered dietitian, social worker, pharmacist, and occupational therapist.

In evaluating the patient for discharge, the registered dietitian must assess and review the nutrition status of the patient along with his or her ability to purchase, store, and prepare food. This evaluation includes reviewing nutrition, medical, and social histories, as well as medications for potential drug-nutrient interactions, and performing an oral intake analysis, anthropometric measurements, and biochemical measurements (see Exhibits 4-1 and 4-2). Social support systems at home, such as persons available to shop for and prepare food, assist with feeding, and provide emotional support and encouragement, also should be evaluated.

PREPARATION OF THE PATIENT FOR DISCHARGE

The hospital discharge planner is frequently responsible for decisions regarding the utilization of home health care services for discharged patients. In other circumstances, the hospital may have a hospital-based home care program to which patients requiring home care are referred. In either instance, the registered dietitian in the hospital should work with the designated home caregivers to provide uninterrupted care to the patient.

Whether the patient is to be followed by the hospital nutrition team or a home care company, a home visit should be scheduled. This affords the registered dietitian the opportunity to view the physical surroundings and kitchen facilities and to interact with family members or others who will be assisting the patient at home. In some instances, the registered dietitian will be unable to visit the home. If a nursing or community agency is scheduled to complete a home visit, the registered dietitian should establish a communication system with the agency to obtain information about the home and support system. A system for continued contact with the agency making home visits should be established.

NUTRITION ASSESSMENT—INITIAL AND PERIODIC

A nutrition assessment is completed immediately before discharge to determine the appropriate diet and set a baseline nutrition status. Reassessments should be conducted periodically by the registered dietitian who is responsible for monitoring the patient at home. The Harris-Benedict equation[1] can be used with appropriate injury and activity factors to determine energy needs. (See Chapter 5, Exhibit 5-2.) After any significant weight change, energy needs should be recalculated so that established weight goals can be met. The patient should keep a daily food diary, which can be reviewed during clinic visits or established telephone appointments. The diary may be reviewed as frequently as biweekly in the unstable patient

Exhibit 4-1 Nutrition Assessment Record Form

NAME _____ NO ____ AGE ____ SEX ____ ROOM ____
HEIGHT _____ BODY WEIGHT (usual, current, admitting) _____
WRIST CIRCUMFERENCE _____ BODY FRAME TYPE _____
IDEAL BODY WEIGHT _____ % IDEAL BODY WEIGHT (actual/ideal) _____
TRICEPS SKINFOLD _____ PERCENTILE ____ ARM CIRCUMFERENCE ____
ARM MUSCLE CIRCUMFERENCE _____ PERCENTILE _____

PHYSICAL FINDINGS:
Hair _____
Face _____
Skin _____ Nails _____
Skeletal _____ Nervous _____
Internal _____ Other _____

MEDICAL/SOCIAL HISTORY (factors which may affect nutritional status):
_____
_____
_____
_____
_____
_____

DIETARY INFORMATION: (days NPO, calorie count, nutrition history, current diet
order, tube feeding, IV's, etc.): _____
_____
_____
_____
_____
_____
_____
_____
_____

LABORATORY VALUES:	normal		normal
sodium	_____	hematocrit	_____
potassium	_____	hemoglobin	_____
calcium	_____	other	_____
glucose	_____		_____
total protein	_____		_____
serum albumin	_____		_____
alkaline phosphatase	_____		_____
BUN	_____		_____

DRUGS, SUPPLEMENTS:
_____   _____
_____   _____
_____   _____
_____   _____

DATE _____ DIETITIAN _____

Source: Reprinted from *Nutritional Assessment Guidelines Handbook*, by A. Grant, with permission of A. Grant, Seattle, Washington, ©1979, p. 109.

Exhibit 4-2 Nutrition Assessment Summary Form

NAME _____ NO ____ AGE ____ SEX ____ ROOM ____

NUTRITIONAL IMPLICATIONS OF PATIENT HISTORY (medical, social, dietary):

_____
_____
_____
_____
_____
_____

NUTRITIONAL IMPLICATIONS OF PHYSICAL EXAM (anthropometric, weight, clinical findings):

_____
_____
_____
_____
_____
_____

NUTRITIONAL IMPLICATIONS OF LABORATORY VALUES:

_____
_____
_____
_____
_____

NUTRITIONAL IMPLICATIONS OF FOOD AND DRUG INTERACTIONS:

_____
_____
_____
_____
_____
_____

RECOMMENDATIONS (chart entry):

_____
_____
_____
_____
_____
_____
_____
_____
_____

SIGNED _____ DATE _____

Source: Reprinted from *Nutritional Assessment Guidelines Handbook,* by A. Grant, with permission of A. Grant, Seattle, Washington, ©1979, p. 110.

or less frequently in stable patients. Food diaries are particularly valuable in patients in transition from tube feedings to oral diets (see Exhibit 4-3). Oral diets should make up about two thirds of estimated needs before tube feedings are discontinued.[2]

Weight and laboratory data should be monitored frequently. Weight change should be compared to hospital discharge weight and desirable weight. In elderly persons, percentage weight loss should be based on usual body weight as opposed to ideal body weight.[3] Patients should be instructed to record weights once or twice weekly and to weigh themselves at the same time of day, preferably in the morning (after urination and bowel movement and before breakfast). An unintentional weight change of two pounds or more in one week should be reported to the registered dietitian or physician.

Measurements of midarm muscle circumference and triceps skinfold, two anthropometric parameters, provide estimates of changes in somatic protein and fat stores, respectively, and can be helpful in long-term nutrition care and follow-up of home patients. These measurements can demonstrate depletion of muscle or fat mass in the patient who continues to lose weight.

Biochemical measurements should assess concentrations of serum albumin, creatinine, sodium, potassium, chloride, and bicarbonate, and blood urea nitrogen; hemoglobin level; hematocrit; white blood cell count; and percentage of lymphocytes. If feasible, assessments should be performed about every three weeks. Changes in serum albumin levels may reflect adequacy of diet and nutrition status.

Vitamin and mineral deficiencies may occur independent from major metabolic and nutrition abnormalities in the patient (see Table 4-1). Physical assessment of patients and evaluation of risk factors for deficiencies should be incorporated into the nutrition evaluation process. Physical signs of nutrient deficiencies should be discussed and referred to the patient's physician for further evaluation and supplementation.

A therapeutic multivitamin supplement may be considered, depending on nutrient needs, intake and any drugs that may impair vitamin or mineral utilization (see Table 4-2). Many multivitamin preparations do not contain all the vitamins to meet established recommended dietary allowances (set forth by the Food and Nutrition Board, National Research Council). All multivitamin preparations should be reviewed carefully to ensure that needed nutrients are included. More than one supplement may be provided if one vitamin preparation lacks specific nutrients required by the patient. In many instances, generic substitutes are available that may be equal in value and lower in cost than brand-name preparations.

Regular appointments for home nutrition support patients should be established. Initially, at least, visits should be frequent (one week after

Exhibit 4-3 Food Intake Record

INSTRUCTIONS:

Please record your intake of food and beverages for the next 7 days. Include:

1. Item consumed
2. Method of preparation
3. Amount consumed:

    Liquid—cups or fluid ounces

    Meat, Cheese, Fish, Poultry—in ounces, specifying if the amount given is in cooked or raw weight

    Vegetables—cups or individual units (1 tomato)

    Fruits—cups or individual units, including diameter of fresh fruits (apple, orange) or length (banana)

    Bread—number of slices

    Cereal, Pasta, Rice, Potatoes—cups

    Pancakes, Waffles—number and diameter

    Crackers—number

    Margarine or Butter—teaspoons or pats

    Dressings, Mayonnaise—teaspoons or tablespoons

    Gravy—tablespoons or cups

    Bacon, Sausage—number of slices or links

    Jam, Jelly, Honey, Sugar, Syrup—teaspoons or tablespoons

    Candy—number of bars, number and size of pieces

    Jello, Pudding, Ice Cream—cups

    Cookies—number

    Pie, Cake—number of pieces, length and width at largest end

Record each entry as soon as possible after each meal or snack. Attempt to keep your intake as normal as possible. Do not write in last 3 columns on form.

Day # _____ *

Items Consumed	How Prepared	Amount	Protein	Fat	CHO
Breakfast _____					
Snack _____					
Lunch _____					
Snack _____					
Dinner _____					
Snack _____					

*Sample form for one day

Source: Reprinted from *Enteral and Tube Feeding* by J.L. Rombeau and M.D. Caldwell, p. 161, with permission of W.B. Saunders Company, ©1984.

Table 4-1 Disease States and Historical Features Associated with Micronutrient Deficiences

Disease State or Historical Feature	Associated Deficiency
Gastrointestinal Disorders	
Pancreatic insufficiency	Vitamins A, D, E, K
Gastrectomy	Vitamins A, D, E, B_{12}, folic acid, iron, calcium
Liver disease, alcoholism	Vitamins A, D, C, riboflavin, niacin, thiamine, folic acid, magnesium, zinc
Short bowel syndrome, ileal resection	Vitamins B_{12}, folic acid, calcium, magnesium
Blind loop syndrome	Vitamin B_{12}
Sprue, gluten enteropathy	Vitamin A, folic acid
Bile salt depletion, cholestyramine ingestion	Vitamins A, K
Obstructive jaundice	Vitamins A, K
Prolonged antacid therapy, peptic ulcer disease	Thiamine, vitamin C
Endocrine Disorders	
Thyrotoxicosis	Vitamins A, B_6, B_{12}, C, thiamine, folic acid
Diabetes mellitus	Magnesium, chromium
Cardiorespiratory Disorders	
Chronic obstructive pulmonary disease	Vitamin A
Congestive heart failure	Vitamins A, C, thiamine
Cystic fibrosis	Vitamin A
Hematopoietic Disorders	
Sickle cell anemia	Folic acid
Leukemia	Folic acid
Renal Disorders	
Chronic renal failure	Magnesium, calcium, vitamin D*
Miscellaneous Disorders	
Prolonged antibiotic therapy	Vitamin K
Fever	Vitamins A, C, thiamine, riboflavin, folic acid

*Inability of renal tissue to synthesize the metabolically active form of vitamin D.

Source: Reprinted from *Enteral and Tube Feeding* by J.L. Rombeau and M.D. Caldwell, p. 128, with permission of W. B. Saunders Company, © 1984.

discharge for the first visit). Appointments serve as a control mechanism, allowing the registered dietitian and patient to review the diet for appropriateness and compliance. Problems with weight loss and poor diet tolerance may be decreased with scheduled home care appointments. For the nonambulatory patient, regular follow-up by telephone or home visits should be arranged.

Table 4-2 Some Drugs That Impair Utilization of Vitamins and Minerals

Drugs	Vitamins	Minerals	Drugs	Vitamins	Minerals
Alcohol	Thiamine	Magnesium	Isoniazid	Pyridoxine	Iron
	Pyridoxine	Zinc		Vitamin B$_{12}$	
	Vitamin B$_{12}$			Niacin	
	Folacin		Levodopa	Pyridoxine	Sodium
Aluminum hydroxide	Vitamin A	Phosphorus		Vitamin C	Potassium
(antacid)	Vitamin D		Methotrexate	Vitamin B$_{12}$	
Anticonvulsants	Pyridoxine	Calcium		Folacin	
	Vitamin B$_{12}$	Magnesium	Mineral oil	Vitamin A	Calcium
	Folacin			Vitamin D	Phosphorus
	Vitamin C			Vitamin E	
	Vitamin D			Vitamin K	
	Vitamin K		Neomycin	Vitamin B$_{12}$	Calcium
Cathartics	Vitamin D	Calcium		Folacin	Iron
		Potassium		Vitamin A	Sodium
Cholestyramine	Vitamin B$_{12}$	Calcium		Vitamin D	Potassium
	Folacin	Iron		Vitamin E	
	Vitamin A			Vitamin K	
	Vitamin D		Penicillamine	Pyridoxine	Iron
	Vitamin K				Copper
	Vitamin E				Zinc
Clofibrate	Vitamin B$_{12}$	Iron	Prednisone	Folacin	Calcium
Colchicine	Vitamin B$_{12}$	Sodium		Vitamin C	
	Folacin	Potassium		Vitamin K	
Corticosteroids	Pyridoxine	Calcium	Probenecid		Calcium
	Folacin	Zinc			Magnesium
	Vitamin C	Potassium			Sodium
	Vitamin D	Phosphorus			Potassium
Coumarin	Vitamin K				Phosphorus
Digitalis	Thiamine	Calcium	Salicylates	Thiamine	Iron
		Magnesium			Potassium
		Potassium	Sulfasalazine	Folacin	Iron
Estrogen	Thiamine	Magnesium	Tetracycline	Riboflavin	Calcium
	Riboflavin	Zinc		Folacin	Magnesium
	Pyridoxine			Niacin	Iron
	Vitamin B$_{12}$			Vitamin C	Zinc
	Folacin			Vitamin K	
	Vitamin C		Thiazides	Riboflavin	Calcium
Ethacrynic acid		Calcium			Magnesium
		Magnesium			Zinc
		Potassium			Sodium
Furosemide	Thiamine	Calcium			Potassium
	Pyridoxine	Magnesium	Thyroxine	Riboflavin	
		Zinc	Triamterene	Vitamin B$_{12}$	Calcium
		Sodium		Folacin	Sodium
		Potassium			

Source: Reprinted with permission of Ross Laboratories, Columbus, OH, 43216, from *Nutrition in Long Term Care*, p. 9, © 1987 Ross Laboratories.

The periodic collection of objective data is essential to provide appropriate and continued nutrition support. It also has other benefits. We have found that readily available objective data can help in obtaining reimbursement for services and products from third-party payers.

EVALUATION OF THE HOME

Availability of space for food storage, cleanliness of the kitchen and home, availability of a refrigerator and other kitchen equipment for food preparation, and the presence of a significant other to assist with food purchasing, shopping, and preparation should be evaluated by the registered dietitian and the social worker.

Instructions provided to patients should emphasize general cleanliness and proper food and formula storage. The following are guidelines for formula storage.

- Store canned and packaged goods at room temperature before opening.
- Refrigerate contents after opening.
- Discard any open products not used within 24 hours of opening.
- Check expiration dates on all products for shelf life.

COMMERCIAL FORMULAS

Patients may require modifications in nutrient composition and form as a result of disease states and gastrointestinal function. Commercially available enteral formulas are used often to supplement an oral diet, or as a meal replacement when solid foods are not well tolerated or when nutrient needs cannot be fully met by foods alone.

Formulas available range from meal replacement formulas containing intact carbohydrate, protein, fat, and vitamins and minerals to elemental diets, formulas for renal and liver disease, and modules that contain a protein, a carbohydrate, or a fat component to supplement specific nutrient needs. Formula palatability ranges from bland to sweet and is often dependent on the taste acuity of the patient. Many formulas are available in a variety of flavors. Modules in particular may benefit the home patient. Fat and carbohydrate modules can be incorporated readily into most home foods and fluids without increasing volume. Protein modules can be added to fluids.

When determining appropriate oral supplements for the patient at home, cost is an important factor. The registered dietitian should be familiar with product costs in the retail market. Patients should be advised to look for stores that periodically have sales on supplements, as well as price wars, and to purchase products in bulk if finances and storage space permit. Food stamp recipients may purchase selected products in supermarkets. Pharmaceutical companies may be willing to work out payment schedules for persons with limited financial resources. In some areas of the country there are formula banks for financially disadvantaged patients. The banks are developed by obtaining donations of products from patients and families who no longer need the products. Many patients are happy to donate supplies they are unable to use and cannot return. Local representatives of pharmaceutical companies and hospital social service departments may be familiar with area formula banks when they are available in a community.

When finances do not allow for purchase of commercial products and charitable donations are not available, patients and families can be instructed to prepare homemade formulas for many of the meal replacement formulas and blenderized diets.

Medicare does not reimburse for oral supplements. Medicaid and certain other third-party payers may reimburse for oral supplements when a physician assigns a prescription number for the supplement.

CONSISTENCY AND NUTRIENT MODIFICATIONS

It is beyond the scope of this chapter to detail all potential modifications of the oral diet that may be needed. The two major categories are consistency modification and nutrient modification. Patient tolerance of individual foods, consistencies, and meal patterns, as well as the necessary macronutrient and micronutrient modifications, may change over time. The importance of continued follow-up and monitoring of the patient while he or she is on home nutrition support cannot be overemphasized. The registered dietitian needs to work with the continual change in needs of the patient and assist the patient and significant others in adjusting meal patterns and diet to meet those needs. Commercial supplements may not always be required to boost calorie and protein intake. A high-calorie, high-protein diet may be achieved without using supplements by incorporating multiple small meals.

Consistency modifications range from simply cutting or chopping foods into appropriate size pieces to providing purees and blenderized foods, depending on the patient's ability to chew and swallow. Chewing may be altered by poor-fitting or lack of dentures, oral surgery, or gum disease, or because effects of chemotherapy or radiation therapy have altered the oral environment. Swallowing difficulties may occur as a result of progressive or intermittent dysphagia (or both) or chemotherapy or radiation therapy. Essential components of all consistency-modified diets include adequate calories, protein, and other macronutrients and micronutrients to meet established needs, as well as adequate fluid and sufficient fiber to avoid constipation. Visual and taste appeal are important in planning these diets. Patients and caregivers need instructions on the proper way to make consistency modifications and in planning menus and meals that have a variety of colors, tastes, and flavors to stimulate and enhance the patient's appetite.

TYPES OF DIETS

Blenderized Oral Diet

Blenderized oral diets may be needed for patients whose oral environment has been modified (e.g., the patient with wired jaws), or when disease or disability compromise the ability to chew or swallow solids. Commercially available blenderized diets are nutritionally adequate but lack appeal in appearance, palatability, and variety.

Nutritional adequacy can be achieved with regular table foods or a combination of table foods and formulas. Sufficient fiber should be incorporated into the diet to prevent constipation. Fiber sources include fruits and vegetables (blenderizing changes the form but not the amount of fiber), whole wheat products, and grains. Almost any food can be incorporated into the blenderized diet. All foods, however, should be blended, strained, and thinned to an appropriate consistency before serving

Bacterial contamination is a major concern with the use of homemade blenderized diets. Raw eggs should not be used. The preparation area and utensils should be clean and free from rust. All foods should be refrigerated after preparation if they are not going to be used immediately. Foods can then be reheated before serving. Recipe resources for blenderized diets, as well as other diets, are listed in Exhibit 4-4.

Soft or Mechanical Soft Diets

Consistency modifications for soft or mechanical soft diets may be transitional for persons advancing from a liquid diet or tube feeding. They can be used for those patients who need pureed, minced, or soft foods because of head and neck trauma from radiation therapy, surgery, or accidents and those with an inability to chew or swallow well. The diet can be nutritionally complete without the use of commercial formulas. A blender or food processor can be used to prepare regular table foods at the desired consistency. Juices and broth can be used to thin and flavor foods.

Exhibit 4-4 List of Commercially Available Recipe Booklets

American Diabetes Association and American Dietetic Association, *Family Cookbook, Volume II* (Englewood Cliffs, N.J.: Prentice-Hall, 1984).
American Heart Association, *The American Heart Association Cookbook* (New York: Random House, 1984).
Jane E. Brody, *Jane Brody's Good Food Book* (Englewood Cliffs, N.J.: W.W. Norton, 1985).
Michael E. DeBakey, *The Living Heart Diet* (New York: Raven Press, 1984).
Diet and Nutrition (Bethesda, Md.: U.S. Department of Health, Education and Welfare, National Institutes of Health, 1979).
Diet for a Healthy Heart (East Hanover, N.J.: Nabisco Brands, 1985).
Eating Hints: Recipes and Tips for Better Nutrition During Cancer Treatment (Bethesda, Md.: U.S. Department of Health and Human Services, National Institutes of Health, 1984).
Eating Well with Pulmonary Disease (Columbus, Ohio: Ross Laboratories, 1986).
Nutrition: An Ally in Cancer Therapy (Columbus, Ohio: Ross Laboratories, 1985).
Taste-Tempting Recipes To Improve Nutrition (Columbus, Ohio: Ross Laboratories, 1987).
J. Randy Wilson, *Non-Chew Cookbook* (J. Randy Wilson, 1985).

Liquid Diets

Clear-fluid diets are rarely used in the home. They provide minimal calories and protein and contain primarily electrolytes and some carbohydrate. The clear-fluid diet may be used temporarily when patients experience severe nausea and vomiting for a day.

Full-liquid diets usually are used in the home as a transition from a tube feeding to a solid diet or during periods of dysphagia. Patients who have had head and neck surgery or those with esophageal cancer may benefit from full liquids, especially while undergoing radiation to the head and neck area, which may compromise swallowing. The diet is usually milk based and includes cereals, juices, strained cereals, eggs, and custard-type products. Commercially available oral supplements can be incorporated into this diet. Nutritional adequacy can be achieved with careful planning to meet individual calorie and protein needs and the Recommended Daily Allowances for vitamins and minerals. Because of the high lactose content of this diet persons with known or suspected lactose intolerance may exhibit bloating, cramping, and diarrhea. Elderly persons, many of whom are not milk drinkers, and persons of African, Afro-American, American Indian, Mediterranean, or Jewish heritage are known to be at high risk for lactose intolerance. Lactose-reduced or soy-based formulas can be substituted to achieve adequate nutrition for persons with lactose intolerance. Tofu (soy) drinks, puddings, and ice creams can also be used. Fiber-supplemented formulas also are available.

Low-Fiber/High-Fiber Diets

A low-fiber diet may be needed for persons with radiation enteritis. It also may be used as a transitional diet for patients with new colostomies or ileostomies. Patients should be counseled to avoid any foods they find offensive, regardless of the fiber content.

A high-fiber diet (25-30 grams of dietary fiber) may be useful when medication, bedrest and inactivity, or disease (or all of these) cause constipation. Often the combination of bed rest, which leads to inactivity, and poor diet causes constipation, which may only further reduce appetite. Elderly persons are more prone to constipation. Adequate fluid intake (more than two quarts per day) is important, along with gradually increasing fiber in the diet. Dietary fiber should come from a variety of sources, including fruits, vegetables, and grain or bread products. Fiber-enriched oral supplements are available.

Low-Lactose Diet

As previously discussed, lactose intolerance may have resulted primarily or secondarily from abdominal radiation therapy, disease, or malnutrition. It may be pre-existing or arise in a patient who is at risk for intolerance after the introduction of a high-lactose diet.

Milk, milk products, and food prepared with milk products should be avoided. Lactose-reduced milk and cheese products, soy drinks, and tofu products can be substituted with equal or greater caloric and protein density. In addition, most of the commercial meal replacement supplements offer another lactose free, but expensive alternative.

Diets To Restrict Specific Nutrients

Sodium-, potassium-, cholesterol-, or fat-restricted diets are used for a variety of chronic diseases or are needed after surgery. The appropriateness of the type and degree of restriction should be determined for the home patient by the registered dietitian and the physician. In patients whose intake may already be compromised by nausea and anorexia, additional restrictions may further reduce intake. When the nutrient restriction is essential to prevent potentially life-threatening conditions or further problems, it cannot be avoided. The registered dietitian is responsible for working with the patient and significant others to assist in incorporating restrictions into the diet, helping plan menus, working to develop supplements that are in accordance with restrictions, and providing additional help as needed. As mentioned earlier, special diet recipe booklets are available and can provide appealing menu alternatives (see Exhibit 4-4).

Diets for the Diabetic Patient

The American Dietetic Association and the American Diabetic Association have developed exchange lists that can be used for and by the patient with diabetes mellitus.[4] They also have developed *Guidelines for Healthy Eating,*[5] which is a simplified diet without the exchange groups, as an alternative. The registered dietitian and physician should work together to prioritize the need for the diabetic diet for chronically ill patients or for any patient on home nutrition support who may already be consuming a restricted diet because of anorexia. A no-concentrated-sweet diet, which is not based on exchanges but simply avoids sweets and added sugar, may be appropriate for the chronically ill patient at home as an alternative to achieve a more desirable level of nutrient intake. The diet should be individually tailored by the registered dietitian on the basis of nutrient needs with the desired goal of achieving adequate nutrient intake and not exacerbating hyperglycemia.

High-Calorie, High-Protein Diet

The high-calorie, high-protein diet provides for nutrition repletion of the malnourished patient and prevents weight loss and tissue wasting in conditions in which calories and protein requirements are increased. The diet is frequently used at home for the postoperative patient or the patient with cancer. A diet of small, frequent, calorically dense meals should be tried first before oral supplements are added. Commercial meal replacement formulas or modules, however, may be necessary to achieve estimated nutrient needs.

Low-Fat Diet

A low-fat diet is used to treat steatorrhea in disorders that interfere with fat digestion, absorption, or transport. In patients with pancreatitis a fat-restricted diet is used in conjunction with enzyme replacement therapy to control steatorrhea and losses of fat-soluble vitamins. Medium-chain triglyceride oil can be used to increase fat calorie intake. The diet can be nutritionally adequate when fat calories are replaced with additional carbohydrate, protein, or medium-chain triglyceride (or with all three) calories to meet estimated needs and fat intake is sufficient to prevent an essential fatty acid deficiency. Minimal- and low-fat supplements can be prepared with modular ingredients, juice-type beverages, and skim milk if lactose is tolerated.

GENERAL DIETARY GUIDELINES

Detailed verbal and written guidelines should be provided to the patient and significant others before discharge. Instruction should begin as early as possible before discharge to allow adequate time for teaching, assessment of knowledge, questions, and review. Short- and long-term goals should be established and nutrient requirements should be determined. Variables in eating that may contribute to nutrition depletion or repletion (or both) should be reviewed with the patient and significant others. The rationale for the specific diet; an individualized meal plan, including portion sizes and a sample meal plan; and suggested recipes or preparation tips will give structure and shape to the diet plan for home. Commercial formulas should be included as needed, with consideration for patient finances and product availability. Patients should be able to taste-test products in the hospital before discharge to determine favored brands and flavors.

The registered dietitian should try to be creative to stimulate and motivate persons involved with food preparation at home. A communication network should be established to deal with postdischarge problems, questions, or concerns for the patient or significant other.

Patient documentation at home should be discussed before discharge. The patient or significant others (or both) should be instructed on the importance of and how to keep a food diary, when to do weight checks, and the need to alert the dietitian and physician of any dramatic changes in intake, tolerance, and weight. The first postdischarge visit should be scheduled before discharge.

Guidelines for the patient and significant others regarding oral nutrition at home are important. Compliance with these guidelines will provide support for the patient through the "rough times" and help to achieve the best possible intake. Exhibit 4-5 provides an example.

For the elderly patient at home, the old adage, "a little bit of what you fancy," is the best advice, with emphasis on mealtimes and balancing the diet. Often, overemphasis of diet modifications can discourage elderly patients from eating. The necessity of diet modifications should be reviewed by the physician and the registered dietitian.

The registered dietitian is vital to the optimal nutrition management of the patient receiving oral nutrition support at home. Education, follow-up, and continuous monitoring of patient and significant other are essential to provide optimal nourishment and promote nutrition repletion. The importance of a closely managed, registered dietitian–based home care oral nutrition program should be emphasized to health care team members and home care company providers.

Exhibit 4-5 Sample Guidelines for a Patient Requiring Oral Nutrition Support

1. Eat small meals and eat more frequently than three times a day. Small meals are digested more readily, decrease gastrointestinal distress, decrease the possibility of cardiac overload, and are less overwhelming psychologically.

2. Include a protein source at each feeding to assist in meeting daily protein requirements.

3. Have a significant other prepare foods if you fatigue easily. Prepare them in advance, when feeling stronger, if you live alone.

4. Try preparing finger foods. They are small, create less waste, and do not require utensils.

5. Take advantage of times when hunger prevails and eat.

6. Keep open minded about trying new and different recipes. Use recipe booklets provided by registered dietitian.

7. Eat in a positive atmosphere; at a favorite table, for example, and with family or friends when possible.

8. Make use of kitchen convenience appliances such as blenders, microwave ovens, food processors (see Exhibit 4-6).

9. Give different foods a chance. Foods that sound unappealing or that you disliked may taste differently now because of changes in taste acuity. Avoid foods that do not taste as they did before you became ill, and substitute other food choices. Taste aversions occur with chronically reduced nutrient intake and with chemotherapy and radiation therapy.

10. Consider joining a food club or participating with Meals on Wheels. Social contact can be enjoyable and increase interest in eating.

Exhibit 4-6 Helpful Kitchen Appliances

Blender:

Very important and useful for soft and liquid food preparation. A simple inexpensive model with three speeds is good enough to mix, blend or make liquid most foods. Easy to use and clean and takes little counter space.

Electric frying pan:

Versatile, helpful time and energy saver. It simplifies meal preparation for the single person or small family. Can warm, fry, simmer and bake. Some newer models even have a broiler in the lid. Usually lightweight, it takes up little space and is easy to clean.

Steamer:

Inexpensive. Fits into existing pot. Does not overcook food. Makes food more attractive without loss of minerals and vitamins.

Pressure cooker:

Can be used to steam, soften or tenderize any amount of food in a short period of time. Somewhat noisy. Use a timer to insure proper cooking for there is a tendency to overcook. Takes practice to operate correctly. Heavy but cleans easily.

Toaster-broiler oven:

Valuable for any size family, as it warms, toasts, broils, and bakes. Comes in many different models and sizes. Requires some counterspace, is lightweight and relatively easy to clean.

Electric crockpot:

Makes soft, simmered food. Useful for "no fuss" soup, stews and similar cooking. Look for one that handles and cleans easily.

Food processor:

It can chop, slice, shred, blend, and puree foods as well as mix batters for baking. Takes some practice to operate correctly, but it is easily cleaned and stored. Can be an expensive appliance, depending on manufacturer.

Microwave oven:

Expensive. Time and energy saver as defrosting and cooking time is much faster. Paper, plastic or glassware can be used for cooking and eating. Cleaning is minimal.

Dishwasher:

Expensive but great energy saver for everyone, even the single person. Smaller machine with one or two cycles is adequate.

Source: Reprinted from *Eating Hints: Recipes and Tips for Better Nutrition During Cancer Treatment*, pp. 31-32. U.S. Department of Health and Human Services, National Cancer Institute, Bethesda, Maryland 1984.

NOTES

1. Calvin Long et al., "Metabolic Response to Injury and Illness: Estimation of Energy and Protein Needs from Indirect Calorimetry and Nitrogen Balance," *Journal of Parenteral and Enteral Nutrition* 3 (1979): 452–456.

2. Annalynn Skipper, "Transitional Feeding and the Dietitian," *Nutritional Support Services* 2 (1982): 45–46.

3. *Suggested Guidelines for Nutrition Management of the Critically Ill Patient* (Chicago, Ill.: American Dietetic Association, 1986), 76.

4. *Exchange Lists for Meal Planning* (Chicago, Ill.: American Diabetes Association, American Dietetic Association, 1986).

5. *Guidelines for Healthy Eating* (Chicago, Ill.: American Diabetes Association and American Dietetic Association, 1986).

BIBLIOGRAPHY

Diet and Nutrition: A Resource for Parents of Children with Cancer. Bethesda, Md.: U.S. Department of Health, Education and Welfare, National Institutes of Health, 1979.

Eating Hints: Recipes and Tips for Better Nutrition During Cancer Treatment. Bethesda, Md., U.S. Department of Health and Human Services, National Institutes of Health, 1984.

Exchange Lists for Meal Planning. Chicago, Ill.: American Diabetes Association and American Dietetic Association, 1986.

Handbook of Clinical Dietetics. New Haven, Conn.: Yale University, 1981.

Krey, Susanna H., and Rebecca L. Murray. *Dynamics of Nutrition Support: Assessment, Implementation, Evaluation.* Norwalk, Conn.: Appleton-Century-Crofts, 1986, 361–71.

Long, Calvin, N. Schaffel, J. Geiger, W.R. Schiller, and W.S. Blackmore. "Metabolic Response to Injury and Illness: Estimation of Energy and Protein Needs from Indirect Calorimetry and Nitrogen Balance." *Journal of Parenteral and Enteral Nutrition* 3 (1979): 452.

Rombeau, John L., and Michael D. Caldwell. *Enteral and Tube Feeding.* Philadelphia, Pa.: W.B. Saunders Co., 1984.

Schneider, Howard A., Carl E. Anderson, and David B. Coursin. *Nutritional Support of Medical Practice.* 2nd ed. Philadelphia, Pa.: Harper & Row, 1983, 382–84.

Skipper, Annalynn. "Transitional Feeding and the Dietitian." *Nutritional Support Services* 2 (1982): 45.

Suggested Guidelines for Nutrition Management of the Critically Ill Patient. Chicago, Ill.: American Dietetic Association, 1986.

Chapter 5

Enteral Nutrition Management

Susan W. Cooning, Maureen E. Laflam, and Carol E. Lang

INTRODUCTION

Enteral feeding has become an increasingly more common method of providing home nutrition support. With increased medical costs, there has been a trend toward shorter hospital stays and extended outpatient convalescence and nutrition rehabilitation. Many of the inpatient enteral techniques and equipment, including cyclic feeding and sophisticated pumps, have been modified for home use.

Criteria for Patient Selection

Tube feeding on an outpatient basis is an option for patients with treatable or controllable disorders. It allows these patients to maintain an adequate quality of life at home. In addition, it may be appropriate for the critically or terminally ill patient, for whom parenteral feeding may be inappropriate and costly. General indications for home tube feeding are listed in Exhibit 5-1 and Table 5-1.

Psychosocial Issues

Tube feeding may involve a significant adjustment in role function and interdependent relations.[1] In addition thirst, taste deprivation, and an unsatisfied appetite for favorite foods are commonly associated with tube feeding.[2] To compensate for some of the negative features social aspects of mealtime can be maintained by encouraging patients to participate, such as by sitting at the table with family members. If oral intake is feasible, patients should be encouraged to consume foods as desired and to view tube feeding as nutrition "insurance." (The psychosocial issues that home nutrition support patients face are discussed in detail in Chapter 9.)

Exhibit 5-1 Clinical Indications and Contraindications for Home Tube Feeding

---

Indications

Physiologic ability to absorb nutrients from the gastrointestinal tract but inability to consume a nutritionally adequate diet by mouth

Absence of other medical conditions that would necessitate continued hospitalization

Compromised nutritional status as a result of an underlying disease process or a medical or surgical intervention (or both)

Continued need for tube feeding for three to four weeks or longer

Contraindications

Evidence of bowel obstruction or ileus

Severe diarrhea

Severe malabsorption or maldigestion

ASSESSMENT OF NUTRITION NEEDS

Nutrition Requirements

Nutrition assessment of the home patient differs little from that of the inpatient. Patients on feedings in the hospital should be evaluated fully before discharge to establish baseline values for monitoring progress. Patients who begin feedings in the home should be evaluated comprehensively in an outpatient clinic. Nutrient recommendations are based on knowledge of nutrition status, including pre-existing deficiencies and current requirements related to clinical status.

The tube feeding must be nutritionally adequate because the patient may require enteral support for an extended period. Reassessment of all nutrient needs is essential and requires the development of an ongoing monitoring system to ensure adequacy of the nutrition support provided.

Table 5-1 Diseases or Disorders For Which Home Tube Feeding Is Potentially Appropriate

Disease/Disorder	Examples
Gastrointestinal diseases	Short-bowel syndrome, inflammatory bowel disease
Cancer	Obstructive diseases, terminal supportive care
Neurologic conditions	Cerebrovascular accidents, head injuries
Psychologic disorders	Anorexia nervosa, chronic depression
Systemic disorders	Chronic renal, cardiac, or liver disease

Fluid

Fluid requirements vary from patient to patient. Medical conditions (e.g., fever, renal disease, diarrhea, and gastrointestinal fistulas), as well as normal fluid losses (insensible water loss, excretion in urine and feces), may lead to a fluid imbalance, with potential sequelae if uncompensated. Dehydration and hyperosmolar diuresis or diarrhea can be life threatening in the comatose or severely debilitated patient, because these persons are unable to consume additional water voluntarily or signal that they are thirsty.

There are several guidelines for determining water requirements. Ideal body weight can be used in calculations for the obese patient; actual weight is used for others. Most adults will require 35 ml/kg/day. Elderly persons generally require 25 ml/kg/day, and younger, active adults may need up to 40 ml/kg/day.[3]

Enteral formula volume should not be equated with free water. Products with caloric densities of 1.5 cal/ml or less are 80 to 90 percent free water; those with greater densities are approximately 60 percent free water. Enteral products providing 1 cal/ml generally are recommended for patients who are unable to report thirst or achieve adequate water intake voluntarily.

Hydration status can be monitored at home by measuring intake and output, evaluating urine frequency and color, monitoring weight, and checking the patient for dry skin and mucous membranes and altered skin turgor. If the enteral product does not meet estimated fluid requirements, it can be diluted, or water can be added directly to the feeding tube after each feeding or periodically during the day.

Electrolytes

Electrolyte imbalances may result from insufficient or excessive formula delivery or incorrect nutrient administration. In the absence of abnormal losses, kidney dysfunction, dehydration, or pre-existing salt depletion, the average adult requires approximately 75 milliequivalents of sodium and 80 milliequivalents of potassium per day.[4] Estimated safe and adequate intakes for chloride are 48 to 144 milliequivalents per day.[5] The electrolyte content of enteral products should be reviewed in light of patient needs, especially in clinical states that predispose the patient to imbalances.

Energy

Predicting and calculating energy needs are often difficult. Inpatients may be evaluated by direct or indirect calorimetry during their hospital stay.

Approximations often are necessary when dealing with the outpatient. Exhibit 5-2 summarizes the use of the Harris-Benedict equation to predict caloric expenditure.

The mechanisms that human beings use normally to regulate food intake and maintain body weight over time are bypassed with tube feeding. The possibility of overfeeding is great, and even a relatively small excess of energy (calories) over a period of several months will lead to a steady gain in weight. Equally possible is underfeeding, in which slightly inadequate intake over an extended period may result in a steady weight loss, which may increase the risk of morbidity and mortality.

Macronutrients

Carbohydrate

A minimum of 100 to 150 grams of carbohydrate should be provided daily to facilitate protein sparing and avoid ketogenesis.[6] The type and amount are necessary considerations when determining carbohydrate requirements.

Protein

Protein requirements vary with age and state of health. Quantity and quality of protein are the two main concerns, because a full complement of amino acids, provided in the appropriate proportions, is required for protein synthesis. A food or formula containing at least 40 percent of its amino acids as essential amino acids is considered to be of high biologic value.

The following is a guide to estimate protein needs.[7]

Status	Estimated Requirements
Normal, average activity	0.8 to 1.0 gm/kg/day
Moderately stressed	1.0 to 2.0 gm/kg/day

Exhibit 5-2 Energy Expenditure Equations

Basal energy expenditure (BEE) =
  66.47 + 13.75W + 5.0H − 6.76A (men)
  665.1 + 9.56W + 1.85H − 4.68A (women)
  where W = weight (in kilograms)
        H = height (in centimeters)
        A = age (in years)
BEE × Activity Factor = Total Energy Expenditure. Activity factors: 1.2 bedridden patient, 1.3 ambulatory

Alternatively, 16 to 20 percent of total calories can be provided as protein.[8] The protein needs of most stable patients on home enteral nutrition programs can be met with 0.8 to 1.0 gm/kg/day. Periodic reassessments of nutrient needs are necessary to ensure adequate intake over time.

Fat

The estimated requirement for essential fatty acids, specifically linoleic acid, is approximately 3 to 4 percent of total calories. Essential fatty acid deficiencies are unlikely to occur in patients on enteral formulas because most contain vegetable oils.[9]

As a source of fat calories, medium-chain triglycerides are beneficial because they are absorbed easily. They are often well tolerated by patients with short-bowel syndrome, inadequate absorptive surface, pancreatic or biliary insufficiency, bowel disease, enteritis, or bacterial overgrowth. Medium-chain triglycerides, however, do not provide essential fatty acids. Enteral formulas with both long-chain and medium-chain triglycerides provide essential fatty acids and retain the ease of absorption provided by medium-chain triglycerides. In specialized formulas (e.g., low-fat formulas or those that contain medium-chain triglycerides only) care should be taken to ensure that adequate essential fatty acids are provided.

Micronutrients

Vitamin and mineral status should be evaluated before the patient begins a home enteral program. Although most formulas supply 100 percent of the recommended dietary allowances in 1,500 to 2,000 milliliters, a vitamin and mineral elixir may be necessary if the patient is receiving a dilute formula or quantities less than 1,500 milliliters daily. Therapeutic doses of vitamins should be considered if the patient demonstrates increased needs or a suspected vitamin deficiency.

ENTERAL PRODUCT SELECTION

General Considerations

Results of the nutrition assessment and clinical status of the patient will dictate the selection of an enteral product. Ideally, the product will provide adequate nutrients in a well-tolerated form and volume. Characteristics such as osmolality, viscosity, nutrient adequacy, cost, and convenience are important considerations. Gastrointestinal tract function, administration route, and patient history of food intolerance should not be overlooked.

Regardless of product type, nutrition requirements are the most important determinants of formula selection.

Convenience of preparation and cost are important. Questions to be considered include

- Is the patient or caregiver able to mix or dilute a formula if necessary?
- Is a refrigerator and storage space available?
- Is preparation space adequate?
- Will formula costs be reimbursed through the patient's insurance?
- What lower cost products are available for those who have to pay on their own?

The disease process may influence not only the patient's nutrition requirements but also the ability to digest and absorb nutrients. Products containing intact nutrients generally are well tolerated when the gastrointestinal tract is functional. Patients with malabsorption or short-gut syndrome may require an elemental or predigested product.

The effects of nutrient composition and physical characteristics on patient tolerance may be difficult to predict in certain patients. For example, pancreatic insufficiency may necessitate the use of a low-fat formula. The selected product, however, may be hypertonic and thus poorly tolerated in patients sensitive to changes in osmolality. Therefore product selection requires prioritizing the requirements dictated by disease within the constraints of individual needs and tolerances.

Types of Enteral Products

A summary of enteral nutrition products appears in the chart supplied by Sherwood Medical.*

Intact-Nutrient Formulas

Standard Tube Feedings. Standard tube feedings are used in patients without unusual nutrient needs. Generally, they are ready to use, provide 1 kcal/ml of energy, and are lactose free. They are composed of complex and simple carbohydrates, intact proteins, and long-chain or medium-chain triglycerides (or both). The unflavored products tend to have a low osmolality and viscosity, which promotes tolerance and easy flow through the narrow lumen of the feeding tube. Vitamin, mineral, and fluid needs usually can be met in 1,500 to 2,000 milliliters of formula.

Calorically-Dense Formulas. Calorically-dense products are concentrated to provide more calories, 1.5 to 2.0 kcal/ml, in less volume. Pro-

---

*See enclosure. *Source*: Sherwood Medical, St. Louis, Missouri. © 1989 Sherwood Medical.

portionately, their nutrition composition is similar to that of standard formulas. Patients who benefit from concentrated feedings include those with fluid restrictions, an intermittent or shortened infusion schedule, increased caloric needs, or the ability to take in additional fluids by mouth or tube. Hydration status should be monitored closely by noting changes in body weight and fluid imbalances to help prevent dehydration or overfeeding.

Milk-Based Products

Lactose-containing products may be appropriate for home enteral feeding because of their low cost and availability in food markets and drugstores. These products can be used only if the patient has a functional gastrointestinal tract, and symptoms of bloating, cramping, and diarrhea may be indicative of lactose intolerance. If symptoms occur after introduction of a milk-based product, lactose-reduced milk or a lactose-free product should be substituted.

Blenderized Food Products

For psychosocial reasons, patients may prefer to prepare a tube feeding from table foods. The patient should be given a recipe to follow and be instructed in formula preparation and storage, so that nutrition needs will be met. Careful attention to preparation and storage also is necessary to prevent bacterial contamination. A large-bore feeding tube may be required to minimize clogging. Commercial products also are available and usually are less viscous than blenderized foods prepared in the home, allowing easier flow through the narrow-lumen feeding tube.

Homemade or commercial blenderized formulas may provide trace nutrients as yet unidentified. Dietary fiber in these products may help prevent constipation and fecal impaction, common complications of long-term tube feeding.[10]

Specialized Products

Fiber-Containing Formulas. In addition to those products in which fiber is supplied through the natural food sources in the formula, commercial products are available to which a fiber source has been added. Patients on long-term enteral nutrition support who have normal digestive and absorptive capabilities may benefit from these products, because they may minimize the occurrence of both diarrhea and constipation. The patient with diabetes mellitus may benefit because of the role of fiber in improving glucose tolerance and slowing gastric emptying.[11]

Formulas for Patients with Renal Failure. Products used for patients with renal failure contain a high proportion of essential amino acids and minimal amounts of nonessential amino acids. Their caloric density ranges from 0.7 to 2.0 kcal/ml. Home patients receiving renal formulas must be monitored closely because these products have a high osmolality and low concentrations of several electrolytes, vitamins, and minerals.

Formulas for Patients with Hepatic Failure. Products used for patients with hepatic failure provide comparatively higher levels of branched-chain, and lower levels of aromatic, amino acids than standard formulas. Like renal formulas, they have a high osmolality and are nutritionally inadequate.

Elemental and Predigested Formulas

Patients with impaired digestive and absorptive capabilities or severe malnutrition, as well as those on bowel rest, require chemically-defined elemental formulas. These products need minimal digestion and decrease secretions into the gastrointestinal tract. They are low residue and lactose free, provide 1 kcal/ml of energy, and meet the recommended dietary allowances in 1,500 to 2,000 milliliters. Protein is in the form of free amino acids or peptides (or both). The high solute and carbohydrate loads in the formulas increase osmolality and may cause diarrhea and glucose intolerance. They contain very little fat, generally 1 to 12 percent of total calories, as medium-chain triglycerides and essential fatty acids. Small amounts of an essential fatty acid-containing oil may be added as tolerated if essential fatty acid needs are not met by the formula alone. Disadvantages of this formula category include cost and high osmolality.

Modulars

A module comprises single or multiple nutrients—protein, fat, carbohydrate, vitamins, and minerals—that can be combined to produce a nutritionally complete feeding or used individually to enhance an existing product. With this type of enteral product the dietitian requires a sophisticated knowledge of the effects of osmolality, caloric density, nutrient composition, and undesired nutrient interactions. Extensive patient or caregiver education on recipe preparation is essential.

PREPARATION AND STORAGE
OF ENTERAL PRODUCTS

Before discharge from the hospital, the patient or caregiver should be instructed on formula preparation and storage, including

- hand washing before preparation
- evaluation of product usability (i.e., recognizing damaged products and avoiding the use of opened or dented containers)

- proper cleansing of cans and can openers
- interpretation of expiration dates
- safe storage times and temperatures
- maximum hang-times
- use of common household measures in recipes for home use (cups rather than milliliters and teaspoons rather than grams), with approximate equivalents calculated in advance by the dietitian
- availability of suitable mixing equipment
- recipe review with validation of understanding (i.e., patient or caregiver able to repeat instruction in their own words)
- guidelines for adding medication, if necessary, and flushing tubes

Recipes for reconstituting powdered products should include the volumes of water for mixing and of the final formula, expressed in common household measures. Rounding off or approximating may be necessary to facilitate measurement. Use of household measures may cause slight variance in product density, but may be necessary in providing instructions for the home setting. Recipe adjustments should be as small as possible and weighed carefully against the patient's condition and tolerances.

Recipes for adding modulars to commercially available products should be stated in terms of formula unit volume. For example, if 8 ounces of tube feeding are used, the patient can be instructed to add a given number of teaspoons of a powdered module to each 8 ounces of formula. This instruction method minimizes confusion and error.

Custom-designed tube feedings that utilize all modular components must be used with great caution in the home. Confusion surrounding the numerous additives and measurements may lead to serious consequences, such as fluid and electrolyte imbalances. Inadvertent omissions of key modular components may not only cause these complications but also create nutrient deficiencies. Success depends on a physically and intellectually capable patient or caregiver, a well-defined recipe, adequate instruction, and ongoing monitoring by health care professionals to ensure proper product preparation and tolerance.

As mentioned previously blenderized products can be prepared in a safe, sanitary and nutritionally complete manner in the home. Types of fluids to be used to dilute pureed or blenderized foods should be defined, as should approximate quantities of foods and fluid volumes necessary to ensure adequate nutrition and hydration. Use of a liquid multivitamin supplement is often recommended with blenderized feedings because of the variability of nutrient density. It is useful to define easily blenderized sources of protein (other than eggs and milk) to ensure adequate protein intake and avoid a high-cholesterol, high-fat product. The four food groups can be used as a teaching tool to assist in ingredient selection.

MODALITIES FOR ENTERAL NUTRITION SUPPORT

Routes of Administration and Tube Selection

A variety of administration modalities are suitable for and encountered in home nutrition support. As an advantage over the parenteral route, enteral routes utilize the normal metabolic processes of the gut and maintain the function and integrity of the gastrointestinal system. In addition, nasogastric, nasoduodenal, and nasojejunal feedings are relatively non-invasive and benefit patients who require only short-term enteral nutrition support.

Factors to consider in tube selection include the amount of functioning gut and its absorptive capacity, the anticipated duration of enteral feeding, the type and viscosity of the enteral feeding, the volume of formula to be delivered, the administration rate, whether an infusion device will be used, and the patient's level of cooperation and comfort. In the alert and active home patient, cosmetic appearances also should be considered. Two common routes of administration are nasal tubes (temporary) and feeding ostomies.

Nasal Tubes (Temporary)

Tube Selection. Selecting the appropriate nasal tube can be an overwhelming task. Decisions regarding distal feeding site placement and tube length are based in part on the patient's underlying medical problems. Specific choices must be made:

- What material should the tube be made of?
- Is a bolus tip or stylet (or both) needed?
- What lumen size will best accommodate the formula and type of infusion?
- Should the tube remain in place, be inserted intermittently for feeding times, or be inserted only at night?

Nasal tubes are available in a variety of materials and sizes. The polyvinyl chloride tube is the least expensive. It can be reinserted easily and does not require a stylet for placement. Although this tube may be ideally suited for more viscous formulas, or for patients who insert their own tubes, its large bore and rigidness increase the risk of gastric reflux from reduced competency of the esophagogastric sphincter. Use of this tube also has been associated with esophageal fistula formation.

Use of pliable, small-bore, polyurethane or silastic transnasal tubes reduces the likelihood of mechanical complications. They are moderately to expensively priced and suitable for long-term feeding. Usually, they cannot be reinserted and used after removal. A bolus tip and stylet are included features. Prelubricated tubes facilitate insertion, and radiopaque tubes help in confirmation of proper placement. Despite these features, they still may be difficult to insert, and placement may be difficult to verify as well. Also, flow of more viscous formulas may be impeded. Mechanical complications of all transnasal tubes include dislocation after coughing and vomiting, obstruction, pharyngeal and mucosal irritation, otitis media, and discomfort.

Variations in tube length offer a number of advantages to the patient. The short nasogastric tube can be removed or clamped off between intermittent or bolus feedings. Thus the patient has more freedom and can lead a relatively normal life. Long nasoduodenal and nasojejunal tubes can be used to bypass a malfunctioning upper gastrointestinal tract and reduce the risk of reflux and aspiration.

Insertion Considerations. When inserting transnasal tubes in the home setting, the patient or caregiver must take special care with tubes that have stylets or weighted boluses. The stylet-guided tubes may inadvertently be positioned in the airway or may perforate the gastrointestinal tract during insertion. Weighted tips help prevent coiling and serve as an anchor for placement of nasoduodenal and nasojejunal tubes. Coughing or vomiting, however, can cause displacement of all types of tubes.

The home patient and caregiver must not become complacent in checking tube position. Regurgitation of the formula may occur if the tube is misplaced. Placement should be verified by aspirating gastric or intestinal contents with a syringe before every feeding. Because some of the small lumen tubes may collapse when aspiration is attempted, a second check with the use of the auscultation method is recommended. Nasoduodenal and nasojejunal tubes usually remain in place. Placement should be verified with x-ray films after initial insertion in the hospital.[12]

The features to look for in a home enteral tube can be summarized as follows.[13] The tube must

- be of small enough diameter (10 F or less) to avoid mucosal irritation, but be large enough to allow free flow of formula and resist twisting and kinking
- be made of a clear material to allow for monitoring of flow and to indicate when the tube is dirty
- be made of a flexible material such as silicone or polyurethane
- be available in a variety of sizes to accommodate individual patient needs
- have a smooth bolus to prevent trauma on insertion or removal

- have a stylet that is stable during insertion, well lubricated, and easy to remove (the stylet should be a flow-through type to allow for aspiration of gastric contents when checking for initial placement with the stylet still in place)
- have clear markings at designated lengths for measuring depth of tube insertion
- be radiopaque to verify placement
- have a weighted tip to prevent dislodgement after placement, particularly in transpyloric tubes (disposal of mercury tips requires special handling—incineration creates harmful vapors—but tungsten and silicone tips are nontoxic and require no special precautions)
- have distal feeding ports adequate in size and number to allow smooth infusion, facilitate aspiration through the tube, and avoid clogging
- adapt to the feeding system without modification

Feeding Ostomies

Feeding ostomies may be used when prolonged feeding is anticipated or transnasal formula administration is contraindicated. Gastrostomies and jejunostomies are the most common; esophagostomies have been associated with laryngeal nerve damage, fistula formation, and aspiration.[14]

Gastrostomies. Gastrostomies are indicated in patients with obstructive head, neck, or esophageal lesions, or with impaired swallowing as a result of a central nervous system disorder. Advantages of a standard gastrostomy include tube stability, a large lumen for medications and thicker formulas, and patient comfort. Disadvantages include the potential for aspiration, skin excoriation from leaking gastric secretions, peritonitis, bowel obstruction, and gastrocutaneous fistula formation.[15]

Two standard types of gastrostomy tubes are (1) the Malecot self-restraining tube with a basket-type end for holding the feeding tube in place and (2) the balloon-tip Foley catheter.[16] Some Foley-type tubes have a plastic disk that rests against the skin on the abdomen at the stoma site, which prevents tube migration and helps hold the internal balloon against the stomach wall. Patients and caregivers should measure the length of external tubing or mark the tube with tape or ink to maintain placement.

The percutaneous endoscopic gastrostomy tube is inserted nonsurgically with the aid of an endoscope or fluoroscope. In comparison with standard gastrostomy tubes, it is less expensive, reduces the length of hospitalization after insertion, and has been associated with few complications. Outpatient clinic visits are required for periodic medical check-ups and for catheter replacements if the tube clogs or cracks. Dislodgement of the feeding catheter may occur, but a well-formed tract remains open for approximately

24 hours, allowing reinsertion in an outpatient setting. As with the standard gastrostomy tube, aspiration and intraperitoneal leakage with tube dislodgement are potential complications.[17]

Jejunostomies. Jejunostomy tubes offer less risk than gastrostomies of gastric overload and aspiration. Indications for the jejunal route include obstructions of the stomach, duodenum, and proximal jejunum. Use of clean technique during jejunal formula administration is especially important to the home patient because the antimicrobial gastric secretions are bypassed with the use of this tube.[18] Jejunal tubes can migrate with bowel peristalsis, become plugged or dislodged, and have been associated with volvulus, diarrhea, and intraperitoneal leakage.[19]

The nonsurgical insertion of a needle catheter jejunostomy is a safer alternative to the standard procedure, but the small-bore tube used usually requires the use of elemental solutions administered by pump. Kinking or dislodgement can also occur with this tube.[20] Narrow jejunostomy tubes are prone to clogging but can be cleared at home with careful irrigation.

The surgically inserted K-tube catheter is large enough to facilitate flow of most commercial formulas. Tube placement is more stable through surgical attachment of silicone wings to the abdominal wall and a tunneled Dacron cuff.[21]

ADMINISTRATION TECHNIQUES AND FEEDING APPARATUS

Decisions regarding rate, volume, and frequency of administration depend on the patient's underlying medical problems, the enteral feeding site, and the type of formula. Selection of the appropriate container and feeding set for enteral use in turn depends on the type of feeding, as well as the viscosity of the formula, the feeding schedule, and whether a pump is needed. With the proliferation of home care companies, many types of feeding equipment are now available to ensure accuracy, minimize risk of contamination, and maintain affordability.

Bolus Administration

Typically, bolus feedings are administered directly into the feeding tube by means of a large syringe or funnel. Approximately 300 to 400 milliliters of formula must be provided over a short period of time and repeated four to six times per day to meet the patient's nutrient needs. Patients with head and neck cancer and other patients with relatively normal digestion and absorption usually tolerate bolus feedings well. It may be possible to begin a patient on intermittent or continuous feedings, transferring them to gravity feedings once they tolerate rapid infusion rates. Bolus administration is convenient for patients who desire minimal disruption of their work or school day. The potential side effects of bolus feeding include diarrhea, nausea, and vomiting, with the potential for aspiration, distention, and abdominal cramps.

Intermittent Feedings

With intermittent feedings many of the problems associated with bolus delivery methods are avoided. A portion of the gastric or jejunal feeding is delivered over at least 30 minutes and up to several hours by gravity drip or controlled pump infusion. This slower method more closely simulates gastric emptying, generally is better tolerated, and allows the home patient more freedom between feedings. Some home patients may be able to tolerate nocturnal feedings administered over 8 to 10 hours, leaving daytime hours free.

Intermittent feedings may be controlled by a gravity drip system. Gravity infusions are relatively inexpensive. They may cause aspiration, however, and are cost ineffective for patients who require around-the-clock feedings. During nocturnal feedings, the patient's movements and positioning may significantly slow or speed the gravity system.

Some patients have complex nutrition needs and metabolic requirements that necessitate a continuous infusion of nutrients. A pump is more desirable for the consistent delivery necessary for duodenal and jejunal feeding to prevent dumping and rapid transit. Complications associated with the sudden delivery of a nutrient load are minimized. Pumps also are appropriate for narrow-lumened feeding tubes and thick formulas, as well as for patients who do not tolerate variations in administration rate.

Feeding Containers

Rigid and flexible bag containers are designed for convenience and adaptation to individual needs. A feeding set with a screw cap can be attached to the manufacturer's premixed, sterile-packaged formula, inverted, and delivered by means of a pump or by gravity. This set is safe, convenient for home use, and decreases the potential for bacterial contamination. Reusable, rigid containers suitable for home use have a flat-bottom surface and wide mouth to permit filling by one person.

Flexible bag systems are designed for pump or gravity use. Some are prefilled. Gravity sets include a roller clamp for rate regulation and may be vented if prefilled. Sealed bags are disposable after one use and minimize formula contamination. Other containers are designed with the formula spout at the top to facilitate refilling without interrupting a continuous infusion.

All feeding containers come in a range of sizes from 150 to 1,500 milliliters. Container size is a consideration for patients on large-volume intermittent or nocturnal enteral feedings. Feeding containers that hold 250 milliliters are available for patients receiving small or supplemental enteral feedings. Exhibit 5-3 describes the ideal feeding container for home use.

In the home setting, continuous feeding sets should be changed every 48 hours; tubing should be changed every 24 hours to prevent bacterial contamination and clogging. Reuse of enteral sets may be cost saving; however, unless managed carefully it can greatly increase risk of bacterial contamination.

Enteral Pumps

The choice of an enteral feeding set and container may be dictated by the type of pump used. Intravenous infusion devices can be adapted but are more expensive, larger, heavier, and have added features not usually needed for tube feeding. Two types of enteral pumps are (1) volumetric or peristaltic pumps and (2) gravity-dependent controllers.

Volumetric or peristaltic pumps can deliver precise volumes to the patient requiring a constant, accurate formula flow. The volumetric pump is highly accurate and requires a special administration set to deliver a measured volume of fluid under a specified pressure. The peristaltic pump also requires its own administration set with a section of special tubing that is alternately squeezed and released by a set of rollers to propel the formula. Both pumps exert gentle, steady pressure, which makes them safe and effective for use with delicate, narrow-lumened tubes.

Exhibit 5-3 Characteristics of Home Feeding Containers

Available in a variety of sizes
Made of nonleaching materials
Easy to open, fill, close, and hang
Closed during use to prevent contamination
Nonleaking
Clearly calibrated for measuring volume
Easily washed and reused
Easily filled by one person
Compatible with the required infusion method

Controllers merely count drops of formula delivered. The delivery rate varies with formula viscosity, tube lumen size, and patient position and activity. They are less accurate than other enteral pumps but are inexpensive and easy to operate. Controllers are not recommended for home patients who require accurate flow rates or who are receiving thick formulas and have a narrow lumen feeding tube.

Certain pump features are recommended for home use. The ideal enteral pump should have empty bottle, occlusion, and low battery alarms. An overly sensitive pump that has frequent false alarms can be disruptive to patient life style. Pumps with a battery option allow patient mobility; the battery should last at least 8 hours and be rechargeable. Other alarms signal that formula flow has ceased and are essential for the patient who is asleep during feedings or who is unable to monitor the infusion. The pump should have an accurate volume delivery system and should be inexpensive, quiet, sturdy, lightweight, and portable (i.e., on a pole, strap, or carrying device, such as a backpack or vest). Pumps should provide a broad range of delivery rates and increment changes to allow use with home pediatric patients on small hourly volumes and with others requiring relatively rapid infusions.

OTHER USES OF THE ENTERAL SYSTEM

Feeding tubes and containers may be used to deliver medications or bulking agents. Care must be taken to avoid clogging the narrow lumen tubes with medications, especially those with a syrup base. Solid additives should be crushed or diluted carefully to facilitate smooth administration. The delivery system should be flushed with fluid to prevent coating or clogging of the tube. If the set is not flushed between medications, incompatible drugs may mix and form precipitates. If the tube becomes clogged, a 20 milliliter syringe or larger should be used to clear tubing. Smaller syringes create pressure, which will rupture the tube.

CONCLUSION

Home enteral nutrition support is a rapidly growing area in this era of medical cost containment and shifting of health care to the home setting. The importance of the dietitian's role in planning, coordinating, and modifying home tube feeding programs cannot be overemphasized.

NOTES

1. B.L. Rains, "The Non-Hospitalized Tube-Fed Patient," *Oncology Nursing Forum* 8 (1981): 8–13.

2. Geraldine V. Padilla et al., "Subjective Distress of Nasogastric Tube Feeding," *Journal of Parenteral and Enteral Nutrition* 3 (1979): 53–57.

3. Henry Randall, "Fluid, Electrolyte, and Acid-Base Balance," *Surgical Clinics of North America*, 56 (1976): 1019–1058.

4. Cynthia L. Rohde and Terri M. Braun, *Home Enteral/Parenteral Nutrition Therapy* (Chicago, Ill.: American Dietetic Association, 1986), 12–15.

5. Ibid.

6. George Cahill, "Starvation in Man," *New England Journal of Medicine* 282 (1970): 668–675.

7. ASPEN, *Regional Seminar: Nutritional Support of the Hospitalized Patient.* (Seattle, Wash.: Virginia Mason Medical Center, 1979).

8. George Blackburn et al., "Surgical Nutrition," in *Quick Reference to Clinical Nutrition*, ed. S. Halpern (Philadelphia, Pa.: J.B. Lippincott, 1979), 152–73.

9. *Comparison of Foods, Fats, and Oils*, Agriculture Handbook No. 8-4 (Washington, D.C.: U.S. Department of Agriculture, 1979).

10. Alan Tsai et al., "Effect of Soy Polysaccharide on Gastrointestional Functions, Nutrient Balance, Steroid Excretions, Glucose Tolerance, Serum Lipids, and Other Parameters in Humans," *American Journal of Clinical Nutrition* 38 (1983): 504–511.

11. James Anderson and B. Sterling, "High-Fiber Diets for Diabetics: Unconventional but Effective," *Geriatrics* 36 (1981): 64–75.

12. Victoria Haynes-Johnson, "Tube Feedings Complications: Causes, Prevention and Therapy," *Nutritional Support Services* 6 (1986): 17.

13. Deeann Del Rio, Karen Williams, and Becky Miller, *Handbook of Enteral Nutrition: A Practical Guide to Tube Feeding* (El Segundo, Calif.: Medical Specifics Publishing, 1982), 70–72.

14. John L. Rombeau et al., "Feeding by Tube Enterostomy," in *Enteral and Tube Feeding*, ed. John L. Rombeau and Michael D. Caldwell (Philadelphia, Pa.: W.B. Saunders Co. 1984), 275–76.

15. Ibid., 277–80.

16. Elizabeth Ahmann, *Home Care of the High Risk Infant* (Rockville, Md.: Aspen Publishers, 1986), 93–106.

17. John S. Wills, John T. Oglesby, and W. Arthur Burke, "Percutaneous Gastrostomy: A Safe, Cost-Effective Alternative to Surgical Gastrostomy and Intravascular Hyperalimentation," *Nutritional Support Services* 6 (1986): 10.

18. Brad Baldwin, Allen J. Zagoren, and Norman Rose, "Bacterial Contamination of Continuously Infused Enteral Alimentation with Needle-Catheter Jejunosotmy: Clinical Implications," *Journal of Parenteral and Enteral Nutrition* 8 (1984): 30–33.

19. Emma L. Cataldi-Betcher et al., "Complications Occurring during Enteral Nutrition Support: A Prospective Study," *Journal of Parenteral and Enteral Nutrition* 7 (1983): 546–52.

20. Carey P. Page et al., "Safe, Cost-Effective Postoperative Nutrition. Defined Formula Diet via Needle Catheter Jejunostomy," *American Journal of Surgery* 138 (1979): 939–45.

21. Mitchell V. Kaminski, "A New Catheter for Home Enteral Hyperalimentation," *Journal of Parenteral and Enteral Nutrition* 4 (1980): 604.

Chapter 6

Parenteral Nutrition Management

Annalynn Skipper

INTRODUCTION

Home parenteral nutrition is a complex therapy involving careful evaluation, detailed planning, extensive teaching, conscientious follow-up, and tremendous financial resources. It is lifesaving therapy for those who need it, a burden to those who do not, and dangerous when used improperly. For these reasons, it should be provided to patients who have been selected carefully by personnel trained in the technique.

The number of patients receiving home parenteral nutrition has expanded ever since its introduction in 1970.[1,2] In 1986 an estimated 5,500 patients received home parenteral nutrition at a projected expense of $170 million yearly.[3] This number is expected to increase as health care providers become more comfortable with the technique and as pressure to decrease hospital stays continues. Consumer demand is being created as patient advocate organizations and support groups educate patients about parenteral nutrition at home.

PATIENT SELECTION

Successful home parenteral nutrition is predicated on careful patient selection. Evaluation of candidates for home parenteral nutrition is a multidisciplinary effort and occurs on several levels simultaneously. Although the specific discipline that performs each task may vary, the key elements in patient evaluation remain constant.[4]

Medical Evaluation

A complete medical evaluation is necessary to document that gastrointestinal function is inadequate for enteral or oral nutrition. The patient must have adequate renal and cardiac function to tolerate the desired volume of parenteral nutrition, and permanent vascular access must be obtained. Finally, the patient must be stable enough from a medical standpoint to allow for hospital discharge.

Home parenteral nutrition has been used in a variety of diseases and conditions. The American Society for Parenteral and Enteral Nutrition (ASPEN) has published guidelines to aid the clinician in selecting patients for home parenteral nutrition.[5] A brief synopsis of the medical indications for home parenteral nutrition is provided for review.

Gastrointestinal Disease

The most unequivocal indication for home parenteral nutrition is short-bowel syndrome. Superior mesenteric artery infarct or repeated resections may reduce the small bowel to a remnant inadequate for nutrient absorption. Parenteral nutrition is the only means of nutrition support under these circumstances.[6]

Other gastrointestinal diseases for which home parenteral nutrition may be a benefit are severe inflammatory bowel disease, particularly if complicated by fistulas, radiation enteritis, and intestinal motility disorders such as scleroderma.[7-9] For the pediatric patient, congenital bowel defects precluding adequate nutrient absorption are a primary indication for parenteral nutrition.[10]

Neoplasia

Home parenteral nutrition is indicated for patients whose gastrointestinal tract is obstructed by pelvic or abdominal tumors. In most circumstances, home parenteral nutrition is used as adjuvant therapy in patients who are being treated for malignant disease. For those with extensive metastatic disease and for whom there is no treatment, home parenteral nutrition is of little therapeutic benefit. Home parenteral nutrition also may be used in cancer patients with significant gastrointestinal toxicity from radiation or chemotherapy.[11,12]

Pregnancy and Hyperemesis Gravidarum

The safety of parenteral nutrition during pregnancy has been documented as home parenteral nutrition patients have become pregnant and delivered live, healthy infants.[13] For a small number of patients with hyperemesis gravidarum refractory to conservative management, home parenteral nutrition may be of benefit.[14]

Acquired Immunodeficiency Syndrome

Use of parenteral nutrition at home for patients with acquired immunodeficiency syndrome–related enteropathy has been considered.[15] The benefits of parenteral nutrition in these patients must be weighed carefully against increased risk of life-threatening catheter-related infection.

Social Evaluation

The social evaluation of a patient for parenteral nutrition includes a review of emotional, social, and financial resources. Patients or their family members must be lucid, reliable, and motivated enough to learn and to perform accurately required procedures to qualify for home parenteral nutrition. They also must have sufficient strength and dexterity to manipulate syringes, change dressings, and maneuver bags of solutions. A supportive social structure is desirable, as is the availability of another person to learn parenteral nutrient administration. In addition, the patient's residence must have adequate space for equipment and supply storage.[16] For patients who cannot meet these criteria, placement in a skilled care facility may be required to ensure that parenteral alimentation can be administered safely.

A financial review is necessary to determine that adequate resources exist to cover the costs of parenteral nutrition. Third-party payers recognize the benefit of providing parenteral nutrition at home and usually cover the majority of costs with appropriate documentation of medical necessity. For indigent patients, the social worker may be helpful in obtaining grants from government or charitable agencies. Some home care providers absorb the costs incurred by indigent patients as part of a partnership agreement with the referring institution.

Nutrition Evaluation

Nutrition assessment establishes a baseline against which the effects of nutrition therapy are measured. Anthropometric data are collected so that nutrient requirements may be predicted. Evaluation of somatic and visceral protein enables the clinician to determine whether maintenance or repletion therapy is required. Tests that require collection of urine samples or special handling of the specimen should be performed before discharge because samples are difficult to obtain at home.

Determination of Ideal Body Weight

Ideal body weight may be determined with the use of a variety of commonly available formulas or tables. The results are reviewed with the patient to determine if ideal weight is a desirable goal. Many patients with chronic disease view weight gain positively and desire a return to their premorbid weight regardless of whether it was ideal. For other patients the ideal weight is too high and a new weight must be negotiated. In my experience, obtaining patient concurrence on the weight goal improves compliance with therapy.

Calorie Requirements

Energy needs may be predicted with the use of the Harris-Benedict equation (see Chapter 5, Exhibit 5-2) or measured by means of indirect calorimetry. Additions to this figure center on anticipated activity level and attainment of ideal body weight. Increases for fever, stress, surgery, or sepsis are unnecessary because resolution of these conditions is a prerequisite to hospital discharge.

For recovering patients, energy requirements are increased according to projected activity levels.[17] In underweight patients, additional calories are given to promote weight gain of one to two pounds weekly. In nonambulatory patients, care is taken to avoid excessive weight gain because it makes them more difficult to move, interfering with their care.

Protein Requirements

Patients receiving parenteral nutrition in the hospital are often given 1.0 to 2.5 grams of protein (or more) per kilogram of body weight. This amount is frequently required to compensate for surgical losses and to provide muscle repletion to critically ill patients. Because of their more stable medical condition, patients receiving home parenteral nutrition may have nearly normal protein requirements (0.8-1.0 gm/kg).

VASCULAR ACCESS

Administration of parenteral nutrition by peripheral vein is not suitable at home because of the difficulty in maintaining venous access. The central venous catheters used in hospitals for administration of parenteral solutions have been used at home, but permanent vascular access is usually required.

Catheters

Long-term parenteral nutrition may be maintained with the use of a catheter designed specifically for that purpose (Hickman or Broviac catheters). The catheter is inserted surgically, usually in the operating room after a local anesthetic has been administered. Catheters are made of silicone rubber and are distinguished from regular central venous lines in that they are tunneled subcutaneously away from the site of venous access to exit the skin near the xiphoid process or axilla.[18] Another feature of these catheters is a dacron cuff. It is implanted under the skin and facilitates formation of scar tissue and deters bacteria from traveling up the outside of the catheter.

Catheters designed for parenteral nutrition are durable and often stay in place for many months. They can be capped off, allowing for discontinuous nutrient infusion, and are available with single, double, and triple lumens. Presence of an indwelling catheter does not preclude showering or swimming provided precautions are taken to prevent contamination of the connector site. The skin around the catheter exit site is usually dressed daily, and the catheter is flushed regularly with heparin to prevent occlusion.

Implantable Access Devices

Originally designed for intermittent drug infusions, implantable access devices (Port-a-cath, Infuse-a-port) have been used for parenteral nutrition at home.[19] Like parenteral nutrition catheters, these devices are placed surgically after administration of a local anesthetic. They lie completely under the skin near the infraclavicular fossa. When healed, they are almost invisible, which is an advantage to patients with an active life style or for those who are concerned about body image. Dressings are not required, but regular flushing with heparin is necessary to maintain patency.

A disadvantage of this type of access is that the skin must be punctured at the start of each infusion. It also may be complicated to use because its location makes the device difficult for patients to see and access.

NUTRIENT FORMULATIONS

Formulas for home parenteral nutrition are usually similar to those provided in the hospital. The majority of calories are given as dextrose. In normoglycemic patients, the dextrose solution may be concentrated to provide a greater number of calories, thereby minimizing the length of time required for infusion.

Protein is provided as crystalline amino acids according to patient requirements. As with dextrose, concentrated solutions may be provided to minimize infusion time. Modified amino acid solutions are available for patients with liver or renal failure, as well as for increased needs related to stress. The medical stability required for patients to be discharged from the hospital, however, usually precludes the necessity and added expense of these formulas at home.

Fat

Exact fat requirements are unknown, but a minimum of 4 percent of calories from linoleic acid are believed to prevent essential fatty acid deficiency. Essential fatty acid requirements usually can be met in 500 milliliters of 10 percent lipid emulsion given twice weekly. Fat administration is problematic for home patients because it is difficult to provide without increasing infusion time. It is suggested that 10 percent lipid emulsion be given over a minimum of four hours, representing eight additional hours per week of infusion time, to prevent complications. Twenty percent lipid emulsions are frequently used in the hospital, but offer little advantage to the home patient because they require twice the infusion time of less-concentrated solutions.[20]

Lipids may be given as part of a three-in-one admixture, but this practice has limited practical applications at home because three-in-one solutions are stable only for relatively short periods of time.[21] Concomitant infusion of lipids with parenteral nutrition may be accomplished if appropriate administration sets and filters are available.

Before the development of commercially available lipid emulsions, safflower oil was applied topically to alleviate symptoms of essential fatty acid deficiency. This method has been used at times for home patients who are unable to tolerate lipid infusion. Patient compliance is limited because of aesthetic concerns. For patients who are able to tolerate oral intake, the diet is evaluated for essential fatty acid content, and fat sources are prescribed as necessary.

Fluid

In most patients, 30 to 40 milliliters of fluid per kilogram of body weight is adequate to prevent dehydration. Fluid requirements predicted by this method are evaluated in conjunction with intake and output records and clinical signs of hydration status. For patients with vomiting, diarrhea, or fistula losses, additional fluid is usually required. Fluid may be administered orally if the patient tolerates it.[22] Parenteral administration of extra fluid is more reliable, however. Additional fluid needs may be met by including water, with appropriate electrolytes, in the parenteral nutrition solution, and increasing the infusion rate. Fluid also may be administered before or after the parenteral nutrition infusion, but this method increases infusion time and may interfere with the life style of some patients.

Vitamins and Minerals

In 1979 the Nutrition Advisory Group of the American Medical Association (AMA) developed recommended vitamin intakes for patients receiving parenteral nutrition.[23] Commercial multiple vitamin formulations that meet these guidelines are available and maintain adequate serum levels in the majority of patients receiving parenteral nutrition.[24] Initially, vitamin K was not added to parenteral nutrient infusions to allow for individual manipulation of anticoagulation therapy. Home patients, however, are usually stable from this standpoint, and vitamin K may be added to one infusion weekly.

Reports of zinc, copper, chromium, and selenium deficiency have documented the need for these minerals in total parenteral nutrition.[25] Commercial preparations of trace minerals provide zinc, copper, chromium, and selenium according to AMA guidelines.[26] Because of concern for stability, vitamins and minerals are added to the parenteral solution immediately before the infusion is begun.[27] Some centers have reported adding iron to parenteral solutions, but others prefer to administer it by injection as hematologic parameters dictate.[28]

Other Additives

Electrolytes are added to parenteral nutrient solutions as needed to maintain acceptable serum levels. Commercial preparations containing sodium, potassium, acetate, magnesium, calcium, and phosphorus are available. At my institution (Pennsylvania Hospital, Philadelphia, Pa.) a standard electrolyte mix (35 milliequivalents sodium, 40 milliequivalents potassium, 34 milliequivalents chloride, 75 milliequivalents acetate, 17 millimole phosphorus, 8 milliequivalents magnesium, and 5 milliequivalents calcium per liter) has been used to meet the needs of the majority of patients.

Medications

Regular human insulin may be added to the solution by the patient just before infusion. Heparin is given to minimize thrombosis and maintain patency of the catheter or implantable device. The complex medical problems of patients receiving parenteral nutrition at home frequently dictate intravenous medications. Addition of medications to the parenteral nutrient solution is dependent on compatibility data. Cimetidine and morphine are compatible with parenteral nutrition. Lack of long-term stability necessitates that the patient add medications just before beginning the infusion. For those on intermittent antibiotic therapy, infusions are usually administered during hours the catheter is not being used for nutrition.

Self-Mix Formulas

In some programs, patients are encouraged to mix their own formulas, combining dextrose and amino acids, then adding electrolytes, vitamins, minerals, heparin, and medications individually as needed. Proponents of this practice state that it promotes independence, involves the patient in his or her care, and allows for frequent formula changes without waste. It also requires less storage space and less frequent deliveries of supplies. Self-mix formulas are usually considered to be less expensive, but some vendors charge more for individual components of parenteral nutrition than premixed solutions.[29]

Ready-Mix Formulas

Ready-mix formulas contain amino acids, dextrose, and electrolytes. Vitamins, minerals, heparin, and medications are added by the patient just before beginning the infusion. The advantage of this system is the reduced time that the patient has to spend in preparing and giving solutions. Proponents of this system also believe that reduced formula manipulation minimizes the potential for contamination and compounding error. Disadvantages of this system include the potential for waste because of formula changes or rehospitalization and the increased refrigeration space required for storage of premixed dextrose and amino acid solutions.

EQUIPMENT

Provision of parenteral nutrition requires certain equipment, regardless of the setting. A pump is necessary to ensure that parenteral solutions are administered accurately and at a constant rate. In selecting a pump, reliability and ease of operation are key factors. Accuracy also is important, as is size and, for some patients, battery operation.

Some patients use a table top to support their pump, but for the majority, an intravenous pole is ordered. Refrigerator space in the home must be adequate to store parenteral solutions. This may necessitate buying an additional refrigerator if deliveries are infrequent. The supplies needed for parenteral nutrition represent a significant expense and require storage space. Care is taken to order only necessary supplies and to avoid stockpiles of these items. All equipment and supplies are selected with ease of use as a prime factor.

Supply Management Systems

Reliable delivery of equipment, solutions, and supplies ensures the success of home parenteral nutrition. As home parenteral nutrition has developed, several types of supply management systems have evolved. The key to choosing a system is to find one that complements the strengths of the inpatient program, as well as one that can reliably supply the patient at the desired location and frequency.[30] ASPEN has established standards for home care that should be of use in evaluation of services provided by commercial companies.[31]

DETERMINATION OF THE HOME SCHEDULE

In the hospital, a 24-hour infusion of parenteral nutrition is usual. At home, patients may wish to spend some time "off the pump." For this reason, home infusions are frequently given for only part of the day.

The optimum administration schedule is one that minimizes the number of hours required to complete the infusion and is compatible enough with the patient's life style to promote compliance. A collaborative effort is necessary to determine the home infusion schedule. In practice the dietitian calculates the number of hours the patient will receive the infusion, and the patient selects the hours to start and stop the infusion. Night-time schedules for infusion may be preferred so as not to interfere with daytime activities. Some patients, however, object to this schedule as pump alarms or frequent micturition interfere with sleep.

Transition to the Home Schedule

Transition to the home feeding schedule is ideally accomplished before discharge so that tolerance to increased infusion rates, glucose loads, and volume may be assessed. Transition to a home schedule may be accomplished on an outpatient basis, provided adequate follow-up is available.

For patients on a 24-hour infusion, the number of hours the patient receives parenteral nutrient infusion is decreased as the rate of feeding during the remaining hours is increased. This process may be accomplished over three or four days until the desired schedule is achieved. (See Exhibit 6-1.) For patients who have not previously received parenteral nutrition, the infusion is begun for the desired number of hours and the rate is increased gradually over several days. (See Exhibit 6-2.)

Trouble Shooting

During the discharge planning process, there are two or three major concerns that might alert the clinician to potential problems. The first is metabolic intolerance to the parenteral nutrition solution. Because parenteral nutrient solutions are often given at very high rates over short

Exhibit 6-1 Conversion From Continuous to Cyclic Total Parenteral Nutrition (TPN)

	NUTRITION SUPPORT SERVICE
	PENNSYLVANIA HOSPITAL
	Sample Conversion From Continuous to Cyclic TPN
	(for a patient receiving 2,400 milliliters daily of TPN)
Day 1:	Three hours off continuous infusion
8:00 A.M.	Decrease rate to 40 ml/hour for one hour.
9:00 A.M.	Turn off TPN; flush Hickman catheter with
	3 milliliter of heparin solution (100 U/ml).
12:00 M.	Restart TPN at 40 ml/hour for one hour.
1:00 P.M.	Increase rate to 120 ml/hour for 19 hours.
Day 2:	Six hours off continuous infusion
8:00 A.M.	Decrease rate to 40 ml/hour for one hour.
9:00 A.M.	Turn off TPN; flush Hickman catheter.
3:00 P.M.	Restart TPN at 40 ml/hour for one hour.
4:00 P.M.	Increase rate to 140 ml/hour for 16 hours.
Day 3:	Nine hours off continuous infusion
8:00 A.M.	Decrease rate to 40 ml/hour for one hour.
9:00 A.M.	Turn off TPN; flush Hickman catheter.
6:00 P.M.	Restart TPN at 40 ml/hour for one hour.
7:00 P.M.	Increase rate to 180 ml/hour for 13 hours.
Day 4:	Twelve hours off continuous infusion
8:00 A.M.	Decrease rate to 40 ml/hour for one hour.
9:00 A.M.	Turn off TPN; flush Hickman catheter.
9:00 P.M.	Restart TPN at 40 ml/hour for one hour.
10:00 P.M.	Increase rate to 230 ml/hour for 10 hours.

Source: Courtesy of Michael Crivaro, M.D., Resident, Pennsylvania Hospital.

Exhibit 6-2 Initiation of Cyclic Total Parenteral Nutrition (TPN)

NUTRITION SUPPORT SERVICE
PENNSYLVANIA HOSPITAL
Sample Initiation of Cyclic TPN
(for a patient requiring 1,680 milliliters daily of TPN)

Day 1:

8:00 P.M.	Begin at 40 ml/hour for one hour.
9:00 P.M.	Increase TPN to 80 ml/hour for 10 hours.
7:00 A.M.	Decrease TPN to 40 ml/hour for one hour.
8:00 A.M.	Stop TPN.

Day 2:

8:00 P.M.	Begin at 40 ml/hour for one hour.
9:00 P.M.	Increase TPN to 120 ml/hour for 10 hours.
7:00 A.M.	Decrease TPN to 40 ml/hour for one hour.
8:00 A.M.	Stop TPN.

Day 3:

8:00 P.M.	Begin TPN at 40 ml/hour for one hour.
9:00 P.M.	Increase TPN to 160 ml/hour for 10 hours.
7:00 A.M.	Decrease TPN to 40 ml/hour for one hour.
8:00 A.M.	Stop TPN.

Source: Courtesy of Brett Harrison, M.D., Resident, Pennsylvania Hospital.

---

periods of time, the patient may develop previously undiscovered glucose, electrolyte, or volume intolerance.

Glucose intolerance is noted by monitoring urine glucose levels two hours after the beginning and end of each infusion. Blood samples for glucose level determination may also be drawn, but they are not expected to be within normal limits while the patient is receiving the infusion. Hyperglycemia may be managed with the use of hypoglycemic agents, by decreasing the carbohydrate concentration of the formula, or by slowing the infusion rate and lengthening the duration of the infusion.

Electrolyte levels are measured every one or two days until tolerance of the home schedule is established. Electrolyte abnormalities are corrected by adjusting the composition of the solution. Persistent electrolyte abnormalities may require medical evaluation to determine and treat the underlying cause.

Volume intolerance may be managed by increasing the caloric density of the formula, by decreasing the infusion rate, or by administering diuretics.

Another problem that may be recognized during discharge planning is separation anxiety. For the patient who requires significant medical care, the prospect of going home can be frightening. Inability to learn home parenteral nutrition techniques, memory lapses, or unsubstantiated physical complaints may be symptoms of emotional inability to cope with the complexities of home care. Reassuring the patient that there will be support at home, combined with a temporarily less intensive teaching schedule, may be helpful. The psychosocial issues associated with home parenteral nutrition are complex, and some centers retain a psychiatrist to assist patients in dealing with the adjustment to home parenteral nutrition.[32] Failure to recognize and resolve these issues may result in patient noncompliance with therapy and early hospital readmission.

ROLE OF THE DIETITIAN IN HOME PARENTERAL NUTRITION

Hospital dietitians have long participated in the care of patients receiving parenteral nutrition. Expansion of this role into discharge planning and home care is a logical direction for growth. In caring for these patients, the dietitian performs nutrition assessments, determines nutrient requirements, coordinates nutrient intake, and performs patient education.

Coordination of Nutrient Intake

Despite the fact that a nonfunctioning gastrointestinal tract is a prerequisite for parenteral nutrition, food is the societal basis for social interaction, and patients on parenteral nutrition often continue to eat. The challenge for the dietitian is to determine the appropriate oral intake for patients receiving parenteral nutrition, to determine what, if any, of the oral intake is absorbed, and to adjust the nutrient concentration of the parenteral nutrient solution so that optimum nutrition status is maintained.

Oral Intake

In general, parenteral nutrition produces feelings of satiety, and patients receiving it report diminished appetite. For some patients who receive parenteral nutrition over time, appetite may disappear entirely. Conversely, hyperphagia has been reported with the use of long-term parenteral nutrition for patients with short-bowel syndrome.[33]

Some patients should be discouraged from eating. Because of the risk of pneumonia, patients with persistent aspiration should be counseled to avoid eating altogether. Patients with bowel obstruction also should not take nutrients orally because this usually causes vomiting, aggravating fluid and electrolyte imbalances. Patients with malabsorption or inflammatory bowel disease may tolerate oral intake as limited by tolerance of subsequent pain or diarrhea. If the desire for food persists, the patient may be instructed to suck on hard candies or rinse the mouth with flavored liquids.

SUMMARY

Effective management of home parenteral nutrition is a major undertaking. A successful program requires collaboration among the patient and physicians, nurses, pharmacists, social workers, and dietitians. Growing experience with this population will increase knowledge, improve equipment, and streamline procedures resulting in improved quality of life for patients receiving parenteral nutrition at home.

NOTES

1. Maurice Shils et al., "Long-term Parenteral Nutrition Through an External Arteriovenous Shunt. Report of a Case," *New England Journal of Medicine* 283 (1970): 341–44.

2. Belding H. Scribner et al., "Long Term Total Parenteral Nutrition: The Concept of the Artificial Gut," *Journal of the American Medical Association* 212 (1970): 457–63.

3. OASIS, *Annual Report: 1985 Data* (Silver Spring, Md.: Oley Foundation and American Society for Parenteral and Enteral Nutrition, 1987).

4. Ian L. Mackenzie, "Evaluation of the Patient for Home Parenteral Nutrition" *Nutritional Support Services* 2 (1982): 16–19.

5. ASPEN Board of Directors, "Guidelines for Use of Home Total Parenteral Nutrition," *Journal of Parenteral and Enteral Nutrition* 11 (1987): 342–44.

6. George F. Sheldon, "Role of Parenteral Nutrition in Patients with Short Bowel Syndrome," *American Journal of Medicine* 62 (1979): 1021–29.

7. Bruce M. Wolf et al., "Experience with Home Parenteral Nutrition," *American Journal of Surgery* 146 (1983): 7–14.

8. C. Richard Fleming et al., "Home Parenteral Nutrition for Management of the Severely Malnourished Adult Patient," *Gastroenterology* 29 (1980): 11–18.

9. Stanley J. Dudrick et al., "100 Patient-Years of Ambulatory Home Total Parenteral Nutrition," *Annals of Surgery* 199 (1984): 770–81.

10. Cory T. Strobel et al. "Home Parenteral Nutrition: Results in 34 Pediatric Patients," *Annals of Surgery* 188 (1978): 394–403.

11. Lyn Howard, Lenore L. Heaphey, and Maryann Timchalk, "A Review of the Current National Status of Home Parenteral and Enteral Nutrition from the Provider and Consumer Perspective," *JPEN. Journal of Parenteral and Enteral Nutrition* 10 (1986): 416–24.

12. J.C. Tunca, "Impact of Cisplatin Multiagent Chemotherapy and Total Parenteral Hyperalimentation of Bowel Obstruction Caused by Ovarian Cancer," *Gynecologic Oncology* 12 (1981): 219–21.

13. M.M. Mughal et al., "Nutritional Management of Pregnancy in Patients on Home Parenteral Nutrition," *British Journal of Obstetrics and Gynaecology* 94 (1987): 44–49.

14. Donald F. Kirby, Vittorio Fiorenza, and Robert M. Craig, "Intravenous Nutritional Support During Pregnancy," *Journal of Parenteral and Enteral Nutrition* 12 (1988): 72–80.

15. Maria E. Garcia, Candy L. Collins, and Peter W.A. Mansell, "The Acquired Immune Deficiency Syndrome," *Nutrition in Clinical Practice* 2 (1987): 108–11.

16. Cathleen Marein et al., "Home Parenteral Nutrition," *Nutrition in Clinical Practice* 1 (1986): 179–92.

17. Calvin Long et al., "Metabolic Response to Injury and Illness: Estimation of Energy and Protein Needs from Indirect Calorimetry and Nitrogen Balance," *Journal of Parenteral and Enteral Nutrition* 3 (1979): 452–56.

18. Michael M. Meguid, Samuel Elder, and Ashe Wahba, "The Delivery of Nutritional Support: A Potpourri of New Devices and Methods," *Cancer* 55 (1985): 279–89.

19. Susan L. Beck, Norman R. Rose, and Allen J. Zagoren, "Home Total Parenteral Nutrition Utilizing Implantable Infusion Ports: A Retrospective Review," *Nutrition in Clinical Practice* 2 (1987): 26–29.

20. T. Peter Stein, "Fat Requirements for Parenteral Nutrition," *Nutritional Support Services* 1 (1981): 19–20.

21. C.R. Pennington and J.M. Richards, "Three-Liter Bags Containing Intralipid for Parenteral Nutrition," *Journal of Parenteral and Enteral Nutrition* 2 (1983): 304.

22. R.A. MacMahon, "The Use of The World Health Organization's Oral Rehydration Solution in Patients on Home Parenteral Nutrition," *JPEN. Journal of Parenteral and Enteral Nutrition* 8 (1984): 720–21.

23. American Medical Association, Department of Foods and Nutrition, "Multivitamin Preparation for Parenteral Use. A Statement by the Nutrition Advisory Group," *Journal of Parenteral and Enteral Nutrition* 2 (1979): 258–62.

24. Maurice Shils, H. Baker, and O. Frank, "Blood Vitamin Levels of Long-Term Adult Home Total Parenteral Nutrition Patients: The Efficacy of the AMA-FDA Parenteral Multivitamin Formulation," *JPEN. Journal of Parenteral and Enteral Nutrition* 9 (1985): 179–88.

25. Daniel Rudman and Patricia Jo Williams, "Nutrient Deficiencies during Total Parenteral Nutrition," *Nutrition Reviews* 43 (1985): 1–13.

26. American Medical Association, Department of Foods and Nutrition, "Guidelines for Essential Trace Element Preparations for Parenteral Use: A Statement by an Expert Panel," *Journal of the American Medical Association* 24 (1975): 2051–54.

27. Russell Brown, Robert A. Quercia, and Robert Sigman, "Total Nutrient Admixture: A Review," *Journal of Parenteral and Enteral Nutrition* November/December (1986): 650–57.

28. J.A. Norton et al., "Iron Supplementation of Total Parenteral Nutrition: A Prospective Study," *Journal of Parenteral and Enteral Nutrition* September/October (1983): 457–61.

29. Richard J. Baptista et al., " The Cost of Home Total Parenteral Nutrition," *Nutrition in Clinical Practice* February (1987): 14–22.

30. John R. Wesley et al. "Home Parenteral Nutrition: A Hospital-Based Program with Commercial Logistic Support," *Journal of Parenteral and Enteral Nutrition* September/October (1984): 585–88.

31. ASPEN Board of Directors, *Standards for Nutrition Support: Home Patients* (Rockville, Md.: American Society for Parenteral and Enteral Nutrition, 1985).

32. A. Dale Gulledge et al., "Psychosocial Issues of Home Parenteral and Enteral Nutrition," *Nutrition in Clinical Practice* October (1987): 183–94.

33. Sara DiCecco et al., "Nutritional Intake of Gut Failure Patients on Home Parenteral Nutrition," *JPEN. Journal of Parenteral and Enteral Nutrition* 11 (1987): 529–32.

Chapter 7

Preparing the Patient for Home Enteral Management

Abby S. Bloch

Home care has been facilitated by advances in medicine, as well as in equipment technology. This progress has had a profound effect on nutrition management, and patients now can and should be kept in sound nutrition balance, regardless of condition or requirements. This chapter focuses on training methods for the home enteral patient.

EDUCATION—A STEPWISE PROCESS

Successful education, from the time of initial patient referral to the point at which feedings can be managed independently, requires careful and ongoing assessment in three areas: (1) patient/caretaker readiness for the current step, (2) competence in performing a designated activity, and (3) readiness to move on to the next step. Stepwise assessment allows the trainer to identify and work on problem areas and to ensure that the patient and caretakers are ready mentally, psychologically, and educationally, to manage enteral feeding at home.

Enteral training can be separated into distinct segments. During the initial screening, potential stumbling blocks in attitude, ability, and home environment can be identified. The goals of information gathering and intervention at this stage are to assess the appropriateness of the enteral prescription plan. Demonstration of all equipment and procedures before hands-on training sets the stage for learner readiness to handle the system. Modification of the training schedule is made based on patient and caretaker participation. The final stage of readiness guarantees that the home environment has been adapted to meet the patient's needs and that all aspects of care can be coordinated.

Many dietitians evaluate patient and caretaker readiness on an informal basis. Certainly time constraints on schedules and lack of adequate notice of a patient's discharge may preclude stepwise assessment. Appreciation of readiness at all stages of training, however, increases the effectiveness of education and, as a result, patient management.

STEP ONE—INITIAL SCREENING

Initial screening determines the parameters by which the patient will need to be managed. Although feeding regimens usually are determined before referral for home training, it is not unusual for the dietitian to identify aspects of the prescribed system that are incompatible with the patient's home life style. For this reason, the initial screening can be an opportunity to fine tune the feeding program before training. Assessment of the patient's physical, medical, and psychosocial status allows the enteral trainer to adapt the feeding regimen to the patient's needs and modify the training process to ensure comprehension, manipulation, and compliance.

Physical Status

An evaluation of the patient's physical status assesses mobility, dexterity, strength and vision. Mobility and range-of-motion limitations may reduce the number of options for delivery systems, affecting the selection of bolus, slow-drip gravity, or continuous feedings. For example, placing of the feeding bag on a fully extended intravenous pole may be physically impossible, thereby necessitating either bolus feedings or patient training on alternate hanging systems.

Dexterity is necessary for particular manipulations required by the different feeding techniques. Patients with impairment of the fingers, hands, and arms may not be able to use the roller clamp on the bag tubing, open the top spout of the bag to pour in formula, or pop open the tops of ready-to-use cans. Arthritis, medications, muscle degeneration, and other factors can compromise dexterity, making simple movements extremely difficult and frustrating.

Strength may be separate from but not necessarily independent of dexterity. If the fingers, hands, and arms are weak from muscle degeneration or general body weakness, then strength may be affected to the point that feeding tasks are difficult. Modifications must be made for the person who is too weak to stand and prepare the feeding, open caps, or hold and fill the bag. A family member or other caretaker can prepare formula or set up the system. Devices can be created to hold the feeding bag for filling if it becomes too heavy for the patient to hold. The formula can or bottle may be rested on a hard surface and tipped over to pour.

Vision may be distorted and limited in an elderly or debilitated patient. It must be assessed before planning patient education so that potential problems with measuring, pouring, and equipment handling can be addressed. Accommodations in feeding management then can be made. For example, if letter or number acuity is problematic, print can be enlarged and darkened on the equipment, as well as in the instruction sheets. Colors may be used for markers to replace lines or words. Coding by means of textural materials, such as Velcro or fabric tape, help identify specific parts of the system.

Mental Status

Once the patient's physical abilities have been evaluated, mental status must be considered.

- Is the patient cogent?
- Is the patient appropriate in his or her awareness of the situation and surroundings?

A patient's mental capabilities may be impaired by senility, medications, preoccupation with illness, or fear of death. It may be possible to train the patient after medications such as sedatives have worn off or after the patient has undergone psychiatric counseling by a social worker. Family members or other caretakers must be involved with the training process if the patient's mental functioning is such that successful training and consistent management cannot be ensured.

If the patient is extremely depressed, noncompliance with enteral management must be seriously considered. The patient who does not agree philosophically with enteral feeding may not cooperate and may require reevaluation for other feeding modalities.

Medical Status

Medical status also must be a part of the initial screening.

- Is the patient an appropriate candidate for the feeding technique, or does the medical condition warrant a different approach?
- Should the patient be on modified foods by mouth with oral supplementation or, conversely, on total parenteral nutrition?

- If home tube feeding is indicated, which type and site of tube feeding is appropriate?
- Should discharge be postponed if a gastrostomy or jejunostomy feeding tube is to be placed?

The rate and method of delivery will be affected by the medical condition of the patient. If the gastrointestinal tract is intact and functional, bolus feedings at intervals throughout the day to meet the total daily requirements of the patient can be used as the method of choice. The patient requiring slow, but not continuous, feeding may be trained on a gravity infusion. Continuous slow-drip feeding may be more appropriate and effective for the debilitated, significantly malnourished, or malabsorbing patient. It may be feasible to train this patient on more than one approach if a simpler method (e.g., bolus feeding) can be used once the patient has reached a high enough feeding rate by pump or gravity. Transition and then crossover to the simpler method of feeding can thus be accomplished easily at home.

Home Environment

The home environment and family life style impact on formula selection; daily infusion rate, volume, and progression over time; method of feeding; and selection of equipment, on the basis of need, ability, and prevailing circumstances. Logistics such as delivery and purchase of equipment and supplies must be worked out, as well as storage in the home setting. The feeding trainer and social worker often explore the psychosocial aspects of home care during their early interactions with the potential outpatient. Major adjustments in the feeding regimen, including schedule and equipment, should be established before training is started.

While screening for discharge, the physical facilities and attitudes and availability of caretakers must be evaluated. Consider the following situations:

Mr. S., a candidate for home feeding, lived in a hotel room without cooking and refrigeration equipment. He was trained to infuse full cans of formula to eliminate the problem of leftovers.

Mrs. B. lived with relatives and was concerned about inconveniencing them with all her equipment and supplies. In her case, equipment needs were streamlined and smaller deliveries were scheduled on a more frequent basis.

If a supportive home environment is not available, successful management becomes more difficult. Patients living alone pose different considerations. The health care trainer should be sensitive to the existing situation before discharging the patient home.

Once the goals and objectives are clearly defined and established, the initial training and preparation for the patient's home discharge can proceed.

STEP TWO—DEMONSTRATION

Most patients are intimidated and overwhelmed by the thought of going home with enteral feedings. It is foreign and alien to them, and they may doubt their ability to use the equipment correctly. A gradual, nonthreatening introduction to the system helps minimize apprehension. Most inpatients will have received some type of tube feeding while hospitalized and may be somewhat familiar with the infusion system. Others are started on tube feeding one or two days before discharge and have not had an opportunity to master the technique fully.

Outpatients may be started on enteral management in a clinic setting. Those who come into the clinic hoping to get a "magic bullet," such as a vitamin pill or a special drink, to cure their nutrition problem can be shocked and unreceptive when they learn that tube feeding is being considered. To lessen this adverse reaction, some patients receive counseling on a high-calorie diet and are given a one-week trial to improve their intake. This also provides one week for the patient to adjust to the concept of enteral feeding and to become psychologically ready to undergo training. Other patients are started on tube feeding during the first visit.

The enteral system is introduced (by a dietitian experienced in tube feeding training and management) to the patient, family, or other caretakers. Each piece of equipment is described and passed around for touching and familiarization. Next, the trainer physically demonstrates the step-by-step feeding process, explaining the rationale for each action. It is important to allay fears regarding handling of the feeding set and tubing, which may be viewed as potentially dangerous. Most important, the patient and family members must be assured that air bubbles in the tubing, unlike those in intravenous feeding, are not serious.

Likewise, it is explained that the feeding technique is merely a convenience to provide nutrients because oral intake alone is insufficient to meet all nutrition needs. The analogy of the use of straws for those who cannot drink from a cup or the use of a blender to puree foods for those who cannot chew or consume solids to compare with tube feeding for those who cannot eat is easily understood by patients. The tube feeding is presented as an alternative route to eating, rather than a highly technical piece of medical equipment, such as a respirator or ventilator. This approach makes the entire system less threatening.

As each component of the system is demonstrated and explained, the patient or caretaker is encouraged to ask questions. If early discharge planning permits several training sessions, repeated exposure to the enteral system allows adjustment to the feeding method and assimilation of all the information provided. From experience, dietitians involved in training know that patients absorb about one fourth of the instructions given to them at any given sitting. Therefore the more often material is reinforced, the more successful is the learning process. It must be recognized that patients and families often focus on other things unrelated to the training session, preventing them from comprehending much of the material covered.

Unfortunately, training may be required on very short notice. It is not unusual for inpatients to be cleared for discharge without adequate training. Outpatients may receive a tube during a clinic visit and be expected to initiate feedings at home after a single training session. For these patients, it is imperative that the trainer provide as much assurance and support as possible during that session. Written materials, as well as telephone numbers of team members to call for assistance, are helpful to the patient trained on short notice.

STEP THREE—PARTICIPATION

Training

The next phase of training, whether during a single session or a second meeting, includes a review by the trainer and then patient and family of the assembly and operation of the system, step by step. It is helpful to ask them to explain to the instructor, while setting up the system, what each task is and why it is being performed. This process allows the trainer to assess understanding and readiness for independent operation. Supervised practice once or twice before discharge home builds confidence and a sense of familiarity.

The training session should replicate closely the actual home setup. Better reinforcement will be possible by using the same equipment, formula, and feeding bag that will be used at home rather than improvising on a different system. This is not always possible because of availability of equipment and supplies during training. Photographs, illustrations, and instruction materials for a different home system are useful in demonstrating the similarities and differences between the hospital and home equipment and infusion procedures.

Many patients on nasal enteric tubes are taught by a nurse or physician to pass their own tubes for each feeding. If a team exists, the nutrition support team nurse inserts the tube initially while explaining the procedure to the patient. Instructions should include measuring the length of tubing to be inserted, ensuring patency, and swallowing the tube to allow passage beyond the gag reflex.

Because daily chest films are costly and impractical in the home setting, patients must learn other methods for confirming tube placement. Patients at Memorial Sloan-Kettering Cancer Center learn a three-step procedure.

1. Insert air into the tube and observe for patency.
2. Place the adapter end of the tube in a cup of water, inhale and exhale, and check for bubbles. (This is referred to as the Jacques Cousteau test, after the famous marine explorer, because bubbles resemble those produced by an underwater diver.)
3. Inject 10 milliliters of water and monitor for coughing or feeling water in the throat or mouth.

A positive response to any test suggests that the tube is not placed properly, may be lodged in the throat or bronchus, and must be reinserted.

The next step in training is to remove the tube and allow the patient to replace it. After the initial insecurity about the procedure abates, the patient begins to appreciate the ease with which the tube can be inserted and removed.

Reinforcement

Reinforcement of procedures should be a multidisciplinary process. A dietitian instructor can develop a training schedule with the hospitalized patient's primary nurse, allowing the patient and caretakers to set up actual feedings under the nurse's supervision. The nurse or stoma therapist is consulted to teach and reinforce tube site care, especially for patients with feeding gastrostomies and jejunostomies. In conjunction with the nurse, the dietitian explains to the patient what is entailed in the care and use of the tube, including methods of checking for proper placement and flushing to maintain patency and cleanliness. If a percutaneous endoscopic gastrostomy tube is used, care of the dressing site and tube or button should be reviewed by the nurse and dietitian together so instructions and follow-up care are consistent among the team members who monitor the patient at home.

STEP FOUR—LOGISTICS

Equipment and Supplies

A brief discussion about care of the equipment and cleaning of the feeding bag or container must be included. While introducing this issue, home facilities and space allowances can be discussed in greater detail. For instance,

- Where can the patient hang the bag if a pump and pole are not being used?
- Is a picture hook or door available near where the patient will be fed?
- Where will the supplies of bags and formula be stored?
- What arrangements can be made for bag refilling and icing during an overnight feeding?

A discussion of mobility will minimize problems once the patient arrives home. Many patients try to roll the pole and pump into the bathroom. If there is thick carpeting in the room or the bathroom has a door saddle, maneuvering of the pole may be difficult. The patient can disconnect from the pump tubing temporarily, but any break longer than approximately 15 minutes requires flushing of the feeding tube to prevent clogging.

Patients are encouraged to assume as normal a life style as possible. Their training may include suggestions on creative bag hanging with the use of paper clips, lamp shades, or coat racks to facilitate feeding in different rooms without the pole. (One patient at Memorial Sloan-Kettering Cancer Center, who was an artist, was assisted in modifying a backpack to hold his pump and bag while he painted in his studio.) The training period offers an opportunity to explore with the patient and significant others life style issues that may impact on traditional feeding routines.

Other Considerations

Medications and Foods

Another area of concern for the home patient is the administration of medications and foods through the feeding tube. When possible, liquids should be substituted for pills. Those medications for which a liquid form is not available must be pulverized thoroughly and dissolved in water. It is helpful to work with the patient's primary nurse for hands-on practice of medication injection. By showing the patient the size of the formula exit ports on the feeding tube, the dietitian demonstrates the ease with which the ports can be clogged and reinforces crushing and flushing procedures.

Nutrition Goal Setting

During the hands-on aspect of training, all questions about the system should be answered. The patient should be comfortable enough to feel at ease with performing tasks at home. As part of the review, nutrition goals and needs should be clearly identified. Short-range goals to be achieved over the next week to 10 days should be given, as well as long-range goals for the future. Assuring the patient that options to formulas or feeding systems are available if this particular system does not meet his or her needs provides a feeling of comfort and relief.

If oral intake is permitted to augment enteral intake, guidelines about the kinds of foods, the amount of each portion, and any restrictions or limitations should be presented. Patients may be more motivated to eat if told that tube feeding will be cut back or discontinued once oral intake alone is adequate.

Monitoring

Home monitoring must be reviewed near the end of the training session, once the patient and family feel comfortable with all procedures. Discussion of potential complications before patient readiness increases fear and apprehension about the feeding process. A check sheet with monitoring concerns should be provided and explained to prepare the patient for potential complications. (See Exhibit 7-1.) By teaching the patient to maintain a home log of weights, intakes, and problems, the clinician ensures that appropriate management information is available.

A telephone call schedule may be established to monitor the patient between clinic visits. At Memorial Sloan-Kettering Cancer Center patients are called within two days of discharge and then on a weekly or biweekly basis. The patient should be provided with a list of team and vendor telephone numbers for questions and emergencies.

Weight changes and bowel habit patterns also should be reviewed with the patient. An understanding of weight management and of how many calories are needed to gain a pound reinforces the importance of compliance. Patients should be instructed to weigh themselves on a regular basis to monitor their progress. If a scale is not available in the home, other assessment tools, such as tape measures and belts, can be used.

Exhibit 7-1 Complications To Be Reviewed in Training

Weight changes	Tube obstruction
Stool and urine changes	Tube site infection
Nausea and vomiting	Pain
Productive cough	Edema
Unexplained fever	

Activity

The patient also should be instructed on activity limitations. How much bed rest or ambulation is recommended? Should the patient resume normal activities? Most will be hesitant to engage in physical activity but might need to begin a modest program of exercise to regain muscle mass. Working with a physical therapist may be helpful for those patients who need professional assistance.

EDUCATION MATERIALS AND METHODS

Several approaches are used in considering the patient's educational needs during the training process. Hands-on practice with the system is invaluable to familiarize the patient with the individual components of the delivery system and feeding tube. Allowing the patient to perform each task involved with the feeding identifies problem areas. For example, when the trainer demonstrates the pulling of water into the syringe for flushing, the patient does not always discern that the plunger must be closed first and then pulled back to allow the water to enter the barrel. Explaining that the amount of water going into the barrel is arbitrary allays concern about getting the exact amount of water into the syringe. Also, many patients do not realize that the cap of the syringe must be removed before use. Simple manipulations may seem trivial to the experienced clinician but may cause great frustration to the neophyte.

Written material is useful for later referral and as a security measure once the patient is at home. Patients should be trained fully before they are provided with written information. Handouts and publications should be concise and in language that is understandable to the patient, regardless of educational level. Medical jargon can intimidate even the most highly educated lay person. Written instructions should duplicate, in identical order, the procedures demonstrated and practiced during the training sessions. If materials being used were prepared by another center or a commercial vendor, the trainer must eliminate discrepancies to prevent patient confusion.

Nutrition information sheets or diet plans should be offered to patients for whom oral intake is indicated. Foods included and excluded, as well as portion sizes, should be stated clearly. Instructions in weighing, blending, mixing, and measuring of food items and modular ingredients assist the patient in modifying a formula to prescription.

Additional information on the care of ostomy tubes, nasogastric tubes, and percutaneous endoscopic gastrostomy sites should replicate in-house practices. Materials developed with the input of all team and ancillary staff members ensure that comprehensive and consistent procedures will be maintained.

Patients taking medications should receive written information on dosages, side effects, drug-nutrient interactions, and other relevant information that may impact on feeding. Insulin administration varies with changes in the enteral prescription and may necessitate patient training on dose adjustment. Pain medications are likely to cause constipation, a side effect often unexpected by the patient.

Printed material explaining the procedure, techniques used, and care of the system provides an overall view of the feeding method. If videotapes are available, demonstration of the system (similar to the first training session) allows the patient to view the demonstration as often as needed. Viewing the tapes after the training reinforces techniques and permits learning at the patient's own pace.

Encouraging the patient to work with the feeding apparatus in the hospital under the supervision of the nursing staff services as a reinforcement and confidence builder. When time and circumstances permit, this practice alleviates much of the fear experienced by patients. Like any new process, such as turning on a computer without previous knowledge, familiarity comes with practice.

MANAGEMENT AT HOME

The nutrition and medical status of the patient will change over time. Depending on the length of enteral management, the patient may go through significant changes medically and nutritionally. As part of follow-up, updating the care to be consistent with needs may require retraining to reflect changes in feeding method, rate, or formula. Retraining by telephone, if feasible and successful, eliminates the need to schedule a special patient visit. Nevertheless, new materials and instruction sheets may have to be prepared and mailed.

Good communication and interaction between the patient and family and the medical staff is the key to successful management of the patient in the home. Although frequent contact becomes time consuming and laborious to the clinical staff, it is crucial for proper care. Only with continual interaction can good rapport be established, letting the patient know that concern and interest exists from the clinical staff. Patients appreciate this touchstone with the professional once at home.

SUMMARY

Home enteral management is an important component of health care today and will become even more important in the future. Commercial and technologic advances have already provided the means to implement such a program effectively in the home setting without inconvenience or risk to the patient. With proper preparation, training, planning, and communication, this management option not only becomes a viable one but the most desirable choice in many instances. When the health care team sends a patient home with all the tools to perform feeding without complications or inconveniences, they provide a meaningful service, as well as feel a sense of satisfaction in serving the best interests of all.

Chapter 8

Patient Management and Monitoring

Jo Ann Davey-McCrae

Home enteral and parenteral nutrition is a rapidly growing field. In 1985 almost 20,000 patients were receiving enteral nutrition and 5,000 patients were receiving parenteral nutrition therapy.[1,2] Two events in particular have contributed to the increasing demand for home nutrition services. First, new access devices, formulas, and supplies allow for safe nutrient provision on an outpatient basis. Second, there is a strong cost-containment incentive to discharge patients from the hospital earlier when similar therapy can be provided at home, resulting in more persons receiving home nutrition support. Home care providers have developed monitoring systems to ensure that safe and quality care can be given in the home.[3,4]

HOME NUTRITION CANDIDATES

When oral intake is inadequate or not possible, the best alternate mode of therapy is selected. The criterion for enteral therapy is a functional gastrointestinal tract. If this cannot be met, parenteral nutrition is indicated. Conditions for which home enteral and parenteral therapy are indicated are listed in Table 8-1 and Exhibit 8-1. Of the two therapies enteral nutrition is the preferred method of treatment because it is less expensive, more similar physiologically to eating, safer, and easier for the patient or caregiver to learn to prepare and administer.[5]

Metabolic Requirements

Before discharge from the hospital, assessment of the patient's nutrition status and metabolic requirements, as well as determination of short- and

Table 8-1 Candidates for Home Enteral Nutrition

Inability to Swallow	Impairment of Gastrointestinal Tract
Neurologic Disorders	*Disease Processes*
Alzheimer's disease	Cystic fibrosis
Cerebrovascular accident	Crohn's disease
Myasthenia gravis	Ulcerative colitis
Guillain-Barré syndrome	Pancreatic dysfunction
Organic brain syndrome	
Amyotrophic lateral sclerosis	*Malignancy*
Parkinson's disease	Gastrointestinal cancer
Achalasia	Gastrointestinal tumor obstruction
Head injury	Pancreatic cancer
Multiple sclerosis	
	Other
Other	Radiation enteritis
Wired or fractured jaw	Abdominal fistulas
Head, neck, esophageal cancers	Malabsorptive disorders
	Failure to thrive
	Side effects of cancer therapy

long-term goals of therapy, is needed to plan and monitor nutrition therapy at home.

Indirect calorimetry or the Harris-Benedict equation (see Chapter 5, Exhibit 5-2) can be used to assess resting energy expenditure. Five hundred to one thousand calories are added daily to produce an increase in weight of one to two pounds per week. A more rapid weight gain may indicate peripheral edema or an excessive amount of calories. Therefore calorie requirements and weight changes are reassessed continuously. A goal weight for the patient may be the same as the usual or ideal body weight, or it may be a weight agreed on by the team and patient.

Protein requirements generally range from 0.8 to 1.5 grams per kilogram of body weight. After the patient's protein status is at an adequate level, protein intake is reassessed to prevent infusion of excessive amounts. In parenteral nutrition, lipids generally supply approximately 30 percent of the caloric intake, whereas in enteral nutrition fat content may vary as a result of malabsorption or the disease state. Carbohydrate, fat, and protein substrates can be modified to a greater extent in enteral nutrition to promote optimal absorption and assimilation. In all cases a detailed diet history is taken to determine the amount of each nutrient obtained from the oral route. The parenteral or enteral prescription is adjusted to take this into account.

Exhibit 8-1 Candidates for Home Parenteral Nutrition

Disturbances of Intestinal Motility
Intestinal pseudo-obstruction
Scleroderma
Collagen vascular disease
Hereditary and acquired disorders of intestinal motility
Postoperative intestinal obstruction adhesions

Malabsorption
Intractable sprue syndromes
Short-bowel syndrome
Ischemic bowel (mesenteric infarct)
Carcinoid tumors
Advanced cystic fibrosis
Chronic diarrhea
Inflammatory bowel disease
Radiation enteritis
Graft-versus-host disease

Malignancy
Bowel obstruction
Intra-abdominal pelvic malignancy

Other
Enterocutaneous and enteroenteric fistulas
Pancreatitis
Side effects of radiation therapy and chemotherapy

Discharge Record

A discharge record (Exhibit 8-2) is helpful not only for future outpatient clinic visits but also as a communication tool for the home care agency and other referrals. All diagnoses, nutrition prescriptions, therapies, physical examination notes, and laboratory tests and procedures results are charted and filed for easy access. Lists of contact persons in hospitals/home care agencies and available support groups/resources (with addresses and telephone numbers) at home care agencies also are included. A review of this information before each outpatient visit is helpful.

Home Parenteral Prescription

The discharge nutrient prescription for parenteral nutrition should list the amount of macronutrients and micronutrients, along with the amount

Exhibit 8-2 Discharge Sheet

Patient's Name: _____ Address: _____
Telephone No. _____ Admission   Discharge
Primary Caretaker: _____ Date: _____   Date: _____

Primary Diagnosis: _____
Allergies: _____

Discharge Problems:	Ongoing Problems:
1. _____	1. _____
2. _____	2. _____
3. _____	3. _____
4. _____	4. _____
5. _____	5. _____

Access: Hickman/Port/Esophagus/GT/JT/PEG/PEGJ/Nasoenteral/Self-intubate
    Inserted by: _____ Date: _____ Catheter/Tube: _____ French: _____
Resting Energy Expenditure: _____ kcal/day (estimated/measured)
Nutrition Goals: Weight_____ (repletion/maintenance/reduction)
                Protein _____ (repletion/maintenance/reduction)
    Requirements: KCAL _____ % REE _____ Fluid _____ ml/kg Total Fluid _____ ml
    CHO _____ gm FAT _____ gm % FAT _____ PRO _____ gm _____ gm/kg
RESTRICTIONS: _____

Home Schedule: _____
Diet:

	VOL	KCAL	%REE	CHO	FAT	%FAT	PRO (gm)	PRO (gm/kg)
Oral								
Enteral								
Parenteral								

	Na	K	Mg	Ca	Cl	Acetate	Phosphorus	Vitamins
Enteral								
Parenteral								

Enteral Brand: _____ Concentration: _____ Extra Water: _____ Total Volume: _____
    Rate: _____ Schedule: _____ Additives: _____

Parenteral Type: _____
Additives: _____
    Heparin _____ IU Insulin _____ IU Cimetidine _____ mg Albumin _____ gm
    Trace Elements: _____
    Schedule: _____ Rate: _____

Discharge Nutrition Status:
HT: ___ WT: ___ IBW: ___ %IBW: ___ UBW: ___ %UBW: ___ Goal WT: _____
Anthropometrics: MAC _____ MAMC _____ TRI _____
Visceral Proteins: Albumin _____ Transferrin _____

Social Factors: _____ Family Support: _____

Discharge Training Summary:
    Training Days: _____ Competency: _____

Exhibit 8-2 continued

Home Nutrition Vendors: Home Nursing:
Agency: _____   _____
Contact Person: _____   _____
Address: _____   _____
Telephone No.: _____   _____

Outpatient Laboratory: _____ Telephone No.: _____
    Address: _____

Insurance: (Medicaid/Medicare/Private Insurer/HMO)
    Social Security No.: _____ Policy/Group No.: _____ Telephone No.: _____
    Address: _____ Employer: _____

Primary Physician: _____
    Address: _____ Telephone No.: _____
Referral Physician: _____
    Address: _____ Telephone No.: _____

Medications:

Type	Dose	Frequency
1.		
2.		
3.		
4.		
5.		

Summary of Hospitalization: _____
_____
_____
_____
_____

Abbreviations: CHO, carbohydrate; GT, gastrostomy tube; IBW, ideal body weight; JT, jejunostomy tube; MAC, mid arm circumference; MAMC, mid arm muscle circumference; PEG, percutaneous endoscopic gastrostomy; PEGJ, percutaneous endoscopic gastrojejunostomy; PRO, protein; %REE, percentage of resting energy expenditure; TRI, triceps skinfold; UBW, usual body weight; VOL, volume.

Source: Courtesy of the Hospital of the University of Pennsylvania, Nutrition Support Service, Philadelphia, Pennsylvania.

of fluid. Prescriptions vary among patients, depending on the disease state, nutrition status, losses from ostomies and drainages, results of laboratory studies, and renal function. All changes in parenteral therapy are dated and entered on a standardized form. Special consideration is given to trace elements, vitamins, and additives, such as insulin and heparin (Exhibit

Exhibit 8-3 Home Parenteral Prescription

	Date	Date	Date	
Formula				
Volume				
Schedule				
(ml/kg)				
KCAL				
%REE				
CHO (gm)				
FAT (gm)				
%FAT				
PRO (gm)				
Pro (gm/kg)				
Sodium (mEq)				
Potassium (mEq)				
Magnesium (mEq)				
Calcium (mEq)				
Chloride (mEq)				
Acetate (mEq)				
Phosphorus (mmol)				
Vitamins (ml)				
Vitamin K				
Iron				
Copper (mg)				
Zinc (mg)				
Chromium (μg)				
Manganese (mg)				
Molybdenum				
Selenium				
Iodine				
Insulin				
Cimetidine				
Albumin				
Lipid (concentration)				
Schedule				

Abbreviations: CHO, carbohydrate; PRO, protein; %REE, percentage of resting energy expenditure.

8-3). Most patients receive 6- to 16-hour cyclic infusions at home, and, again, these instructions, along with total volume and infusion rate, are documented (Exhibit 8-4). Tapering instructions are included for patients who experience hypoglycemic-like symptoms after discontinuation of total parenteral nutrition (TPN).

Exhibit 8-4 Parenteral Nutrition Cycle Schedule

Home Parenteral Nutrition Solution:
   No. of hours: _____ From _____ To _____
   Infusion Rate: _____ From _____ To _____
   *At _____ the infusion rate will be changed to _____,
   from _____ to _____.
Lipids:
   No. of Hours: _____ From _____ To _____
   Infusion Rate: _____

   *If applicable.

In home parenteral nutrition lipids can be incorporated into the home nutrient prescription plan in many ways. Most often, lipids are given through an infusion line separate from the main parenteral infusion line and are administered as 10 percent or 20 percent concentrations on a daily basis. For some patients the frequency of infusion may be decreased to two to three times per week, just enough to prevent an essential fatty acid deficiency. Admixture formulas (solutions containing a combination of fat, amino acids, and glucose) have also been used in the home setting. Use of admixtures is advantageous because it decreases manipulation of the solution, catheter, and administration tubing and may improve compliance. With separate infusions through two lines, risk of contamination and costs increase. Also, when compared with lipid emulsions alone, admixtures have been shown not to increase significantly microbial growth.[6-8] Disadvantages of admixtures are inability to inspect visually the formula for precipitation, and greater refrigerator storage space and more frequent home deliveries are required.

The parenteral solution can be mixed at home or premixed by the hospital or the home care pharmacy. Home mix, in which the patient adds a portion of the nutrients at home, is generally less expensive but requires great care in preparation to prevent contamination of the solution. In contrast, premixed solutions are more costly but easier to administer and beneficial for those with manual dexterity difficulties or physical limitations.

Home Enteral Prescription

A home enteral regimen may change several times during the course of therapy. Therefore it is important to maintain up-to-date records for com-

Exhibit 8-5 Home Enteral Prescription

	Date	Date	Date	
Formula				
Volume				
Extra water				
Strength				
Rate				
Schedule				
Route				
Final volume				
CHO (gm)				
FAT (gm)				
PRO (gm)				
KCAL				
Sodium (mEq)				
Potassium (mEq)				
Magnesium (mEq)				
Calcium (mEq)				
Phosphorus (mmol)				
%RDA				
Tube				
Additives				
Comments				

Abbreviations: CHO, carbohydrate; PRO, protein; %RDA, percentage of recommended dietary allowances.

parison (Exhibit 8-5).[9] All additives and medications are listed for easy reference.

OUTPATIENT VISITS

Generally, periodic outpatient visits are scheduled by the discharging hospital. Facilities that do not have a home enteral and parenteral nutrition clinic refer patients to one that can provide the necessary care. The optimal clinic visit incorporates the expertise of a dietitian, nurse, pharmacist, and physician.[10] Responsibilities for each discipline are shown in Exhibit 8-6.

Clinic Assessment

Patients receiving parenteral nutrition are usually seen within two weeks after discharge, or earlier if they are unstable. After the first visit, they are assessed on a regular basis until their metabolic course is stabilized. Patients receiving enteral nutrition are generally seen two to four weeks after discharge, again depending on stability. The patient is expected to bring in a record of temperatures, weights, urine checks (for glucose) and fluid balance, as well as a three-day food intake record when appropriate.

Members of the health care team evaluate the patient at each clinic visit. The dietitian takes a detailed diet, enteral, and parenteral history. This information is used to evaluate weight gains or losses, abnormal laboratory test values, and compliance with the nutrient prescription. A major role of the nurse is to reassess the patient for catheter care, as well as his or her psychosocial and environmental status. A medication history, ideally performed by a pharmacist, is also important to determine drug compliance. All of this information is recorded in an outpatient flow sheet (Exhibit 8-7). Careful assessment of fluid status is always necessary because excessive urine output may indicate the patient is receiving too much fluid, necessitating a volume reduction (approximately 500 milliliters to start). Conversely, an increase in diarrhea or stoma output may require an increase in fluid. Laboratory indexes should be monitored (Exhibit 8-8), with

Exhibit 8-6 Functions of the Home Care Team

Dietitian	*Nurse*
• Assessment	• Assessment
1. Nutrition status	1. Physical status
2. Metabolic goals	2. Psychosocial status
3. Diet history	• Review
• Review	1. Catheter care
1. Enteral orders	2. Enteral/parenteral technique
2. Parenteral orders	3. Nursing care plan
3. Diet instruction	• Recommendations
4. Enteral technique	
5. Nutrition care plan	
• Recommendations	
Pharmacist	*Physician*
• Assessment	• Assessment
1. Medication history	1. Physical examination
2. Compliance	• Review
• Review	1. Medical history
1. Parenteral orders	2. Prescription orders
2. Other drug therapy	3. Plan of care
• Recommendations	• Recommendations
	1. Nutrient prescription
	2. Medications
	3. Therapy
	4. Final plan of care

Exhibit 8-7 Outpatient Clinic Flow Sheet

Name: _____ Date: _____ Calorie/Protein Goal: _____

Wt.: Wt. Change: _____ %IBW: _____ %UBW: _____ %Goal: _____

Diet History Summary:

　Diet: _____ Fluid: _____

　KCAL: _____ CHO: _____ FAT: _____ PRO: _____ (gm) PRO: _____ (gm/kg)

　Supplements: _____

　Vitamin/Minerals: _____

　Comments: _____

Enteral and Parenteral Summary:

　Prescription: _____

　Schedule: _____

　Compliance: _____

　KCAL: _____ CHO: _____ FAT: _____ PRO: _____ (gm) PRO: _____ (gm/kg)

Current Problems:

　1. _____

　2. _____

　3. _____

　4. _____

　5. _____

Medications:

	Type	Dose	Frequency
1.			
2.			
3.			
4.			
5.			
6.			

No. of Stools/Day: _____ (loose/formed)   Nausea: _____   Vomiting: _____

Drainage/Day: _____   Catheter Site: _____   Dressing Changes: _____

Fluid Balance: _____

Vital Signs: _____ Temp.: _____ BP: _____ Pulse: _____ Resp. Rate: _____

Physical Examination: _____

Changes: _____

Diet: _____

Enteral: _____

Parenteral: _____

Medications: _____

Therapy: _____

Next Clinic Visit: _____

Abbreviations: BP, blood pressure; CHO, carbohydrate; %IBW, percentage of ideal body weight; PRO, protein; %UBW, percentage of usual body weight.

abnormal values addressed through corrections to the solutions. After the physician has examined the patient, the nutrition care plan is modified to correct any abnormal parameter and to make changes in the enteral or parenteral solution. It is convenient to have the home formula and supply delivery coincide with the clinic visit so the home care agency can incorporate the most recent changes and prevent wastage of nutrition supplies.

Weight Changes

Metabolic goals are set before discharge and at each clinic visit. Often, a patient is sent home on a nutrition repletion plan. It should be reviewed on a regular basis to prevent excessive weight gain. Once a desired weight is achieved, a maintenance nutrition plan is presented. Excessive fluctuations in weight can be due to fluid imbalances and should be corrected immediately. Patients with excessive fluid losses, as with gastrointestinal losses (vomiting, diarrhea, fistulas, ostomies, nasogastric drainage) should be monitored closely. Parenteral formulas can be readily concentrated; enteral formulas are available as 1.0, 1.5, and 2.0 calories per milliliter. Calories can always be added or subtracted from a feeding regimen to achieve a weight goal.

Home Care Agencies

Home care agencies should be evaluated for their ability to meet the needs of the patient and the referring hospital. Twenty-four hour availability is critical for safe home care. Some agencies allow nurses to draw blood samples for monitoring of laboratory values. A communication system between the referring hospital and the agency is important for good patient care.

LONG-TERM FEEDING: MONITORING AND COMPLICATIONS

Over time, enteral and parenteral feedings may produce many unique side effects, the pathophysiologies of which often are not fully understood. Careful monitoring of the patient is essential to prevent the occurrence of these complications or to lessen the symptoms. The following is a review of the most common complications associated with long-term home parenteral and home enteral nutrition support.

Exhibit 8-8 Home Enteral and Parenteral Monitoring

	Enteral	Parenteral	Comments
Date	x	x	
Weight	x	x	
REE	x	x	
MAC	x	x	
MAMC	x	x	
TRI	x	x	
Sodium	x	x	
Potassium	x	x	
Glucose	x	x	
Blood urea nitrogen	x	x	
Creatinine	x	x	
Chloride		x	
Carbon dioxide		x	
Calcium	x	x	
Phosphorus	x	x	
Magnesium	x	x	
Albumin	x	x	
Transferrin	x	x	
White blood cell count	x	x	
Prothrom bin time	x	x	
Hemoglobin	x	x	
Hematocrit	x	x	
Alkaline phosphatase	x	x	
Aspartate amino transferase	x	x	
Gamma-glutamyltranspeptidase	x	x	
Total bilirubin	x	x	
Triglycerides	x	x	
Cholesterol	x	x	
Ferritin	x	x	
Iron	x	x	
Zinc		x	
Copper		x	
1,25 Vitamin D		x	
25 Vitamin D		x	
Other			
Tube site	x		
Residuals	x		
Catheter site		x	
Patency	x	x	
Temperature	x	x	
Bone density		x	
Urine checks		x	

Abbreviations: MAC, mid arm circumference; MAMC, mid arm muscle circumference; REE, resting energy expenditure; TRI, triceps skinfold.

Home Parenteral Nutrition

Metabolic Bone Disease

Metabolic bone disease is one complication of long-term parenteral nutrition. Its cause is unknown. Patients on home parenteral nutrition for six months or longer often complain of periarticular bone pain, which becomes worse on bearing weight. Persons with metabolic bone disease may develop spontaneous fractures of the bones of the feet, the vertebrae, and the ribs. Some are so debilitated that they become nonambulatory and confined to a wheelchair.

Several investigators have studied metabolic bone disease. Results of early studies showed improvement in the disease after withdrawal of vitamin D from the parenteral solution.[11,12] Intravenous vitamin D was reported to be toxic to the bone and removing it decreased urinary calcium and phosphate excretion, reduced bone pain, and allowed fracture healing. Although little is known about the intravenous administration of the parenteral form of vitamin D (ergocalciferol, or vitamin D_2) and whether its bioavailability is the same as vitamin D_3 (7-dehydrocholesterol), these findings have not been confirmed by others.

In some centers patients have been studied for aluminum-induced osteomalacia. Klein and colleagues[13] found elevated aluminum levels in the bone, urine, and plasma of patients on long-term parenteral nutrition support. Seven of eight patients studied had osteomalacia. After substituting crystalline amino acids for casein hydrolysates (which were found to be contaminated with aluminum), aluminum levels in the urine and plasma dropped. Similarly, Ott and others[14] found that all their patients who were receiving home parenteral nutrition with casein hydrolysate had increased bone aluminum levels and reduced bone formation rates. Even though casein hydrolysates have been replaced by crystalline amino acids as a protein source, other additives in the parenteral solution may be contaminated with aluminum. Koo and others[15] measured aluminum levels in TPN additives and found high levels in calcium and phosphorus salts, ascorbic acid, folic acid, a multivitamin preparation, and albumin (25 percent).

The amount of protein infused has been implicated as a cause of metabolic bone disease. A high protein load has been known to cause an increase in calcium excretion. Bengoa and colleagues[16] examined calcium excretion after 1 and 2 grams of protein per kilogram of ideal body weight were administered. At 2 gm/kg, a high excretion of calcium contributed to a negative calcium balance. Der Vernejoul and others[17] also noted a correlation between protein intake and hypercalciuria. Wood and colleagues[18] examined the calciuretic effect of 18- or 12-hour cyclic infusions compared to continuous feeding. Calcium excretion in the 18- and 12-hour infusions was 19 percent and 28 percent, respectively, indicating a calciuretic effect with cycling. Recent studies have shown a decrease in bone matrix formation, rather than a mineralization defect.[19]

Metabolic bone disease remains a complex entity, partly because of its multifactorial nature (Exhibit 8-9). The role of vitamin D in normal bone development is known; less clear is whether the effect of the parenteral form (ergocalciferol, or vitamin D_2) is different from that of the oral form. Furthermore, actual parenteral requirements of calcium, phosphorus, and amino acids have not been defined. A trace element deficiency or suboptimal micronutrient level may also have an effect on bone development. Status of the bones before the initiation of long-term feeding is also an important factor. Many parenterally fed patients have been nutritionally depleted and ill for long periods and may have pre-existing bone disease as a result of malnutrition.

Essential Fatty Acid Deficiency

Linoleic acid is an essential fatty acid and must be supplied in the parenteral solution if adequate amounts cannot be absorbed through oral ingestion.[20] Manifestations of essential fatty acid deficiency are dry, cracked, scaly skin; hair loss; impaired wound healing; and mild diarrhea. Deficiencies of linolenic acid (another essential fatty acid) seldom occur except in the case of home parenteral nutrition. It has been proposed that a diet with two to four percent of the calories derived from linoleic acid will prevent a deficiency. The average patient will receive a sufficient amount with the infusion of 500 milliliters of a 10 percent lipid emulsion two or three times per week, although most patients receive lipids on a daily basis.

Liver Disease

Liver dysfunction develops in a small percentage of patients receiving long-term parenteral feedings.[21] Prematurity and a nonfunctional gastrointestinal tract predispose infants to hepatobiliary dysfunction as a result of cholestasis.[22] In adults, elevated values for liver function tests may be seen two weeks after initiation of TPN and have been attributed to overfeeding and high glucose loads.[23] In a study of patients on long-term parenteral nutrition support, Pitt and colleagues[24] reported a 35 percent incidence of cholelithiasis. Results from a study by Roslyn and others[25] showed a 23 percent incidence of gallbladder disease in patients receiving TPN. The first report of chronic liver disease associated with long-term TPN was that by Craig and colleagues.[26] In 1985 Bowyer et al.[27] studied 60 patients on

Exhibit 8-9 Possible Nutrition Factors in Metabolic Bone Disease

```
Disease State
  Crohn's disease
  Short-bowel syndrome
  Others
Nutrition Status
  Pre-existing bone disease
Macronutrients
  Carbohydrate content
  Protein load
  Solution volume
  Vitamin D and metabolites
  Other vitamins
Trace Elements
  Copper
  Fluoride
  Iodine
  Iron
  Manganese
  Molybdenum
  Nickel
  Selenium
  Silicon
  Zinc
Toxic Elements
  Aluminum
  Arsenic
  Cadmium
  Lead
  Mercury
  Strontium
Hormones
  Corticosteroids
  Insulin
  Parathyroid
  Other
Infusion
  Cyclic versus continuous
Minerals
  Calcium
  Phosphorus
```

long-term TPN and found 15 percent had abnormal liver function test values and steatohepatitis.

Many factors may be involved in TPN-associated liver disease. The administration of only glucose calories promotes fatty liver development. In contrast, the provision of excessive fat increases hepatic triglyceride, phospholipid, and cholesterol content. A protein deficiency that limits lipoprotein synthesis may also promote development of hepatic steatosis. Other factors that may contribute to liver disease are carnitine deficiency, essential fatty acid deficiency, and lack of gastrointestinal hormonal stimulation. Possible methods for prevention are administration of appropriate substrates, avoidance of excessive glucose or fat infusion, avoidance of overfeeding, provision of adequate amino acids, cycled feedings, encouragement of oral intake when appropriate to prevent cholestasis, and cessation of TPN.

Carnitine Deficiency

Carnitine is important in the beta oxidation of fatty acids. Because parenteral solutions do not contain carnitine, it must be synthesized by the liver and kidney. Carnitine deficiency has been associated with the development of hepatic steatosis, muscle weakness, and myopathy, as well as deposition of fat in muscle fibers.

A carnitine deficiency may develop after prolonged TPN therapy. In 1983 Worthley, Fishlock, and Snoswell[28] described a patient whose hyperbilirubinemia, muscle weakness, and reactive hypoglycemia improved after supplementation with L-carnitine. Hahn, Allardyce, and Frolich[29] found plasma carnitine levels were decreased in patients receiving TPN. Bowyer and colleagues[30] measured total and free plasma carnitine levels in a group of patients receiving home parenteral nutrition and found 35 percent had low levels. In 1988 Bowyer et al.[31] examined four patients with liver abnormalities and low total and free plasma carnitine levels. They prescribed carnitine supplementation, and after one month the carnitine levels improved. Values for liver function tests, plasma free fatty acids, and triglycerides, as well as grade of hepatic steatosis, however, did not improve significantly.

Taurine Deficiency

Taurine is not an essential nutrient because it can be synthesized from cysteine. Nevertheless, taurine deficiency can occur in patients receiving long-term parenteral feedings. Geggel and colleagues[32] studied 21 children and found decreased plasma taurine levels (47 percent of normal). Low levels were also seen in adults whose gut absorption was less than 25 percent. Furthermore, electroretinogram findings were abnormal in the eight children tested. (Taurine is important for rods and cones of the retina.)

Choline Deficiency

Choline levels also have been shown to be decreased in prolonged TPN as evidenced by a report by Chawla and others.[33] Although choline is considered nonessential because it can be metabolized from methionine and serine and is available in the diet, it plays an important metabolic role in the production of phospholipids and acetylcholine.

Vitamins and Trace Element Status

Monitoring of vitamin and trace element intake is essential in the home nutrition support patient population. In 1979 the American Medical Association's Nutrition Advisory Group approved multivitamin (Table 8-2) and trace element (Table 8-3) formulations.[34,35] These requirements are less than what is recommended orally because inefficiency of digestion, absorption, and assimilation are not factors.

Unfortunately, assessment of vitamin and trace element levels is difficult. Controversy exists over the best test to use to determine nutrient status. Plasma levels may only reflect recent intake, not total body stores. Urinary levels may be useless because many nutrients are not excreted unchanged.

Table 8-2 American Medical Association's Nutrition Advisory Group Recommendations for Multivitamin Preparations in Parenteral Nutrition

Vitamin	Daily Parenteral Dose
Vitamin A	3,300 IU
Vitamin D	200 IU
Vitamin E	10 IU
Thiamin	3.0 mg
Riboflavin	3.6 mg
Pantothenic acid	15.0 mg
Niacin	40.0 mg
Pyridoxine	4.0 mg
Biotin	60.0 μg
Folic acid	400.0 μg
Cobalamin	5.0 μg
Ascorbic acid	100.0 mg
Vitamin K*	5.0 mg/wk

*Parenteral vitamin K supplementation is not included in the official recommendation because some patients are receiving anticoagulants.

Source: Data from *Journal of Parenteral and Enteral Nutrition*, Vol. 3, pp. 258–262, with permission of American Medical Association, © 1979.

Table 8-3 American Medical Association's Nutrition Advisory Group Recommendations of Trace Element Preparations in Parenteral Nutrition

Trace Element	Daily Parenteral Dose for Stable Adult
Zinc	2.5–4.0 mg
Copper	0.5–1.5 mg
Chromium	10.0–15.0 μg
Manganese	0.15–0.8 mg

Source: Data adapted from *Journal of the American Medical Association*, Vol. 241, pp. 2051–2054, American Medical Association, © 1979.

Functional measurements may be the best, but they are exceedingly difficult to perform and standardize.

Vitamins. The exact parenteral requirement for a vitamin depends on the person. Studies have been designed to evaluate the effectiveness of vitamin mixtures in maintaining plasma levels and body stores. Three vitamins to consider in parenteral nutrition are vitamin A, vitamin E, and vitamin K.

The recommended daily parenteral vitamin A requirement is 3,300 international units. Not all of this is available to the patient, however, because one fourth to one third is lost during delivery. Vitamin A adheres to plastic intravenous bags and administration tubing. It also is light sensitive and undergoes photodegradation. Results of one study[36] showed an 88 percent reduction in vitamin A content after a five-hour period of administration.

The assessment and actual requirements of vitamin A levels in long-term TPN continues to be controversial. Results of one study indicated the recommended dose is insufficient for normalizing serum levels.[37] In a study of 16 patients receiving home parenteral nutrition Shils and others[38] found all values were above the normal range, although some of these patients were also receiving nutrition orally.   Patients with renal insufficiency should be monitored closely because long-term supplementation of vitamin A may produce hypervitaminosis.[39]

Vitamin E (tocopherol) prevents cellular lipid oxidation and protects polyunsaturated fatty acids from free radicals. Again, some of the vitamin E is lost during delivery as it adheres to plastic administration sets and bags. A study by Nicholalds and others[40] showed patients receiving parenteral nutrition had lower than normal vitamin E levels, whereas Davis and colleagues[41] observed that plasma vitamin E levels exceeded the normal range.

Vitamin K generally is not included in multivitamin mixtures and should be added separately as a daily or weekly parenteral dose or be given orally.

Caution should be used when a patient is also receiving anticoagulant therapy.[42]

Trace Elements. The requirements for trace elements are largely unknown. Although many other micronutrients probably are essential for normal nutrition, currently there are parenteral mixtures only for chromium, zinc, copper, molybdenum, selenium, iodine, and manganese.

Chromium is part of the glucose tolerance factor and enhances the sensitivity of insulin to the cell receptor site. Many signs of glucose intolerance have been attributed to chromium deficiency, among them hyperglycemia and insulin resistance. Other signs and symptoms include peripheral neuropathy, encephalopathy, atherosclerosis, and altered lipoprotein ratios. Results of several reports show glucose intolerance is reversed with chromium supplementation.[43-45] In addition, Freund, Atamian, and Fischer[46] observed that metabolic encephalopathy disappeared after chromium administration.

Zinc plays a significant role in cell proliferation, taste acuity, wound healing, and immunocompetence.[47] Because the major excretory routes are pancreatic/biliary and intestinal secretions, low levels may occur in those patients with excessive losses.

Copper deficiency, exhibited by a microcytic hypochromic anemia, neutropenia, and a low reticulocyte count, was one of the first micronutrient deficiencies associated with TPN. Deficiencies have now become rare with the use of trace element mixtures. Patients with copper storage disease and biliary obstruction should be monitored closely.

In a study by Abumrad and others[48] a deficiency of molybdenum produced amino acid intolerance, fatigue and somnolence. All deficiencies were reversed after infusion of molybdenum.

Selenium deficiencies have been well documented in the home parenteral nutrition population. Patients who are receiving parenteral nutrition long term and not receiving selenium supplementation and who also have low body reserves or limited oral intake, or live in low selenium soil content areas, are at risk for developing a deficiency. Watson and colleagues[49] reported low blood selenium levels in a 19-year-old patient with cystic fibrosis who developed myositis and muscle weakness three months after the initiation of TPN. In addition, Brown and others[50] observed low plasma and erythrocyte selenium and glutathione peroxidase levels in a 33-year-old woman with short-bowel syndrome who had been receiving TPN for four years. In another report Baptista and others[51] examined eight patients with short-bowel syndrome who were receiving TPN and found low levels of plasma and erythrocyte glutathione peroxidase. The death of a 24-year-old man with pseudo-obstruction has been attributed to a selenium deficiency.[52] In a recent study of patients receiving home parenteral nutrition,

Davis and colleagues[53] found plasma levels to be low or below the normal range.

Iodine is not routinely added to parenteral solutions because it is thought to be absorbed cutaneously through the use of iodine-containing germacides or by the oral route. Patients not receiving iodine should be monitored with thyroid function tests or assessment of plasma levels.

Because iron is not generally added to home parenteral solutions, many patients have iron deficiency anemia. Iron supplementation is preferentially given orally because parenteral infusion may cause anaphylaxis.[54,55] Before parenteral iron therapy is begun, a test dose should be given under medical supervision. Iron overload should be prevented because it is associated with hemosiderosis and cellular damage.

Catheter-Associated Complications

Catheter-associated complications are the greatest contributor to hospital readmissions associated with home parenteral nutrition support. Catheter breakage, sepsis, and catheter occlusion are among the major complications.

Catheter Breakage. Catheter breakage can usually be prevented if proper precautions are taken. The use of appropriate hemostats and clamps prevents the majority of breakage accidents. Accidental cutting by scissors, repeated clamping at the same site, and excessive pressure when flushing also can cause breakage. Most catheters have repair kits that allow the tubing to be fixed when enough exit tubing is available from the skin entrance site. The risks associated with catheter repair are contamination, migration of the stent at the repair site, and leakage.

Sepsis. The most frequently reported complication and the one that most frequently necessitates hospitalization is sepsis.[56,57] Because catheter related infections can be life threatening appropriate training for prevention is critical. Aseptic technique should be used at all times. The patient should also be reevaluated on a regular basis for appropriate catheter care. Depending on the severity of the case, a patient can be treated as an outpatient or may require hospitalization. Unfortunately, some parenteral antibiotic therapies are not compatible with parenteral solutions. Thus changes in the home parenteral nutrition cycling regimen may be required to incorporate adequate therapy. Some infections may require the removal of the catheter.

Catheter Occlusion. Another frequently reported complication is catheter occlusion as a result of clotting, malposition or kinking of the catheter, and formation of a sheath of fibrin and platelets. The fibrin sheath can cause subclavian vein thrombosis, thromboembolism, and infection. Heparin and warfarin may be prescribed prophylactically. Once an occlusion develops, antifibrinolytic agents such as urokinase may be used. Contraindications include recent surgery, pregnancy, cerebral accident, hematologic disorder, or active bleeding.

Home Enteral Nutrition

Home enteral nutrition is the preferred method of outpatient feeding and is used whenever possible. Complications among the home enteral population, although frequently overlooked, are common and have detrimental consequences. Careful attention and monitoring can prevent many of these complications.

Dehydration

Fluid requirements or limitations should be set before discharge. Alert patients are usually not at risk for dehydration because they can consume water orally or infuse water enterally to satisfy their fluid needs. Patients with neurologic disorders, however, may be unable to verbalize their need for additional fluids. The caretaker must be warned to observe for signs of dehydration.[58] Other patients at risk are those with gastrointestinal losses from vomiting, diarrhea, fistula output, drainage, and high-output ostomies. Signs of dehydration include orthostasis; weak, rapid pulse; concentrated urine; and a decreased urine output.

An estimate of fluid requirements for the adult with normal renal function is 35 milliliters per kilogram of body weight. (For young or underweight patients use more than 35 ml/kg, for elderly persons use less than 30 ml/kg, and for overweight persons base requirements on ideal body weight.[59]) A 1 kcal/ml formula is approximately 80 percent free water, whereas a 2 kcal/ml formula contains 70 percent. It is important to note that the patient receiving 2,000 kcal of a concentrated 2 kcal/ml product takes in only 700 milliliters of fluid. If the volume of formula does not meet the fluid requirements, a patient can dilute the formula, increase the volume or frequency of flushes, or consume fluid orally. At any time dehydration is suspected, electrolyte values should be checked.

Vitamins, Minerals, and Trace Element Status

Requirements for vitamins and trace elements in the home enteral population have been largely undefined. Generally, enteral formulas at a designated volume will provide 100 percent of the recommended dietary allowances. Few studies have addressed whether this will meet the needs of this population. In one study vitamin plasma levels were measured in patients receiving enteral feedings long term. Results showed in many the vitamin intake was in excess of the recommended dietary allowances. This excess, however, did not result in elevated plasma levels, except for biotin.[60] Carotene levels were assessed in three patients and were found to be low normal. Nonessential nutrients should be considered at risk in certain malnourished patients who may be unable to synthesize them, as in the case of choline, which has been shown to be low in patients receiving long-term enteral therapy.[61]

The most frequent metabolic abnormalities in the tube-fed patient are hyperglycemia, hyponatremia, hyperkalemia, and hypophosphatemia, along with iron deficiency.[62,63] Laboratory indexes (see Exhibit 8-8), including electrolyte and glucose concentrations, should be monitored on a regular basis and more frequently in the patient who experiences diarrhea, dehydration, vomiting or excessive drainage. If an electrolyte value is too high, a formula, with the electrolyte adjusted to a lower amount, can be substituted. If the value is too low, electrolytes can be added directly to the formula. In all cases, the patient should be assessed for underlying causes of electrolyte abnormalities. Patients with certain disease states should be monitored more closely for specific nutrient deficiencies. For example, patients with short-bowel syndrome may suffer from a vitamin B_{12} deficiency. Extensive gastrointestinal resections, drainages, fistulas, ostomies, and surgery may predispose patients to excessive vitamin, mineral, nutrient, and fluid losses.

Diarrhea

Diarrhea is a common complaint with enteral feedings. Several causes are listed in Exhibit 8-10.[64-69] Before medical therapy or a change in the enteral prescription, a thorough evaluation should be performed to establish the cause of the diarrhea. Medications can often be implicated. For instance, antibiotics can cause diarrhea by altering intestinal flora. Gastrointestinal hormones secreted by gastrointestinal neoplasms can produce diarrhea.[70] In addition, chemotherapy or radiotherapy can disturb normal intestinal motility, producing malabsorption.

A frequently overlooked cause of diarrhea is bacterial contamination of the formula, occurring as a result of poor hand washing and formula preparation. Ready-to-use commercial formulas are sterile until open. Care should be taken to wipe cans before using and to use clean preparation utensils and a clean technique. If a room is excessively warm (especially in the summer), the formula should be kept as cool as possible by using small volumes of formula, rinsing the bag between refills, or using a bag with an ice pouch. If a patient receives his or her water source from a well, periodic checking for contamination is necessary. If the well water is contaminated, sterile or bottled water must be used.

Exhibit 8-10 Possible Causes of Diarrhea in Patients Receiving Enteral Nutrition

Formula
Bacterial contamination
Improper administration
Hyperosmolar formula

Disease/Therapy
Medication side effects
Gastrointestinal surgery (ileostomy, gastrectomy)
Gastrointestinal disease
Intestinal malabsorption (short-bowel syndrome, atrophy, radiation enteritis)
Hyperosmolar medications
Bacterial overgrowth
Infectious process
Malnutrition
Specific nutrient malabsorption

Antidiarrheals are used to stop diarrhea or decrease it to a tolerable level without causing constipation or a paralytic ileus.[71] A contraindication to the use of these medications is infectious diarrhea, because gastrointestinal absorption of the bacterial toxin may be enhanced. Stool samples should be examined for ova and parasites, and cultured for *Salmonella*, *Shigella*, *Campylobacter*, and *Clostridium difficile* (also tested for toxin) before therapy is instituted.

Soluble fibers have been used to control diarrhea because they provide bulk and water-holding properties to the diet.[72] Formulas and medications containing such fibers can be used to normalize transit time.

Constipation

Patients with a history of constipation may benefit from a formula that contains fiber. The enteral prescription should also be checked for adequate fluid. Medications are available to help control excessive constipation.

Aspiration

The most serious complication of enterally fed patients is aspiration.[73] Aspiration of regurgitated or refluxed acidic gastric contents into the tracheobronchial tree can be life threatening. Neurologically impaired patients are at greatest risk for aspiration because they often do not have a gag reflex. If a patient is at high risk for aspiration, feeding into the small intestine is indicated and a nasoduodenal or jejunostomy tube should be placed. The disadvantage of a nasoduodenal tube is that it can be dislodged easily or migrate upward. Elevation of the head and trunk to at least a 30 degree angle may help decrease the chance of aspiration.

Checking residuals in gastric feedings is necessary to prevent the risk of aspiration. Residuals should be checked before each feeding and all contents returned to the stomach to prevent wastage of electrolytes and gastric contents. Except in the high-risk patient, most feedings are delayed if residuals exceed 150 milliliters. Residuals of 100 milliliters or less may represent the normal gastric volume present at any given time.

Drug–Nutrient Interactions

The enteral access should be used for medication administration only when no other route is available.[74-77] Medications and formulas may be incompatible and cause precipitation, which will ultimately clog the tube. Suspensions, elixirs, and oil and water emulsions are usually more compatible than oleaginous preparations and syrups. It has been shown that iron will react immediately with formulas and start to gel. Feeding tubes should be flushed with water before and after any medication administration.

Even though a medication may be physically compatible with the formula, it is not known whether its absorption or bioavailability will be altered by the formula.[78] Furthermore, medications have not been tested to be administered directly into the small intestine, and the site of delivery may decrease or enhance its therapeutic value by bypassing the natural pathway of drug delivery (mouth, esophagus, and gastric environment). Caution should be used when a prescribed medication is crushed because some drugs when crushed have altered physiologic effects. Another problem with administering drugs by enteral access is their high osmolality.[79] For example, the osmolality of potassium chloride elixir is approximately 3,000 mOsm, which is ten times isotonic. Thus it may cause cramping, bloating, and diarrhea.[80] Cutie, Altman, and Lenkel[81] have reported on the incompatibility of enteral formulas with certain medications.

Enteral Access Complications

Common complications with enteral feeding tubes are occlusion related to formula or medication precipitation or kinking of the tube (or both).[82] A careful flushing regimen is necessary to keep a tube patent. Generally, irrigation with water is the best method. When resistance is noted, gentle flushing should be applied because excessive force may cause the tube to break and cause the patient to aspirate the liquid. The tube should be assessed regularly for patency.

All tubes should be secured to prevent tube migration. If a patient is receiving a nasogastric or nasoduodenal feeding, proper tube placement should be checked before each feeding. Methods to ensure proper placement include examining the length of the portion of the tube that is outside the nose or checking the markers on the tube, checking gastric contents, or auscultating for air as 5 milliliters of air is injected into the tube. If dislodgment of the tube is suspected, the feeding should be delayed until proper enteral placement is verified.

The exit site of all surgically or endoscopically placed tubes should be examined on a regular basis. Swelling, redness, or tenderness may be signs of an infection. If drainage is noticed, the tube should be examined for breakage or migration or should be assessed to ensure proper tube diameter. Drainage at the tube site may cause skin breakdown. Frequent dressing changes, or use of an ostomy wafer or karaya gum, may help protect the skin. If the drainage is excessive, the patient should be evaluated by a physician for intestinal obstruction, which occurs in many patients with abdominal cancer.

SUMMARY

Successful enteral and parenteral therapy requires a systematic method of record keeping and monitoring. Although the cause of many of the long-term complications of forced feedings remain unknown, careful monitoring may decrease their frequency.

NOTES

1. Lyn Howard, Lenore L. Heaphey, and Maryann Timchalk, "A Review of the Current National Status of Home Parenteral and Enteral Nutrition from the Provider and Consumer Perspective," *JPEN. Journal of Parenteral and Enteral Nutrition* 10 (1986): 416–24.

2. OASIS, *Home Nutritional Support Patient Registry. Annual Report—1985 Data* (Albany, N.Y.: Oley Foundation and Silver Spring, Md.: American Society for Parenteral and Enteral Nutrition, 1987).

3. M.C. Gouttebel et al., "Ambulatory Home Total Parenteral Nutrition, *Journal of Parenteral and Enteral Nutrition* 11 (1987): 475–79.

4. Maurice Shils, "A Program for Total Parenteral Nutrition at Home," *American Journal of Clinical Nutrition* 28 (1975): 1429–35.

5. S.A. Chrysomilides and M.V. Kaminski, "Home Enteral and Parenteral Nutritional Support: A Comparison," *American Journal of Clinical Nutrition* 34 (1981): 2271–75.

6. J. Mershon et al., "Bacterial/Fungal Growth in a Combined Parenteral Nutrition Solution," *Journal of Parenteral and Enteral Nutrition* 10 (1986): 498–502.

7. M. Gilbert et al., "Microbial Growth Patterns in a Total Parenteral Nutrition Formulation Containing Lipid Emulsion," *Journal of Parenteral and Enteral Nutrition* 10 (1986): 494–97.

8. M.L. Ebbert, M. Farraj, and J. Hwang, "The Incidence and Clinical Significance of Intravenous Fat Emulsion Contamination during Infusion," *Journal of Parenteral and Enteral Nutrition* 11 (1987): 42–45.

9. H.T. Randall, "Enteral Nutrition: Tube Feeding in Acute and Chronic Illness," *Journal of Parenteral and Enteral Nutrition* 8 (1984): 113–36.

10. *Standards for Nutritional Support, Home Patients, 1985* (Silver Spring, Md.: American Society for Parenteral and Enteral Nutrition, 1985).

11. Moshe Shike et al., "A Possible Role of Vitamin D in the Genesis of Parenteral-Nutrition-Induced Metabolic Bone Disease," *Annals of Internal Medicine* 95 (1981): 560–68.

12. J.V. Seligman et al., "Metabolic Bone Disease in a Patient on Long-Term Total Parenteral Nutrition: A Case Report with Review of Literature," *JPEN. Journal of Parenteral and Enteral Nutrition* 8 (1984): 722–29.

13. G.L. Klein et al., "Aluminum Loading during Total Parenteral Nutrition," *American Journal of Clinical Nutrition* 35 (1982): 1425–29.

14. S.M. Ott et al., "Chronic Parenteral Nutrition," *Annals of Internal Medicine* 98 (1983): 910–14.

15. Winston W. Koo et al., "Aluminum in Parenteral Nutrition Solution—Sources and Possible Alternatives," *JPEN. Journal of Parenteral and Enteral Nutrition* 10 (1986): 591–95.

16. Jose M. Bengoa et al., "Amino Acid-Induced Hypercalcuria in Patients on Total Parenteral Nutrition," *American Journal of Clinical Nutrition* 38 (1983): 264–69.

17. Messing de Vernejoul et al., "Multifactorial Low Remodeling Bone Disease during Cyclic Total Parenteral Nutrition," *Journal of Clinical Endocrinology and Metabolism* 60 (1985): 109–13.

18. Richard J. Wood et al., "Calciuretic Effect of Cyclic versus Continuous Total Parenteral Nutrition," *American Journal of Clinical Nutrition* 41 (1985): 614–19.

19. Moshe Shike et al., "Bone Disease in Prolonged Parenteral: Osteopenia without Mineralization Defect," *American Journal of Clinical Nutrition* 44 (1986): 89–98.

20. R.T. Holman, S.B. Johnson, and T.F. Hatch "A Case of Human Linolenic Acid Deficiency Involving Neurological Abnormalities," *American Journal of Clinical Nutrition* 35 (1982): 617–23.

21. Alfred L. Baker and Irwin H. Rosenberg, "Hepatic Complications of Total Parenteral Nutrition," *American Journal of Medicine* 882 (1987): 489–97.

22. Denis R. Benjamin, "Hepatobiliary Dysfunction in Infants and Children Associated with Long-Term Total Parenteral Nutrition. A Clinico-Pathologic Study," *American Journal of Clinical Pathology* 76 (1981): 276–83.

23. C.C. Roy and D. Belli, "Hepatobiliary Complications Associated with TPN: An Enigma," *Journal of American Clinical Nutrition* 4 (1985): 651–60.

24. Henry A. Pitt et al. "Increased Rate of Cholelithiasis with Prolonged Total Parenteral Nutrition," *American Journal of Surgery* 145 (1983): 106–12.

25. Joel J. Roslyn et al., "Gallbladder Disease in Patients on Long-Term Parenteral Nutrition," *Gastroenterology* 84 (1983): 148–54.

26. Robert M. Craig et al., "Severe Hepatocellular Reaction Resembling Alcoholic Hepatitis with Cirrhosis after Massive Small Bowel Resection and Prolonged Total Parenteral Nutrition," *Gastroenterology* 79 (1980): 131–37.

27. B.A. Bowyer et al., "Does Long-Term Home Parenteral Nutrition in Adult Patients Cause Chronic Liver Disease?" *JPEN. Journal of Parenteral and Enteral Nutrition* 9 (1985): 11–17.

28. L.G. Worthley, R.C. Fishlock, and A.W. Snoswell, "Carnitine Deficiency with Hyperbilirubinemia, Generalized Skeletal Muscle Weakness and Reactive Hypoglycemia in a Patient on Long Term TPN: Treatment with Intravenous L-Carnitine," *JPEN. Journal of Parenteral and Enteral Nutrition* 7 (1983): 176–80.

29. P. Hahn, D.B. Allardyce, and J. Frolich, "Plasma Carnitine Levels during TPN of Adult Surgical Patients," *American Journal of Clinical Nutrition* 36 (1982): 569–72.

30. B.A. Bowyer et al., "Plasma Carnitine Levels in Patients Receiving Home Parenteral Nutrition," *American Journal of Clinical Nutrition* 43 (1986): 85–91.

31. B.A. Bowyer et al., "ʟ-Carnitine Therapy in Home Parenteral Nutrition Patients with Abnormal Liver Tests and Low Plasma Carnitine Concentrations," *Gastroenterology* 94 (1988): 434–38.

32. Harry S. Geggel et al., "Nutritional Requirements for Taurine in Patients Receiving Long Term Parenteral Nutrition," *New England Journal of Medicine* 312 (1985): 142–46.

33. R.K. Chawla et al., "Plasma Concentrations of Transulfuration Pathway Products during Nasoenteral and Intravenous Hyperalimentation of Malnourished Patients," *American Journal of Clinical Nutrition* 42 (1985): 577–84.

34. American Medical Association, Department of Foods and Nutrition, "Multivitamin Preparations for Parenteral Use: A Statement by the Nutrition Advisory Group," *JPEN. Journal of Parenteral and Enteral Nutrition* 3 (1979): 258–62.

35. American Medical Association, Department of Foods and Nutrition, "Guidelines for Essential Trace Element Preparations for Parenteral Use," *Journal of Parenteral and Enteral Nutrition* 241 (1979): 2034–51.

36. Martha A. Riggle and Richard B. Brandt, "Decrease of Available Vitamin A in Parenteral Nutrition Solutions," *JPEN. Journal of Parenteral and Enteral Nutrition* 10 (1986): 388–92.

37. George E. Nichoalds, H.C. Meng and Michael D. Caldwell, "Vitamin Requirements in Patients Receiving Total Parenteral Nutrition," *Archives of Surgery* 112 (1977): 1061–64.

38. Maurice E. Shils, Hermann Baker, and Oscar Frank, "Blood Vitamin Levels of Long-Term Adult Home Total Parenteral Nutrition Patients: The Efficacy of the AMA-FDA Parenteral Multivitamin Formulation," *JPEN. Journal of Parenteral and Enteral Nutrition* 9 (1985): 179–88.

39. Elizabeth E. Gleghorn et al., "Observations of Vitamin A Toxicity in Three Patients with Renal Failure Receiving Parenteral Alimentation," *American Journal of Clinical Nutrition* 44 (1986): 107–12.

40. Nichoalds, Meng, and Caldwell, "Vitamin Requirements in Patients Receiving Total Parenteral Nutrition," 1061–64.

41. A.T. Davis et al., "Plasma Vitamin and Mineral Status in Home Parenteral Nutrition Patients," *JPEN. Journal of Parenteral and Enteral Nutrition* 11 (1987): 480–85.

42. S.D. Krasinski et al. "The Prevalence of Vitamin K Deficiency in Chronic Gastrointestinal Disorders," *American Journal of Clinical Nutrition* 41 (1985): 639–43.

43. R.O. Brown et al., "Chromium Deficiency after Long-Term Total Parenteral Nutrition," *Digestive Diseases and Sciences* 31 (1986): 661–64.

44. H. Freund, S. Atamian, and J.E. Fischer, "Chromium Deficiency during Total Parenteral Nutrition," *Journal of the American Medical Association* 241 (1979): 496–98.

45. K.N. Jeejeebhoy et al., "Chromium Deficiency, Glucose Intolerance and Neuropathy Reversed by Chromium Supplementation in a Patient Receiving Long-Term Total Parenteral Nutrition," *JPEN. Journal of Parenteral and Enteral Nutrition* 30 (1977): 531–38.

46. Freund, Atamian, and Fischer, "Chromium Deficiency during Total Parenteral Nutrition," 496–98.

47. James M. Oleske et al., "Zinc Therapy of Depressed Cellular Immunity in Acrodermatitis Enteropathica: Its Correction," *American Journal of Diseases of Children* 133 (1979): 915.

48. N.N. Abumrad et al., "Acquired Molybdenum Deficiency" (Abstract), *Clinical Research* 27 (1979): 774A.

49. R.D. Watson et al., "Selenium Responsive Myositis during Prolonged Home Parenteral Nutrition in Cystic Fibrosis," *JPEN. Journal of Parenteral and Enteral Nutrition* 9 (1985): 58–60.

50. M.R. Brown et al., "Proximal Muscle Weakness and Selenium Deficiency Associated with Long Term Parenteral Nutrition," *American Journal of Clinical Nutrition* 43 (1986): 549–54.

51. R.J. Baptista et al., "Utilizing Selenious Acid to Reverse Selenium Deficiency in Total Parenteral Nutrition Patients," *American Journal of Clinical Nutrition* 39 (1984): 816–20.

52. C.R. Fleming et al., "Selenium Deficiency and Fatal Cardiomyopathy in a Patient on Home Parenteral Nutrition," *Gastroenterology* 83 (1982): 689–93.

53. Davis et al., "Plasma Vitamin and Mineral Status in Home Parenteral Nutrition Patients," 480–85.

54. J.A. Nortan et al., "Iron Supplementation of Total Parenteral Nutrition: A Prospective Study," *JPEN. Journal of Parenteral and Enteral Nutrition* 7 (1983): 457–61.

55. G. Richard Lee et al., "Iron Deficiency and Iron-Deficiency Anemia, in *Clinical Hematology*, 8th ed., Maxwell M. Wintrobe ed. (Philadelphia, Pa.: Lea & Febiger, 1981), 617–36.

56. Howard, Heaphey, and Timchalk, "A Review of the Current National Status of Home Parenteral and Enteral Nutrition from the Provider and Consumer Perspective," 416–24.

57. C.R. Fleming, D.J. Witzke, and R.W. Beart, "Catheter-Related Complications in Patients Receiving Home Parenteral Nutrition," *Annals of Surgery* 192 (1980): 593–99.

58. W. Kubo et al., "Fluid and Electrolyte Problems of Tube-Fed Patients," *American Journal of Nursing* 76 (1976): 912–16.

59. H.T. Randall, "Fluid, Electrolyte, and Acid-Base Balance," *Surgical Clinics of North America* 56 (1976): 1019–58.

60. Y. Berner et al., "Vitamin Plasma Levels in Long Term Enteral Feeding Patients," *Clinical Research* 36 (1988): 754A.

61. Chawla et al., "Plasma Concentrations of Transulfuration Pathway Products during Nasoenteral and Intravenous Hyperalimentation of Malnourished Patients," 577–84.

62. E. Cataldi-Betcher et al., "Complications Occurring during Enteral Nutrition Support. A Prospective Study," *JPEN. Journal of Parenteral and Enteral Nutrition* 7 (1983): 546–52.

63. S. Vanlandingham, "Metabolic Abnormalities in Patients Supported with Enteral Tube Feeding," *JPEN. Journal of Parenteral and Enteral Nutrition* 5 (1981): 322–24.

64. T.W. Kelly, M.R. Patrick, and K.M. Hillman, "Study of Diarrhea in Critically Ill Patients," *Critical Care Medicine* 11 (1983): 7–9.

65. P.P. Keohane et al., "Relation Between Osmolality of Diet and Gastrointestinal Side Effects in Enteral Nutrition," *British Medical Journal* 288 (1984): 678–80.

66. F.J. Tedesco, "Ampicillin-Associated Diarrhea—A Prospective Study," *Digestive Diseases and Sciences* 20 (1975): 295–97.

67. J.H. Walsh et al., "Gastrointestinal Hormones in Clinical Disease: Recent Developments," *Annals of Internal Medicine* 90 (1979): 817–28.

68. K.R. Anderson et al., "Bacterial Contamination of Tube-Feeding Formulas," *JPEN. Journal of Parenteral and Enteral Nutrition* 8 (1984): 673–77.

69. R.G. Pietrusko, "Drug Therapy Reviews: Pharmacotherapy of Diarrhea," *American Journal of Hospital Pharmacy* 36 (1979): 757–67.

70. Walsh et al., "Gastrointestinal Hormones in Clinical Disease: Recent Developments," 817–28.

71. Pietrusko, "Drug Therapy Reviews: Pharmacotherapy of Diarrhea," 757–67.

72. K.D. Burkitt, A.R. Walker, and N.S. Painter, "Effect of Dietary Fibre on Stools and Transit-Times, and Its Role in the Causation of Disease," *Lancet* 11 (1972): 1408–11.

73. L. Olivares, A. Segovia, and R. Revuelta, "Tube Feeding and Lethal Aspiration in Neurological Patients. A Review of 720 Autopsy Cases," *Stroke* 5 (1974): 654–57.

74. L.A. Bauer, "Interference of Oral Phenytoin in Absorption by Continuous Nasogastric Feedings," *Neurology* 32 (1982): 570–72.

75. K.C. White and K.L. Harkavy, "Hypertonic Formula Resulting from Added Oral Medications," *American Journal of Diseases of Children* 136 (1982): 931–33.

76. P.W. Niemiec et al., "Gastrointestional Disorders Caused by Medication and Electrolyte Solution Osmolality During Enteral Nutrition," *JPEN. Journal of Parental and Enteral Nutrition* 7 (1983): 387–89.

77. A.J. Cutie, E. Altman, and L. Lenkel, "Compatibility of Enteral Products with Commonly Employed Drug Additives," *JPEN. Journal of Parenteral and Enteral Nutrition* 7 (1983): 186–91.

78. Bauer, "Interference of Oral Phenytoin in Absorption by Continuous Nasogastric Feedings," 570–72.

79. White and Harkavy, "Hypertonic Formula Resulting from Added Oral Medications," 931–33.

80. Niemiec et al., "Gastrointestinal Disorders Caused by Medication and Electrolyte Solution Osmolality during Enteral Nutrition," 387–89.

81. Cutie, Altman, and Lenkel, "Compatibility of Enteral Products with Commonly Employed Drug Additives," 186–91.

82. S. Marcuard and A. Perkins, "Clogging of Feeding Tubes," *JPEN. Journal of Parenteral and Enteral Nutrition* 12 (1988): 403–05.

Chapter 9

Developing a Support Network

Karen Londa

INTRODUCTION

For patients and their families, the return home after hospitalization, regardless of cause or length of stay, is filled with intense and conflicting feelings. Although patients usually feel happy, relieved, and encouraged to leave the hospital and return to familiar and reassuring surroundings, they often feel frightened and vulnerable without the supervision provided to them in the hospital by members of the health care team. Fear appears even more pronounced in the patient who has been discharged with special hygiene or nutrition needs requiring active involvement in self-care.

Recent cost-containment efforts and related increased review of and accountability for hospital bed utilization have forced patients to undergo much of their convalescence outside the hospital. "The introduction of prospective payments using diagnosis-related groups in hospitals has resulted in earlier discharge of patients who require supportive care at home."[1] Patients may be considered ready for discharge before they feel fully recovered and able to cope with their needs. Furthermore, relatives often experience a sense of increased responsibility for the patient's well-being and doubt their own coping abilities.

The goal of social work in the health care setting is to facilitate optimal adjustment of the patient to his or her illness, course of treatment, and return to community. Medical social workers are responsible for discharge planning because of their psychosocial perspective, education and training, and knowledge of community resources. Appropriate, effective, and timely discharge planning minimizes the stress that patients and their families experience as they are helped to create and utilize a support network. This network is developed by facilitating the patient's coping, defining family caretaking functions, and using public and private community resources for financial help, home care, and supportive counseling.

ASSESSMENT OF NEEDS

Discharge planning is the process by which hospital staff members assist patients and their relatives in identification of and compliance with the patient's needs after hospitalization. Effective discharge planning requires

1. interdisciplinary collaboration among members of the health care team,
2. assessment of the patient's psychosocial functioning,
3. assessment of the availability of significant others,
4. knowledge of available community resources, and
5. coordinated timing of interventions.

Interdisciplinary Collaboration

Team cooperation is the keystone of a successful home care program.[2] Ongoing discussions enhance the team's awareness of the patient's physical and emotional needs, clarify each member's role in helping meet these needs, minimize duplication and overlap of interventions, and reduce misunderstanding or miscommunication among the team, patient, and patient's family. Effective discharge planning requires interdisciplinary collaboration throughout the patient's hospitalization.

Psychosocial Assessment

Assessment of the patient's psychosocial functioning evaluates past emotional defenses and coping strategies, their present effectiveness, and resolutions of past problems and stresses. This assessment allows the team to differentiate between the usually well-adjusted patient reacting to the stress of a health crisis and the patient with an underlying psychopathology that will interfere with adaptation.[3] Through this process, the team can develop strategies to promote patient compliance with medical recommendations and facilitate active patient participation in the discharge planning process. The facilitation of patient coping requires the patient's involvement in "discussion and a working over of the what and the how and, often, the why of actions to be taken."[4] This involvement promotes the patient's sense of regained control over body and environment.[5] Patient participation also enhances feelings of self-worth by fostering a sense of mastery and promotes patient compliance with hygiene, nutrition, and medical treatment after discharge from the hospital.

Availability of Significant Others

The successful discharge plan must involve both the patient and his or her family. Results of studies in published literature, as well as clinical experience, suggest that family members or friends who understand the need for and encourage patient cooperation with medical recommendations promote compliance. Conversely, caretakers who do not participate in the planning process may interfere with compliance.[6]

Assessment of the patient's support system must include not only evaluation of the needs, strengths, and capabilities of the family, both as individuals and as a collective unit, but also the family's ability to perform the tasks with which the patient requires help. Caretakers often experience frustration, conflict, and feelings of guilt and helplessness from the burden of coping with a stressful, extended illness.[7] In addition, the "inability of a patient or family to seek out and obtain appropriate services and interventions may lead to psychopathological functioning."[8] Therefore the health care team must understand the family's past and present functioning and its current availability to the patient.

Knowledge of Community Resources

An awareness of available community resources requires knowledge of eligibility criteria, referral procedures, and extent and limit of specific services. For example, third-party payers differ in reimbursed home care benefits for patients whose physicians have ordered nursing supervision in the home. Knowledge of resources prevents unrealistic or inappropriate referrals and patient or family disappointment when expectations of help are not to be met.

Interdisciplinary collaboration, assessment of coping mechanisms and support, and knowledge of resources enables the social worker to identify patients at risk for problems after discharge. This identification facilitates the team's development of coordinated interventions to meet the practical and emotional needs of the patient and his or her family. Patient groups at high risk because of unmet home care needs vary from hospital to hospital, depending on the specific populations served. Common risk indicators include the patient's age, marital status, diagnosis, home environment, family support, socioeconomic status, insurance coverage, special care needs, and frequency of hospitalizations.[9]

Timing of Intervention

When should the discharge planning process begin? Social workers believe in both crisis intervention and, more importantly, crisis prevention.

Early referral enables the assessment of patient adjustment and the anticipation, reduction, or elimination of adaptation problems. Not all patients or families are ready to begin the discharge planning process at the same point in time, however. Their overwhelming feelings about the illness, treatment, or home care needs may lead to active avoidance of discharge planning.

Premature discussion of needs after discharge from the hospital (i.e., before the patient and family start to work through their emotional reactions and integrate and accept the realities of the medical situation) can further overwhelm, frighten, or even alienate the patient and his or her family. Furthermore, it can cause a distorted perception of discussions with and recommendations by hospital staff and feelings of being forced out of or abandoned by the hospital. Team members should coordinate their discussions with patients and significant others to promote patient adaptation, compliance with special care requirements, and feelings of regained control.

The team can begin to finalize plans once the physician communicates an approximate discharge date. Dietitians are consulted to review diets, instruct on special enteral feeding procedures, and arrange for home supplies such as formulas or pumps. Nurses reinforce the dietitian's instructions and hygiene practices not yet mastered. Social workers help assess patient adaptation and coordinate supplemental home care services.

FINANCIAL ISSUES

Acute or chronic illness often results in tremendous financial burden. A reduction in or loss of income because of disability or outstanding nonreimbursed expenses can deplete available assets. Financial stress can cause anxiety and exacerbate feelings of helplessness and hopelessness. Although most patients have health insurance, they frequently are unfamiliar with the details of their coverage. It is not uncommon for patients who thought they were well insured to be shocked and angered on learning, in the middle of a health crisis, that their insurance was not as comprehensive as expected. The social worker can help patients clarify and maximize their home care benefits. Unless the cost of private home care is not a problem, it is important that patients understand their benefits before completing home care arrangements.

Third-party payers, such as Medicare, Medicaid, private insurers, and HMOs, reimburse for home care services only when the physician provides written documentation of patient need. Eligibility criteria for services, reimbursable home care agencies, categories of home care personnel, and length and frequency of visits differ among insurers. Similarly, third-party payers vary in their reimbursement of special equipment, transportation, supplies, and formulas. The social worker can help patients understand and use insurance and community resources and advise them of additional sources of income, including public assistance programs, state and federal disability benefits, and veterans' pensions.

It is unrealistic for patients and families to make home care plans on the basis of assumptions of reimbursement. Health care staff must guard against unintentional fostering of unrealistic expectations. Home care services should not be promised until patient resources, insurance benefits, and available services are known.

HOME CARE RESOURCES

Early referral of patients in need of support services enables the social worker to ascertain access to home care personnel. Community resources vary by availability of staff, including housekeepers, home attendants, home health aides, licensed practical nurses, and registered nurses. Cost increases with the level of skill. The number of hours and type of worker contracted for is based on the tasks to be performed and the patient's financial resources. The increased need for home care services and the related expansion of the home care industry has resulted in the development of precise guidelines to define the specific tasks each level of worker can perform. For example, tube feeding operation often is limited to licensed practical nurses or registered nurses. Fee schedules also differ among communities and agencies.

Patients who are independent in their feedings or have adequate assistance with this task from family or friends can use a less skilled and less costly home care worker, as long as the trained relative or visiting nurse provides necessary intermittent skilled care. Patients requiring assistance only with unskilled personal hygiene, such as bathing, grooming, dressing, and housekeeping, employ a home attendant or health aide. Those needing assistance only with domestic chores or supervision of young children employ a housekeeper or homemaker.

Types of Resources

Certified Home Care Agencies

Certified home care agencies, including visiting nurse associations and many hospital-based programs, meet federal and state government guidelines and standards of patient care and are eligible for Medicare, Medicaid, and, frequently, private insurance reimbursement. They usually service patients who require skilled nursing assistance no more than once a day. A registered nurse performs time-limited skilled nursing functions and provides ongoing instruction and supervision. In addition, the nurse can arrange for and supervise a home health aide; coordinate speech therapy, physical therapy, occupational therapy, and social work services; and order supplies, formula, and durable medical equipment. Insurance coverage and availability of staff often determine the number of visits per year that the patient can receive.

Hospices

Eligibility criteria, services provided, and third-party reimbursement for hospices vary from program to program, depending on certification, philosophy of practice, and funding. Hospices provide emotional support and practical help to the family and friends caring for the terminally ill. Hospices also arrange for supplies, food supplements, and durable medical equipment. Some are affiliated with hospitals to facilitate short-term hospitalizations when required.

Proprietary Home Care Agencies

Proprietary home care agencies are privately owned, for-profit businesses that offer a variety of personnel supervised by a registered nurse. Frequently, these agencies verify insurance coverage and bill the insurer directly for services and supplies. These agencies may be costly for patients with limited coverage and personal funds.

Nurse Registries and Employment Agencies

Nurse registries and employment agencies maintain listings of health care staff or domestic workers. They do not supervise these persons, and insurance companies are not billed for their services.

Voluntary Service Agencies

Organizations, such as the American Cancer Society, Cancer Care, Inc., the American Red Cross, and many family service agencies, assist with part-time home care needs, financial aid, outpatient transportation, durable medical equipment, and counseling. Specific services vary among individual chapters of each organization.

Senior Citizen Programs

Senior citizen programs offer low-cost, unskilled home care; individual and group counseling services; aggregate meals or meals-on-wheels; and opportunities for socialization to elderly persons.

EMOTIONAL ISSUES

Patients requiring home enteral or parenteral nutrition have intense reactions to discharge. Sadness, depression, or anger are common responses to anticipated changes in life style or to the inability to participate in family meals. Patients mourn the loss of the oral gratification and the pleasure they experienced from eating, regardless of whether the impairment is temporary or permanent. "By its very nature, tube feeding drastically limits the sensory pleasures which normally accompany eating."[10] Patients also must cope with the altered body image they perceive from a nasal feeding tube, gastrostomy tube, or total parenteral nutrition (TPN) catheter. Cachexia or additional changes in appearance as a result of trauma, tumor, surgery, radiation therapy, chemotherapy, or other health problems may compound the perception of disfigurement. While attempting to cope with these feelings, patients must learn to feed themselves and care for equipment and supplies required for their nutrition regimen.

Assistance from available family or friends is required for patients who are unable to master self-care techniques. It is important to clarify the extent of the designated caretakers' involvement, the specific tasks they are willing to perform, and their availability for instruction in carrying out these tasks. Planning for adequate home care requires the patient's and caretaker's psychologic acceptance of the severity of the problem and acknowledgment of the extent of their needs. Advanced planning helps both parties cope with stress by acknowledging apprehensions and working out solutions to identified problems.

Emotions often impact on relatives' ability to perform practical tasks. Team members should not underestimate the stress of the caretaking responsibility felt by significant others. Strong reactions to the patient's appearance or altered body functions can interfere with their ability to assist. Family members frequently are anxious, depressed, or angry about required adaptations to the patient's nutrition routine, changed roles within the family, or stressed interpersonal relations. Apprehension or doubt about their ability to follow a special diet or regulate tube feedings is common. Significant others can become overprotective, thereby reinforcing the patient's feelings of increased dependence. Ongoing education and counseling by the dietitian, nurse, and social worker help patients and caretakers cope with their feelings.

Creating a Network of Agency and Family Support

Patients, relatives, and health care staff frequently have unrealistic expectations of community resources, which sanction the patient's or family's withdrawal from active planning and often result in the failure of the home care plan. It is imperative that team members guard against premature guarantees of services until the selected agency has accepted the referral. Community agencies may be overwhelmed by and unable to meet the demands for services because of the trend toward home convalescence. For example, a social worker's exploration of available community resources for Mrs. E (a patient who lived alone, was bedridden, and required total assistance with activities of daily living, tracheostomy care, and feedings) indicated that shortages of home care staff in the community, inadequate insurance coverage, and patient finances would preclude a safe discharge home. In this case placement in a long-term care facility was indicated.

The following case illustrates the successful creation of a support network:

> Mr. and Mrs. A, a self-reliant 87-year-old man and his devoted 84-year-old wife, were overwhelmed by Mr. A's planned discharge on tube feedings. He was depressed, unmotivated, and refused to learn feeding procedures. Coordinated interventions by the health care team failed to promote his adaptation. Mr. A's depression lessened when he learned from his surgeon that his swallowing would improve at home. He began to participate in his daily care but still would not set up his tube feedings, although he was able to demonstrate correct procedures to his nurse. Mrs. A was uncertain of her ability to assume total responsibility for the home feedings.

> The social worker assisted Mr. and Mrs. A by helping them understand their feelings and anxieties. She suggested that their adult children become involved in the discharge planning process when Mr. and Mrs. A's continued concern made them unable to proceed with planning. The family agreed to a Medicare-reimbursed visiting nurse to monitor Mr. A's feedings and progress in swallowing and to a home health aide to assist with personal hygiene. Because Mrs. A requested more home care hours than Medicare allowed, the social worker helped her hire a private home health aide, trained in tube feedings, until Mr. and Mrs. A could assume more responsibility. The children paid supplemental home care costs, and Mr. and Mrs. A agreed to referrals to appropriate community agencies for financial assistance.

> After Mr. A's discharge, the social worker remained in contact with the patient, family, and visiting nurse to evaluate the adequacy of the home care plan, assist with changes, and provide supportive counseling. After two weeks at home, Mr. and Mrs.

A were comfortable with the tube feedings and discontinued the private home health aide. Medicare-approved services were maintained until the visiting nurse felt Mr. and Mrs. A were able to function independently.

Nursing Home Placement

Because of shorter hospitalizations, families have had to assume more responsibility for patient home care. Those who are unable to assume this responsibility, alone or with assistance, need help in accepting the limitations of their support and the recommendation for placement. Health care staff need to guard against being judgmental of these families.

Admission criteria for each prospective nursing home must be clarified. For example, skilled facilities may not accept tube-fed patients and will refuse those receiving TPN. The social worker should encourage patient and family to participate actively in the selection process and to visit each facility being considered. The decision for placement can be emotional for patient as well as relative. Obtaining as much information as possible about facilities, costs, sources of reimbursement, and alternatives to placement is an important step to ease this process.

Relatives frequently feel guilty about being unable or unwilling to care for the patient and often need counseling to work through their feelings. Patients experiencing anger toward the family, helplessness, hopelessness, or loss of autonomy also need to express, sort out, and work through their feelings.

Other Support Services

Group meetings offered by hospitals, mental health clinics, family service agencies, and voluntary organizations are important additional sources of emotional help. These groups can be organized and led by a mental health professional, frequently a social worker, and facilitate coping by providing information and counseling. They also can be self-help groups, which are organized and run by people with shared needs and experiences and frequently are action oriented to help others with similar problems.[11]

Self-help groups, such as Alcoholics Anonymous and New Voice Clubs (for laryngectomees), are organized around diseases or health adaptation issues. These groups "have given individuals education, information, and an opportunity to share experience and develop solutions to common problems"[12] and are particularly responsive to the needs of people coping with illness, disability, or change in social role. Education and sharing of experiences decrease feelings of isolation and uniqueness, facilitate problem solving, and result in enhanced feelings of competency, self-worth, and belonging. The social worker can assess the patient's or family's interest in this type of support and assist each with appropriate referral.

Patient volunteers also encourage adaptation by providing information, emotional support, encouragement, and hope to those just beginning to cope.[13] A well-functioning patient who has completed or is undergoing similar treatment is an encouraging role model. Meeting a volunteer enables new patients to ask questions and discuss adaptation related to altered body image, impact of feedings on daily activity or social life, and relations with others.

PATIENTS WITH MODIFIED ORAL DIETS

Any change in diet can be emotionally distressing to the patient. Patients frequently are overwhelmed by diet changes necessitated by impaired chewing, swallowing, or other factors. Health professionals should not disregard requests from these patients or their families for emotional support or practical help. The following case illustrates how the social worker can help secure support services.

Miss B was an 86-year-old woman. Although she had previously functioned independently and did not have special hygiene needs, she had requested home care services. The social worker's evaluation suggested that Miss B's diagnosis, disfiguring surgery, and discharge on a pureed diet had frightened her and exacerbated her fear of loneliness and permanent, increased dependence. She had outlived most of her close friends, lived alone, and had no nearby relatives. Miss B wanted to retain her self-sufficiency. The social worker helped Miss B hire a home health aide for several days after discharge to ease her transition home and referred her to a community-based senior citizens program for further counseling, socialization, and support.

CONTINUITY OF CONTACT

Outpatients find that continued contact with hospital personnel is reassuring and demonstrates ongoing interest and availability. Contact can be maintained through telephone calls, outpatient appointments, or home visits. Follow-up is reassuring and allows patients, families, and members of the health care team to reassess and modify the home care plan. Maintaining a dialogue with the home care agency or home care worker aids the social worker and health care team with this important reassessment process. Home care personnel contribute a valuable perspective on the patient's needs and functioning in the home and on the patient's interactions with family members.

Creating a support network to cushion the patient's transition from hospital to home promotes patient adaptation. Interdisciplinary collaboration, assessments of needs, and utilization of available community resources are coordinated interventions needed to create this network. With a support network in place, patients can leave the hospital with less fear and anxiety, enjoy continuing recovery in familiar and comforting surroundings, and effect a successful adjustment to nutrition support in the home.

NOTES

1. Vincent Mor, Edward Guadagnoli, and Margaret Wool, "An Examination of the Concrete Service Needs of Advanced Cancer Patients," *Journal of Psychosocial Oncology* 5 (1987): 2.

2. Lisbeth Houghton and Anita E. Martin, "Home vs. Hospital: A Hospital-Based Home Care Program," *Health and Social Work* 1 (1976): 91.

3. Grace H. Christ, "A Psychological Assessment Framework for Cancer Patients and Their Families," *Health and Social Work* 8 (1983): 64.

4. Helen Harris Perlman, "In Quest of Coping," *Social Casework* 56 (1975): 213–225.

5. Dorinda N. Noble and Adrianne K. Hamilton, "Coping and Complying: A Challenge in Health Care," *Social Work* 28 (1983): 463.

6. Ibid., 464.

7. Mor, Guadagnoli, and Wool, "An Examination of the Concrete Service Needs of Advanced Cancer Patients," 15.

8. Ibid.

9. For additional high-risk factors see Evelyn G. Hartigan, "Discharge Planning: Identification of High-Risk Groups," *Nursing Management* 18 (1987): 31–32.

10. Geraldine V. Padilla et al., "Subjective Distresses of Nasogastric Tube Feeding," *Journal of Parenteral and Enteral Nutrition* 3 (1979): 53.

11. Joanne E. Mantell, Esther S. Alexander, and Mark Allen Kleinman, "Social Work and Self-Help Groups," *Health and Social Work* 1 (1976): 87.

12. Rita Beck Black and Diane Drachman, "Hospital Social Workers and Self-Help Groups," *Health and Social Work* 10 (1985): 95.

13. Joanne E. Mantell, "The Use of Volunteer Visiting Programs in Life-Threatening Illness Situations," in *The Role of the Volunteer Director in the Care of the Terminal Patient and the Family,* ed. Harriet H. Naylor et al. (New York: Arno Press, 1981), 31.

BIBLIOGRAPHY

Barnet, Elena. "Home TPN—A Social Work Perspective." *Nutritional Support Services* 3 (1983): 42–43.

Becker, Nancy E., and Fred W. Becker. "Early Identification of High Social Risk." *Health and Social Work* 11 (1986): 26–35.

Black, Rita Beck, and Diane Drachman. "Hospital Social Workers and Self-Help Groups." *Health and Social Work* 10 (1985): 45–103.

Christ, Grace H. "A Psychological Assessment Framework for Cancer Patients and Their Families." *Health and Social Work* 8 (1983): 57–64.

Dropkin, Mary Jo. "Development of a Self-Care Teaching Program for Postoperative Head and Neck Patients." *Cancer Nursing* 4 (1981): 103–106.

Haeuser, Adrienne Ahlgren, and Florence Schwartz. "Developing Social Work Skills for Work with Volunteers." *Social Casework: The Journal of Contemporary Social Work* (1980): 595–601.

Hartigan, Evelyn G. "Discharge Planning: Identification of High Risk Groups." *Nursing Management* 18 (1987): 30–32.

Houghton, Lisbeth, and Anita E. Martin. "Home vs. Hospital: A Hospital-Based Home Care Program." *Health and Social Work* 1 (1976): 88–103.

Mantell, Joanne E. "The Use of Volunteer Visiting Programs in Life-Threatening Illness Situations." In *The Role of the Volunteer Director in the Care of the Terminal Patient and the Family*, edited by H.H. Naylor, M.M. Newell, B. Marcus, A.H. Kutscher, D.J. Cherico, and I.B. Seeland, 30–42. New York: Arno Press, 1981.

Mantell, Joanne E., Esther S. Alexander, and Mark Allen Kleinman. "Social Work and Self-Help Groups." *Health and Social Work* 1 (1976): 86–98.

McNett, Susan Cunningham. "Social Support, Threat, and Coping Responses and Effectiveness for the Functionally Disabled." *Nursing Research* 36 (1987): 98–103.

Mor, Vincent, Edward Guadagnoli, and Margaret Wool. "An Examination of the Concrete Service Needs of Advanced Cancer Patients." *Journal of Psychosocial Oncology* 5 (1987): 1–17.

Noble, Dorinda N., and Adrianne K. Hamilton. "Coping and Complying: A Challenge in Health Care." *Social Work* 28 (1983): 462–66.

Padilla, Geraldine V., Marcia Grant, Hilda Wong, Barbara W. Hansen, Robert L. Hanson, Nancy Bergstrom, and Winifred R. Kubo. "Subjective Distresses of Nasogastric Tube Feeding." *JPEN. Journal of Parenteral and Enteral Nutrition* 3 (1979): 53–57.

Perlman, Helen Harris. "In Quest of Coping." *Social Casework* 56 (1975): 217–18.

Polinsky, Margaret L., Patricia A. Ganz, Jacqueline Rofessart-O'Berry, Richard L. Heinrich, and Cyndie Coscarelli Schag. "Developing a Comprehensive Network of Rehabilitation Resources for Referral of Cancer Patients." *Journal of Psychosocial Oncology* 5 (1987): 1–10.

Slevin, Amy P., and Anne S. Roberts. "Discharge Planning: A Tool for Decision Making." *Nursing Management* 18 (1987): 47–50.

Waters, Karen R. "Discharge Planning: An Exploratory Study of the Process of Discharge Planning on Geriatric Wards." *Journal of Advanced Nursing* 12 (1987): 71–83.

Wolock, Isabel, and Elfriede G. Schlesinger. "Social Work Screening in New Jersey Hospitals: Progress, Problems, and Implications." *Health and Social Work* 11 (1986): 15–24.

Chapter 10

Pediatric Nutrition in the Home

Karen Yowell-Warman and Patricia Queen

INTRODUCTION

The goal of nutrition support in the pediatric population (from birth to 18 years of age) is to provide appropriate energy and nutrients for normal growth. Equally important, however, are the fostering of normal feeding skills and the promotion of socialization during mealtimes.

Pediatric nutrition differs in several respects from adult nutrition. First, unlike adults who are fully grown, children are still growing and are at risk for permanent growth stunting if nutrition is inadequate. Poor nutrition can also affect brain growth and learning capability.[1] Second, nutrition requirements for children vary with age and stage of development. Nutritionists must be aware of these differences when determining nutrition needs in pediatric patients. Third, children often are dependent on other caretakers to provide their nutrition. The input and cooperation of these caretakers is essential when formulating and implementing a care plan. Finally, the development of self-image and body image occurs during childhood and adolescence. Nutritionists must recognize the impact of their inventions on these developmental processes.

This chapter describes the requirements for providing enteral and/or parenteral home nutrition support in the pediatric population.

ESSENTIAL QUESTIONS

Beyond the obvious medical questions regarding the need for nutrition therapy, several questions are essential in the initial evaluation of a child for home nutrition support.

- Are the family and patient willing and capable of providing nutrition support at home?

- Are there financial constraints that may limit the type of home therapy implemented?
- How might feeding impact on other aspects of medical care?
- What effect might therapy have on extended family, friends, class-mates, and school personnel? How might this in turn affect therapy?
- What changes may be necessary to facilitate the transition from in-patient nutrition support to that used in the home?

Failure to consider each of these issues before initiating nutrition support in the home environment decreases the chances of success.

INDICATIONS FOR HOME NUTRITION SUPPORT

Nutritionists are responsible for identifying children who may benefit from home nutrition support. In many instances the need for support is obvious. For example, certain metabolic disorders require continuous feed-ings to maintain proper homeostasis and prevent complications.[2] Children with neurologic dysfunction or other conditions that impair the ability to feed by mouth also are obvious candidates for home nutrition support. These patients should be identified and nutrition support instituted even before their decline in nutrition status becomes apparent.

Criteria for implementing nutrition support when it is not the primary therapy for a disorder are not as clearly defined. Nevertheless, nutrition support is indicated in malnourished children who have failed to respond to standard nutrition and behavioral interventions and in children with growth failure as a result of etiologic factors other than heredity or hor-mones. Malnutrition and growth failure may be sequelae of numerous medical conditions. Examples of chronic medical disorders for which en-teral or parenteral nutrition support may be beneficial are listed in Exhibit 10-1.

The extent and duration of malnutrition or growth failure for which nutrition intervention should be implemented remains controversial. The National Center for Health Statistics' percentiles for physical growth (Fig-ures 10-1 to 10-8) and Waterlow's criteria (Table 10-1) are commonly used when assessing malnutrition and growth failure. In children with edema or ascites, in which weight cannot be assessed accurately, the triceps skinfold and arm muscle circumference may also be used.[3]

Nutrition intervention should be strongly considered in a child whose weight is less than 80 percent of standard weight for height (Waterlow's category 2) or whose height is less than 85 percent of standard for age. There are exceptions to this general rule. For example, children with acute weight loss after intermittent chemotherapy may not require aggressive

Exhibit 10-1 Chronic Diseases That Frequently Require Home Nutrition Support

Bronchopulmonary dysplasia
Congenital heart disease
Cystic fibrosis
Inflammatory bowel disease
Liver disease
Renal disease
Oncologic disorders
Acquired immunodeficiency syndrome (AIDS)

therapy if their weight loss is short lived. Children with medical conditions that limit growth potential irrespective of nutrition status may also warrant less aggressive intervention, particularly if their weight for height is normal.

MECHANICS OF HOME NUTRITION SUPPORT

Once it has been determined that a patient is a candidate for home nutrition support, the optimal site, route, and feeding schedule need to be determined. Appropriate equipment also needs to be selected.

The sites for provision of nutrition support in the pediatric population are similar to those in adults. When the gastrointestinal tract is functioning adequately, it should be used. Enteral feedings can be given by means of a tube, inserted nasally (nasoenteric tube) or placed surgically or endoscopically (gastrostomy or jejunostomy tube).[4] Total parenteral nutrition (TPN) administered through an indwelling catheter can be life sustaining when the gastrointestinal tract cannot be used. Peripheral parenteral nutrition is rarely used for the pediatric population in the home.

Delivery Sites

There are several advantages of feeding enterally instead of parenterally.

- Infection and metabolic abnormalities are less likely to occur.
- Restoration of digestive enzymes in the gut and maintenance of mucosal mass may be facilitated.[5]
- Cost is significantly less.
- Psychologic benefits may accrue, as enterally fed patients seem better able to participate in the socialization that occurs during meals.[6]

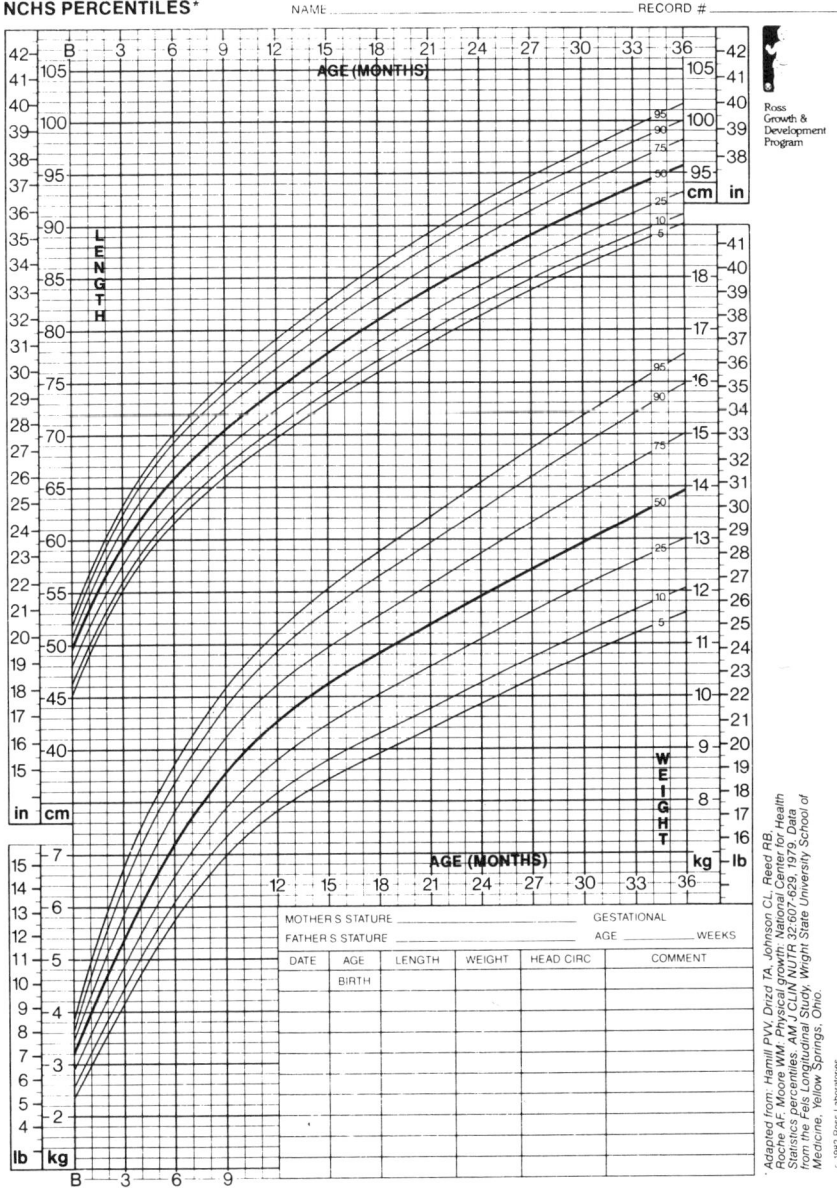

Figure 10-1 National Center for Health Statistics (NCHS) Physical Growth Percentiles for Girls, Birth to 36 Months

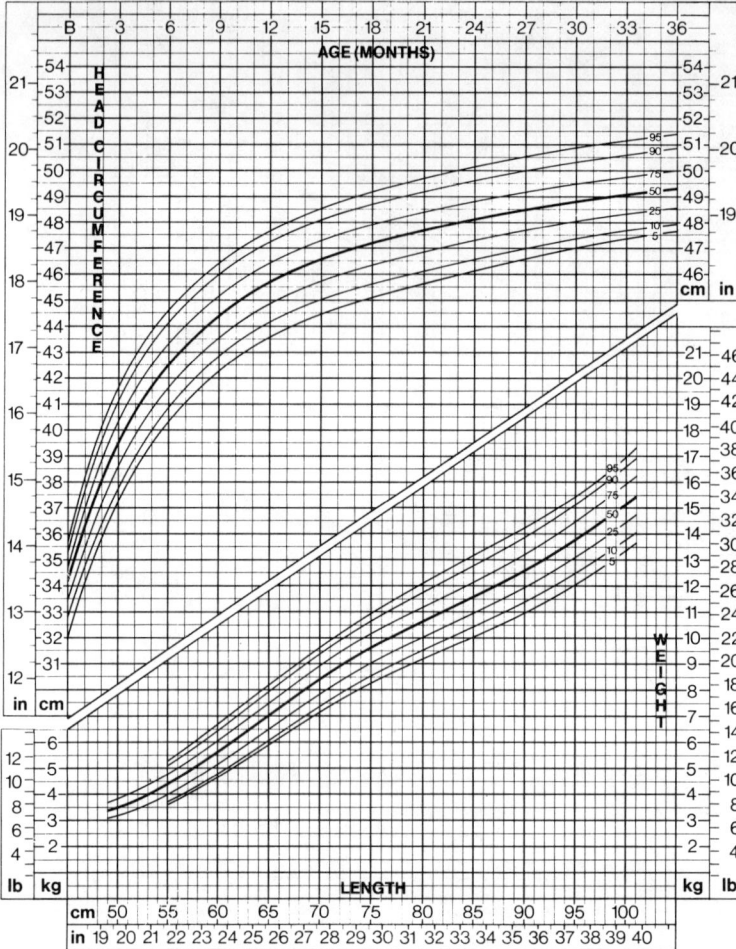

Figure 10-2 National Center for Health Statistics (NCHS) Physical Growth Percentiles for Girls, Birth to 36 Months

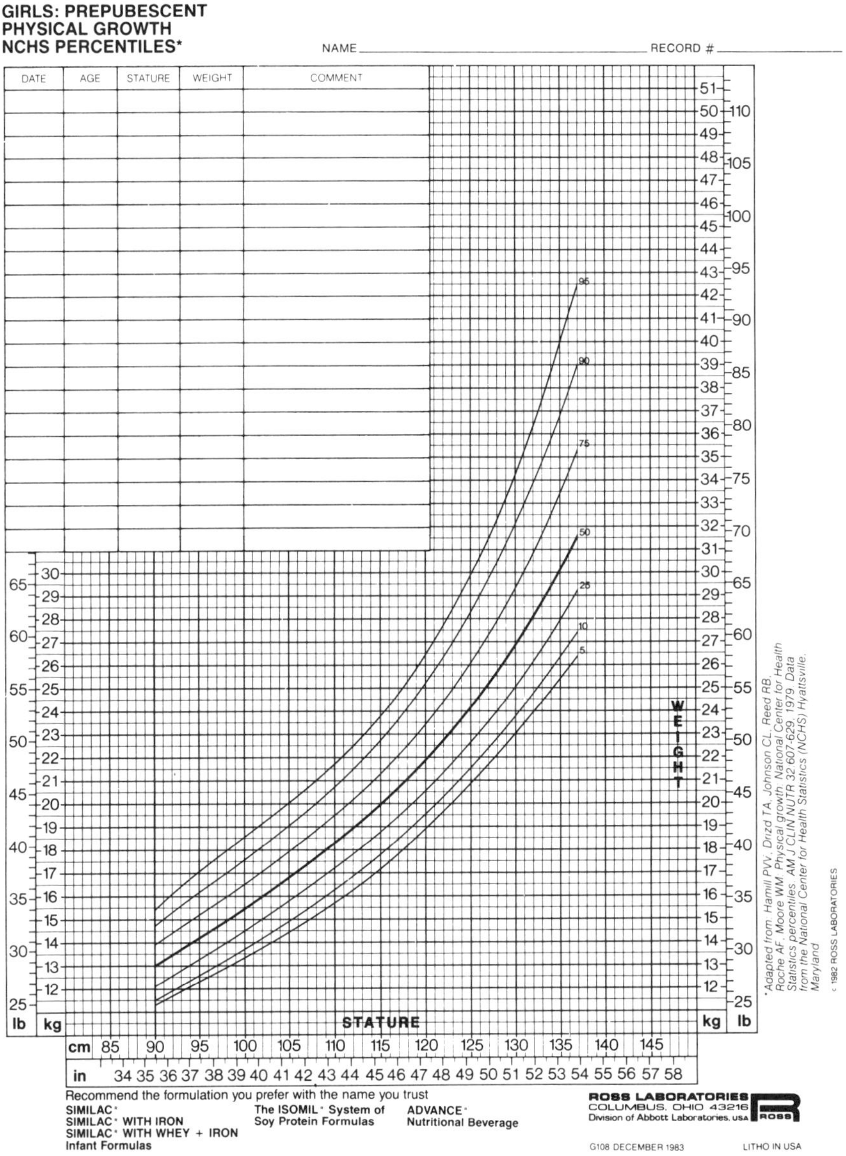

Figure 10-3 National Center for Health Statistics (NCHS) Physical Growth Percentiles for Prepubescent Girls

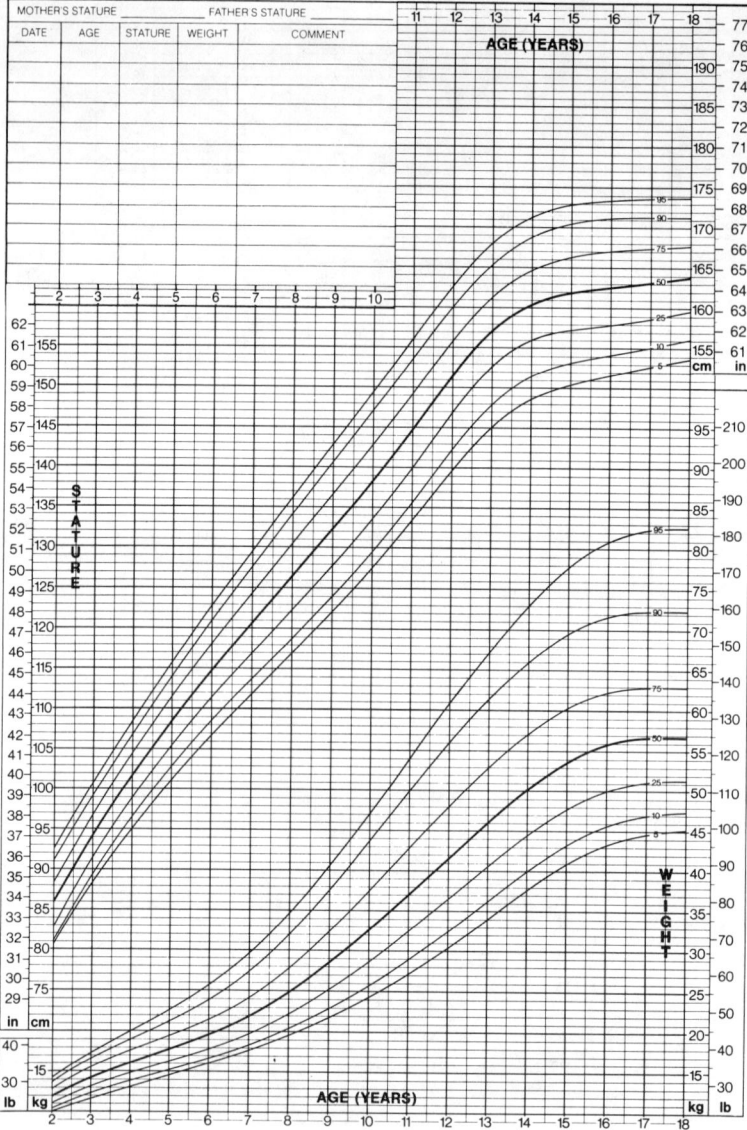

Figure 10-4 National Center for Health Statistics (NCHS) Physical Growth Percentiles for Girls, Aged 2 to 18 Years

BOYS: BIRTH TO 36 MONTHS
PHYSICAL GROWTH
NCHS PERCENTILES*

NAME _____ RECORD # _____

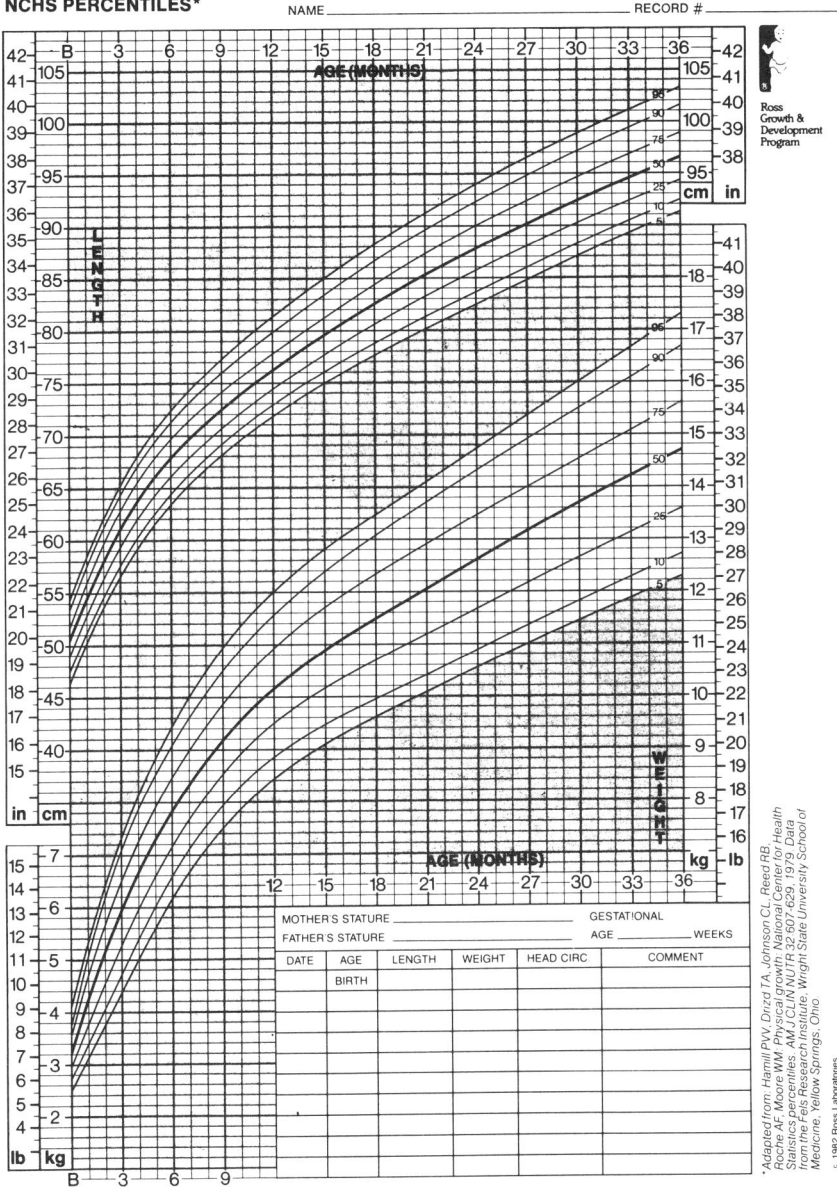

Figure 10-5 National Center for Health Statistics (NCHS) Physical Growth Percentiles for Boys, Birth to 36 Months

**BOYS: BIRTH TO 36 MONTHS
PHYSICAL GROWTH
NCHS PERCENTILES***

NAME_____ RECORD #_____

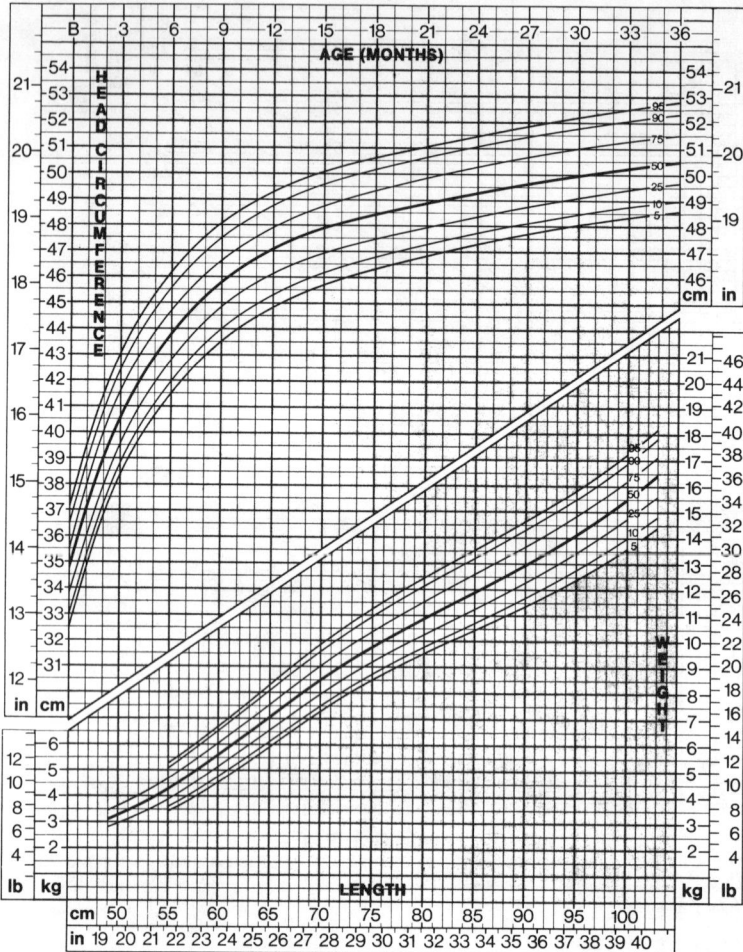

DATE	AGE	LENGTH	WEIGHT	HEAD CIRC	COMMENT

in vivo performance...

SIMILAC® Infant Formula
Closest to mother's milk.

ISOMIL® Soy Protein Formula
When the baby can't take milk.

ADVANCE® Nutritional Beverage

ROSS LABORATORIES
COLUMBUS, OHIO 43216
DIVISION OF ABBOTT LABORATORIES USA

G105 (0.05)/JUNE 1985   LITHO IN USA

Figure 10-6 National Center for Health Statistics (NCHS) Physical Growth Percentiles for Boys, Birth to 36 Months

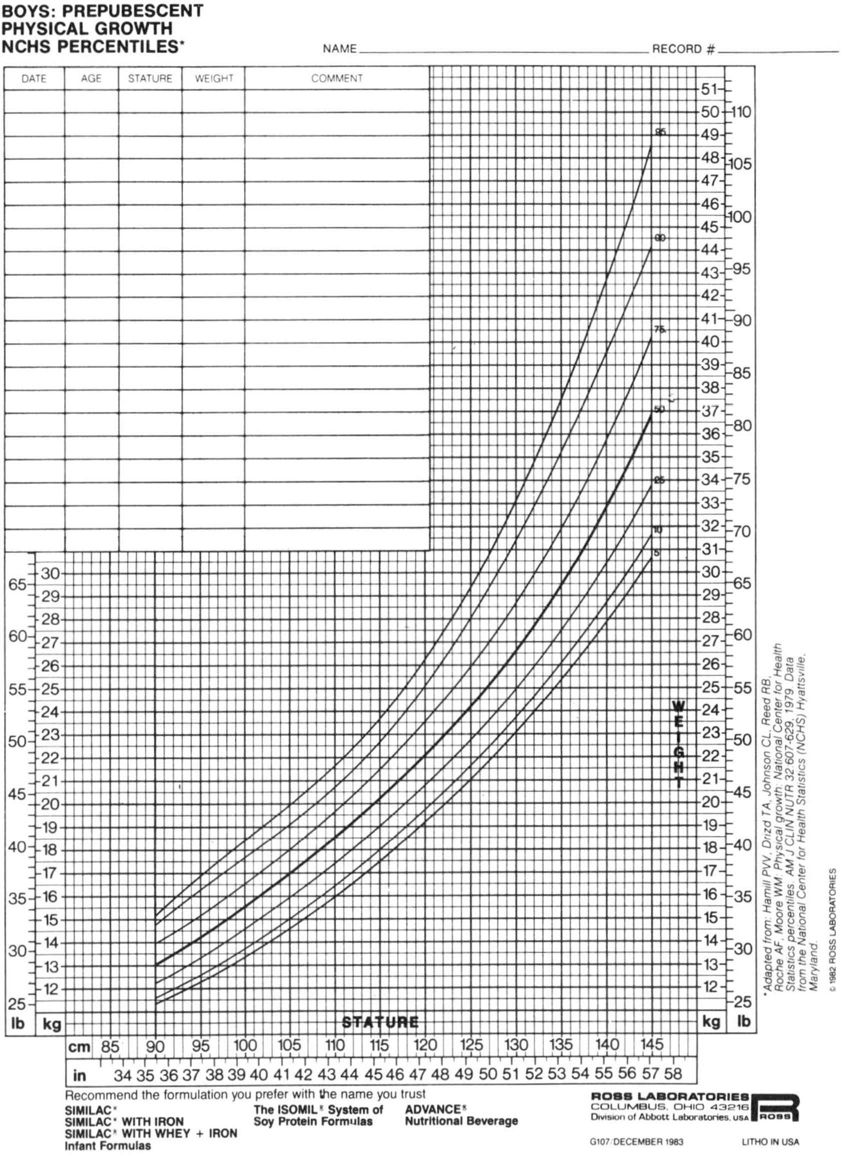

BOYS: PREPUBESCENT PHYSICAL GROWTH NCHS PERCENTILES*

Figure 10-7 National Center for Health Statistics (NCHS) Physical Growth Percentiles for Prepubescent Boys

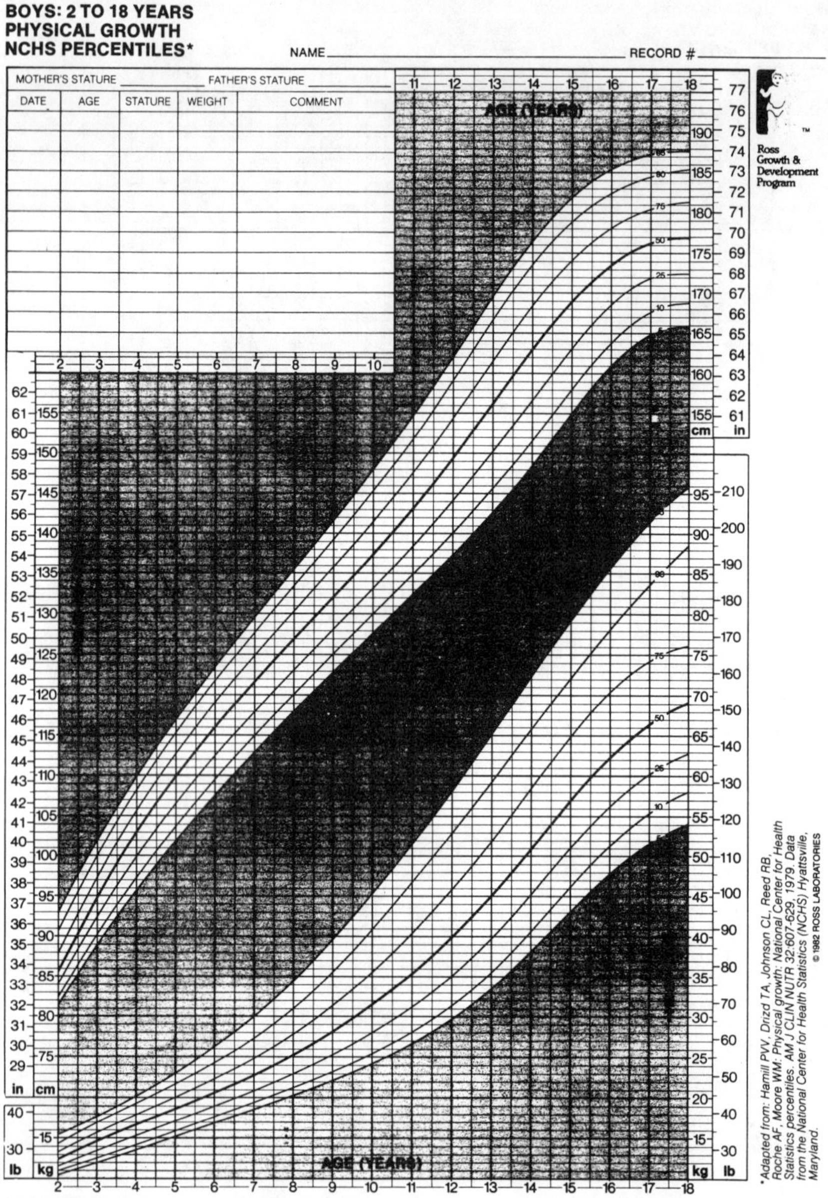

Figure 10-8 National Center for Health Statistics (NCHS) Physical Growth Percentiles for Boys, Aged 2 to 18 Years

Table 10-1 Assessment of Malnutrition—Waterlow's Classification

Grade of Malnutrition	Wt./Ht. % Standard	Ht./Age % Standard
0	>90	>95
1	81–90	90–95
2	70–80	85–89
3	<70	<85

Source: Adapted from *Lancet*, Vol. 2, pp. 87–89, with permission of The Lancet, © 1973.

Among the potential delivery sites for enteral nutrition, the stomach provides the greatest flexibility in feeding schedule and formula choice. Bolus, intermittent, or continuous-drip feedings can be administered. In addition, a broader range of formula composition and osmolality can be tolerated. Gastric contents may provide additional enzymatic activity, aiding in digestion and providing a barrier against many infectious agents.[7]

Two major contradictions for gastric feeding are abnormal gastric emptying and pathologic gastroesophageal reflux. With gastroesophageal reflux the risk of pulmonary aspiration is significant, particularly when a patient has an absent or diminished gag reflex. These problems may be circumvented by altering the feeding schedule or method, or, if needed, by intervening medically or surgically. The latter interventions, however, are not without additional risks, and careful consideration before their implementation is warranted.

With a feeding site distal to the pylorus, such as the duodenum or jejunum, the chance of gastric distention or gastroesophageal reflux is lessened, but feeding schedules and formula choices are limited with these sites. The stomach regulates the osmolality of its contents and the rate at which food enters the small intestine. The combination of bypassing the stomach and administering formulas that are complex or of high osmolality can overwhelm the digestive and absorptive capacity of the small intestine, thereby predisposing to malabsorption and the dumping syndrome.[8] Bolus feedings may also cause a similar effect, even when formulas of low osmolality are used. For these reasons, formulas must be carefully chosen and tested when given by means of continuous or intermittent feedings to children requiring a duodenal or jejunal feeding site.

TPN should be used only in patients who have conditions that preclude the use of the gastrointestinal tract. Examples include severe short-gut syndrome, severe inflammatory bowel disease, and drug-induced damage to the intestinal mucosa.[9] Home parenteral nutrition usually requires surgical insertion of an indwelling intravenous catheter.

Delivery Routes

Once the site of delivery is chosen, the ideal route of delivery is determined. Patients who are expected to need nutrition support for less than three to six months can be intubated nasally. This avoids the need for surgical intervention and provides the patient and family with some flexibility in tube insertion and removal. Caretakers and even patients themselves can be taught to insert nasogastric tubes quickly and safely.

Nasogastric tubes may irritate the nose and pharynx and may stimulate the gag reflex. These problems usually resolve after several days of continuous use. They may be lessened by the use of small caliber, soft, polyurethane catheters. Dislodgment of tubes is another frequent occurrence in young patients, who intentionally pull them out, and in patients with forceful coughs (e.g., those with cystic fibrosis). In patients who require intermittent feedings, nasogastric tubes can be inserted at night and then removed after the feeding the next morning. Despite the advantages of nasogastric tubes, some families have difficulty complying when a tube must be inserted frequently.

If the duration of tube feeding is expected to extend beyond three to six months, placement of a gastrostomy tube is recommended. Although gastrostomy tubes also can become dislodged, they are easily replaced and overall are much easier to maintain than nasogastric tubes. Formula preparation and feeding is the same as for nasogastric tubes. Similar sensations of gastric fullness and satiety, which accompany bolus and intermittent nasogastric tube feedings, appear to occur with gastrostomy tube feedings. In general, feeding by gastrostomy tube is no different than that by nasogastric tube and may be easier in terms of care and maintenance. Some patients and their families, however, prefer nasal intubation even for extended periods of time.

Historically, surgical procedures were necessary for placement of gastrostomy tubes, thus limiting their desirability. Advances in percutaneous endoscopic placement may have eliminated this disadvantage.[10] Another disadvantage of gastrostomy tube feeding appears to be the unexplained increased incidence of gastroesophageal reflux after tube placement.[11] This is particularly problematic in children with a developmental disability or cystic fibrosis. If gastroesophageal reflux occurs, it is prudent to treat this medically before changing to a transpyloric site. Persistent uncontrolled reflux, however, does require a change to a transpyloric site.

Leakage around the insertion site and difficulty in concealing the external portion of the tube under clothing are two other disadvantages of gastrostomy tubes. The latter is also a disadvantage for nasogastric tubes. A gastrostomy "button," which sets flush against the skin, has been described.[12] The cited advantages of the "button" are reduced migration, chance of accidental removal, pivoting action leading to leakage, tissue reaction, and discomfort. The button has the added advantage of being quite appealing to adolescents, who may be self-conscious about having a tube exposed, and to parents of young children, who worry that their children will tug at a tube extending from the stomach.

Similar considerations exist for patients requiring transpyloric feedings. Jejunostomy tube placement is considered when nasojejunostomy tube feedings have been successfully implemented and are anticipated to be required for longer than three to six months.

One difficulty with duodenal and jejunal feeding sites is the placement of the feeding catheter. Passage of a feeding tube into the duodenum or jejunum may take several hours unless done by a radiologist with the assistance of fluoroscopy. Furthermore, the only way to determine accurately the tube's final position is by x-ray films. Thus, the use of jejunal or duodenal tubes for home feeding is limited. Tubes already in place can become displaced as a result of peristaltic activity. Bowel wall perforations are rare complications of tube displacements.

Feeding Schedules

The feeding schedule may be dictated by the patient's medical needs, life style and feeding site. Some patients can maintain an adequate blood glucose level and state of hydration only on continuous drip tube feedings. Other patients may experience significant gastric distention or gastroesophageal reflux, which is relieved only when an intermittent or continuous feeding schedule is used.[13] When medical needs and feeding routes do not dictate the feeding schedule, bolus feedings, every three to four hours given over 15 to 20 minutes, or continuous-drip feedings, given overnight, will frequently fit into a family's daily schedule.

Daytime bolus feedings are recommended for children who cannot take any food by mouth. Bolus infusions may foster a somewhat more normalized life style, as children can be fed at the table during family meal times. Children who experience persistent vomiting after bolus feedings may tolerate better continuous or intermittent feedings, which safeguard against accidental aspiration.

Overnight, continuous-drip tube feedings are recommended for children who are unable to eat enough to promote normal growth. Such children can be given one third to one half of their daily caloric needs at night. The feedings can then be terminated by early morning to promote a good appetite at breakfast. A significant benefit of overnight feedings can be the renewed enjoyment of daytime eating because patients no longer have to eat more than they have an appetite for to receive adequate calories.

The desires of both the patient and the parents should be considered when choosing a feeding schedule. A parent may have obligations during the day that necessitate feeding at night or, conversely, may feel uncomfortable using a pump overnight, thus preferring a daytime schedule. In addition, the patient's involvement in school, physical therapy, or other activities may dictate the choice between receiving optimal nutrition support or complying with other treatments. Therefore the feeding schedule must be earnestly thought through by the nutritionist, patient, and family to ensure the best and most flexible schedule is chosen.

Patients on TPN also should maintain as normal a life style as possible. Cyclic schedules, preferably overnight, allow relatively normal activity during the daytime. Any schedule should be implemented before discharge from the hospital to ensure tolerance. Care must be taken when the patient is weaned from cyclic TPN so that wide shifts in blood glucose levels are avoided.[14] Generally, the last one to two hours of an infusion are used for weaning. During this period the rate is decreased by 50 percent every 15 to 30 minutes. Similarly, when restarting TPN, the first 30 to 60 minutes should be reserved for gradually increasing the rate of infusion. Gradual changes in infusion rates are particularly important in infants and malnourished patients.[15]

Equipment

The equipment needed for nutrition support depends on the site, route, and schedule that have been chosen. Other considerations for determining equipment needs in enterally fed patients include

- length of time the feeding tube is to remain in place before replacement,
- rate at which the formula is to be provided, and
- viscosity of the formula.

Such considerations will enable the nutritionist to choose the optimal tube to meet the patient's needs; that is, one of appropriate material, diameter, and length, as well as one that offers the greatest flexibility and ease of insertion. Tubes that will remain in place for a prolonged period should be made of polyurethane or other materials that remain soft and pliable. Viscous formulas require tubes with a larger diameter. Tubes that extend a great distance externally are more likely to become accidentally dislodged. Adolescents who prefer to pass a tube intermittently at night should have a short, easy to pass tube. Replacement of a Broviac or Hickman catheter with a Port-a-Cath might be considered in the adolescent patient who wishes to have a nonobtrusive site for parenteral nutrition. The Port-a-Cath is inserted under the skin, which limits its visibility and allows for bathing and swimming. (A more thorough review of feeding tubes is provided in Chapter 5.)

Patients receiving continuous, intermittent, or overnight feedings will need infusion pumps. Pumps must be examined carefully to ensure that their rate of delivery can be adjusted to volumes small enough for young children. For infants, pumps should have the capacity to deliver increments of 1 ml/hour. For older children, pumps should be adjustable to deliver increments of 5 ml/hour. The accuracy of the pump also must be ensured. As a rule, pumps accurate to within 10 percent of their predicted rate of delivery are acceptable for enteral feedings.

The equipment necessary for home parenteral nutrition in the pediatric population does not differ significantly from that used in adults, although some new features are particularly useful.

- Some pumps can be programmed to deliver several different rates and volumes during a feeding cycle without the need for manual readjustment. This feature makes feeding schedules easier to accommodate and less time consuming to implement.
- Pumps with safety features that prevent accidental changes in rate or volume during delivery are ideal for toddlers.
- Small, lightweight, portable pumps significantly increase mobility for children who require 24-hour or daytime infusions.

DETERMINATION OF NUTRITION REQUIREMENTS

Enteral Nutrition

A nutrition plan should be formulated while the mechanics of nutrition support are being determined. The patient's fluid, calorie, protein, vitamin, and mineral needs are estimated from basic guidelines for fluid requirements (Exhibit 10-2) and from recommended dietary allowances (Table 10-2). Estimation of the basal metabolic rate is used in determining calorie requirements; however, calorie requirements are modified on the basis of the patient's activity level and medical needs (Exhibit 10-3).

Although recommended dietary allowances are used to determine initial nutrition goals, the patient's current nutrition status and the desired need for "catch-up growth" (Exhibit 10-4) must be considered when formulating

Exhibit 10-2 Fluid Requirements

By body surface: 1,500–1,800 ml/m²/day
By weight:

Body Weight	Maintenance Fluid Needs per Day
1–10 kg	100 ml/kg
11–20 kg	1,000 ml plus 50 ml/kg for each kg >10 kg
>20 kg	1,500 ml plus 20 ml/kg for each kg >20 kg

Average fluid intake is one and one half to two times maintenance needs.

Source: Reprinted from *Manual of Pediatric Parenteral Nutrition* by J.A. Kerner, with permission of John Wiley and Sons, Inc., © 1983.

the final goal for intake. Calories are increased further if growth remains suboptimal despite the provision of catch-up growth calories. An additional 4.4 to 5.7 kilocalories per gram of desired daily lean body weight gain can be given.[16] As calorie goals are increased, protein intake should be monitored closely. In infants, 7 percent to 16 percent of energy requirements should be provided by protein. In children older than one year, 7 percent to 9 percent should be provided by protein.[17,18] Protein intake for young infants should not exceed 5 gm/kg because of their immature renal function.

Formula Selection

Breast milk or commercial infant formulas are recommended for children younger than one year (Table 10-3). Infants taking quantities of breast

Table 10-2 Recommended Dietary Allowances for Children and Adolescents

	Age	Calories/kg/day	Protein (gm/kg/day)
Infants	0–6 months	115	2.2
	6–12 months	105	2.0
Children	1–3 years	100	1.8
	4–6 years	85	1.5
	7–10 years	86	1.2
Boys	11–14 years	60	1.0
	15–18 years	42	0.85
Girls	11–14 years	48	1.0
	15–18 years	38	0.84

Source: Reprinted from "Recommended Dietary Allowances," 9th ed., 1980, with permission from the National Academy Press, Washington, D.C.

Exhibit 10-3 Basal Caloric Requirements

Basal energy requirements (BER) or basal energy expenditure (BEE) refers to an individual's energy requirements under complete physical and mental rest (shortly after awakening and approximately 14 hours after the last food intake).

The BEE does not account for the specific dynamic action of food (SDA), extreme temperatures (including fever), activity level or stress factors such as disease-state, fractures, burns and growth.

To estimate caloric requirements for growth and/or maintenance, the BEE must be calculated and adjusted further to account for an individual's activity level and existing stress factors.

Estimation of Energy Metabolism by Weight
Appropriate for infants-16 years of age
To Calculate BEE:
1. Determine age and weight of patient
2. Read across to appropriate sex
3. Read metabolic rate (Kcal/hr)
4. Multiply metabolic rate × 24 (hrs) to determine daily BEE

Basal Metabolic Rates: Infants and Children

Age 1 wk to 10 mo. Metabolic rate		Age 11 to 38 mo. Metabolic rate			Age 3 to 16 yrs Metabolic rate		
Weight (kg)	(Kcal/hr) Male or Female	Weight (kg)	(Kcal/hr) Male	Female	Weight (kg)	(Kcal/hr) Male	Female
3.5	8.4	9.0	22.0	21.2	15	35.8	33.3
4.0	9.5	9.5	22.8	22.0	20	39.7	37.4
4.5	10.5	10.0	23.6	22.8	25	43.6	41.5
5.0	11.6	10.5	24.4	23.6	30	47.5	45.5
5.5	12.7	11.0	25.2	24.4	35	51.3	49.6
6.0	13.8	11.5	26.0	25.2	40	55.2	53.7
6.5	14.9	12.0	26.8	26.0	45	59.1	57.8
7.0	16.0	12.5	27.6	26.9	50	63.0	61.9
7.5	17.1	13.0	28.4	27.7	55	66.9	66.0
8.0	18.2	13.5	29.2	28.5	60	70.8	70.0
8.5	19.3	14.0	30.0	29.3	65	74.7	74.0
9.0	20.4	14.5	30.8	30.1	70	78.6	78.1
9.5	21.4	15.0	31.6	30.9	75	82.5	82.2
10.0	22.5	15.5	32.4	31.7			
10.5	23.6	16.0	33.2	32.6			
11.0	24.7	16.5	34.0	33.4			

Source: Reprinted from *Metabolism* by P.L. Altman and D.S. Dittmer, p. 344, with permission of Federation of American Societies for Experimental Biology, © 1968.

Exhibit 10-4   Catch-up Requirements

Estimating energy and protein needs for catch-up growth:

$$Kcal/kg = \frac{\text{Ideal Weight for Height} \times \text{RDA kcal/kg Height Age}}{\text{Actual Weight}}$$

$$Protein \ (gm/kg) = \frac{\text{Ideal Weight for Height} \times \text{RDA Protein (gm/kg) Height Age}}{\text{Actual Weight}}$$

Abbreviation: RDA, recommended dietary allowances.

milk or formula (or both) sufficient to meet the recommended dietary allowances for calories will also meet their needs for protein and vitamins. Mineral requirements, with the possible exception of iron and fluoride, will also be met. Infants older than four to six months of age who do not receive either iron-fortified formulas or solid foods high in iron may need supplements.[19] Infants who receive either ready-to-feed formulas or formulas mixed with nonfluoridated water may also require supplements. The Committee on Nutrition of the American Academy of Pediatrics has published recommendations for fluoride supplementation (Table 10-4). Infants who require higher caloric supplementation than can be provided by standard formula alone may benefit from the addition of products such as corn oil, Polycose or Promod to the formula or food. When caloric density is increased beyond that provided by standard products, attempts should be made to maintain a reasonable caloric distribution, osmolality, and vitamin and mineral content in the modified product (Table 10-5).[20]

Children aged one to six years present unique problems. Most commercial products cannot provide adequate vitamins and minerals in an optimal volume for children in this age range. Currently, a commercial formula, PediaSure, is the best formula to meet the needs of this age group (Exhibit 10-5). Fluoride supplements may still be required. Standard adult formulas also may be used; vitamin and mineral supplementation, however, will be necessary

The tendency is to feed standard adult formulas to children older than six years. Again, vitamin and mineral needs must be monitored carefully, particularly in patients who are exclusively formula fed.

Blenderized formulas are used less commonly because of the abundance of commercial products. The known composition and viscosity of commercial formulas and their ease of use, reduced risk of error in preparation, and sanitation are likely reasons for their popularity. Nevertheless, blenderized formulas can be as effective and may be less expensive. Care must

Table 10-3 Infant Formulas

Formula	Indications	Calories/Ounce	Carbohydrate	Protein	Fat	Comments
Milk Based Breast milk	Most preferred for normal infant feeding	20	Lactose	Lactalbumin, 65% Casein, 35%	High in oleic acid; low in volatile fatty acids	Average values for range of 15 days to 15 months postpartum *Note:* Compositional variations because of stage of lactation may be a consideration when breast milk is provided to premature or high-risk infants with increased nutrition needs.
Enfamil (Mead Johnson Nutritional Division, Evansville, Ind.)	Normal infant feeding	20	Lactose	Reduced mineral whey, non-fat milk (60/40)	Coconut oil, 55%; soy oil, 45%	Other uses: sick infant without nutrition problems Lactalbumin:casein ratio close to that in breast milk Also available with iron, 1.25 mg/100 ml
Enfamil Premature (Mead Johnson Nutritional Division)	For the premature and low-birth-weight infant (<2,000 gm)	24	Corn syrup solids, 60%; lactose, 40%	Whey protein concentrate, non-fat milk (60/40)	Soy oil, 40%; medium-chain triglyceride oil, 40%; coconut oil, 20%	High protein (whey:casein 60/40), readily digestible fat and carbohydrate, appropriate calcium, phosphorus, and minerals for rapid growth.
Similac (Ross Laboratories, Columbus, Ohio)	Normal infant feeding	20	Lactose	Non-fat milk	Coconut oil, 53%; soy oil, 47%	Other uses: sick infant without nutrition problems Also available with iron, 1.2 mg/100 ml

continues

Table 10-3 continued

Formula	Indications	Calories/Ounce	Carbohydrate	Protein	Fat	Comments
Similac 24 (Ross Laboratories)	Compensation for limited volume intake	24	Lactose	Non-fat milk	Coconut oil, 60%; soy oil, 40%	Ready-feed formula not available commercially Other uses: recovery from extended illness–induced period of malnutrition, failure to thrive Also available with iron, 1.5 mg/100 ml
Similac PM 60/40 (Ross Laboratories)	Lower sodium and potassium levels; preferred for → renal function	20	Lactose	Demineralized whey, calcium, and sodium caseinate (60/40)	Coconut oil, corn oil	Preferred for renal patients because of lower phosphorus content and 2:1 calcium:phosphorus ratio Low RSL Lactalbumin:casein ratio close to that in breast milk
SMA (Wyeth Laboratories, Philadelphia, Pa.)	Normal infant feeding ↓ sodium and ↓ potassium	20	Lactose	Demineralized whey, non-fat milk (60/40)	Oleo and coconut oil, safflower oil, soybean oil	Other uses: sick infant without nutrition problems; infants with congestive heart failure Lactalbumin:casein ratio close to that in breast milk Low RSL Also available with iron; 0.12 mg/100 ml
Cow's milk	Not recommended for infants <6 months of age	19	Lactose	Casein 81%, lactalbumin 19%	Butterfat	Introduction into infant diet depends on intake of solids Avoid skim milk until 2 years of age
Soy Based Isomil (Ross Laboratories)	Allergy to cow's milk; lactose or galactose intolerance	20	Corn syrup, sucrose	Soy protein isolate	Coconut oil, soy oil	Other uses: recovery stage after mild/moderate diarrhea Also available without sucrose (Isomil SF with 150 mOsm/Kg of water)

Product	Indication	%	Carbohydrate	Protein	Fat/Oil	Other uses
ProSobee (Mead Johnson Nutritional Division)	Allergy to cow's milk; sucrose, lactose, or galactose intolerance	20	Corn syrup solids	Soy protein isolate	Coconut oil, 55%; soy oil, 45%	Other uses: recovery stage after mild/moderate diarrhea; galactosemia
Nursoy (Wyeth Laboratories)	Allergy to cow's milk; lactose or galactose intolerance	20	Sucrose	Soy protein isolate	Oleo, coconut, oleic, and soy oils	Other uses: recovery stage after mild/moderate diarrhea, galactosemia
Nutramigen (Mead Johnson Nutritional Laboratories)	Intact protein intolerance; galactosemia	20	Corn syrup solids	Hydrolyzed casein	Corn oil	Other uses: lactose deficiency, recovery stage after mild/moderate diarrhea, soy intolerance
Portagen (Mead Johnson Nutrition Laboratories)	Fat malabsorption	20	Corn syrup solids, sucrose	Sodium caseinate (intact protein)	Medium-chain triglyceride oil, 86%; corn oil, 11%; soy lecithin, 3%	Minimal lactose content (<0.15%) Fat malabsorption include → pancreatic lipase → bile salt production defect in fat transportation defect in fat absorption
Pregestimil (Mead Johnson Nutritional Laboratories)	Malabsorption, intractable diarrhea	20	Corn syrup solids, modified tapioca starch	Hydrolyzed casein L-tryptophan L-cysteine L-tyrosine	Corn oil, 60%; medium-chain triglyceride oil, 40%	Malabsorption as a result of short-gut syndrome, cystic fibrosis, celiac malnutrition Other uses: intact protein intolerance, sensitivity to hyperosmolar solutions, recovery stage after prolonged diarrhea Less palatable than Nutramigen
RCF (Ross Laboratories)	Carbohydrate intolerance	20, with additional 7% carbohydrate	Dependent on carbohydrate used in preparation	Soy protein isolate	Soy oil, 50%; coconut oil, 50%	Carbohydrate of choice to be added in stepwise progression *Note:* If no oral carbohydrate is tolerated, adequate glucose must be provided intravenously

Table 10-4 Fluoride Supplementation Schedule for Infants and Children

Age (yr)	Fluoride Concentration in Local Water Supply:		
	<0.3 ppm	0.3–0.7 ppm	0.7 ppm
0–2	0.25 mg	0 mg	0 mg
2–3	0.50 mg	0.25 mg	0 mg
3–16	1.00 mg	0.50 mg	0 mg

Source: Reproduced by permission of Pediatrics, Vol. 77, page 758, Copyright 1986.

be taken in determining the appropriate formula, as well as in its daily preparation.

If enteral feeding has not been started before the child is placed in the home care setting, feedings should be started at one to two milliliters per kilogram of body weight per hour, and advanced by five to ten milliliters every 12 to 24 hours until the child's established nutrition needs are met. If the child has been on a nothing-by-mouth status for more than three days, the formula should be started at half strength and increased as tolerated. Care should be taken not to increase volume and strength simultaneously.

Parenteral Nutrition

Parenteral nutrition must be initiated in the hospital for appropriate monitoring for metabolic abnormalities, as well as care of the parenteral access site. At least one to two weeks are required for the child and parents to learn home TPN procedures.

Table 10-5 Recommended Caloric Distribution

	Recommended % Distribution of Major Nutrients		
	Carbohydrate	Protein	Fat
Full-term (normal) infant	35–65	7–16	30–55
>1 year (for individual consideration)	56–58	7–9	35

Sources: Recommended Dietary Allowances by National Research Council Food and Nutrition Board, 9th ed., National Academy of Sciences, 1980; and Infant Nutrition by S.J. Fomon, W.B. Saunders Company, 1974.

Exhibit 10-5 Nutrient Composition of PediaSure

	Per liter*
Energy,Cal	1000
Macronutrients	
Protein,g	30
Carbohydrate,g	110
Fat,g	49.7
Linoleic acid,mg	11,300
Vitamins	
Vitamin A,IU	2570
Vitamin D,IU	505
Vitamin E,IU	23
Vitamin K,mcg	34
Vitamin C,mg	100
Folic acid,mcg	370
Thiamin,mg	2.7
Riboflavin,mg	2.1
Vitamin B6,mg	2.6
Vitamin B12,mcg	6
Niacin,mg	16.5
Choline,mg	300
Biotin,mcg	320
Pantothenic acid,mg	10
Inositol,mg	80
Minerals	
Sodium,mg	380 (16.5mEq)
Potassium,mg	1305 (33.5mEq)
Chloride,mg	1010 (28.6mEq)
Calcium,mg	970 (48.4mEq)
Phosphorus,mg	800
Magnesium,mg	200
Iodine,mcg	95
Manganese,mg	2.5
Copper,mg	1.0
Zinc,mg	12
Iron,mg	14
Conditionally essential nutrients	
Taurine,mg	70
Carnitine,mg	17
Water,g	845

*Calculated from 8-fl-oz label claim values.

continues

Exhibit 10-5 continued

Energy Distribution and Sources of Protein, Carbohydrate and Fat in PediaSure		
Nutrient	% Total Calories	Sources
Protein	12	Low-lactose whey protein and sodium caseinate in an 18:82 blend
Fat	44	High-oleic safflower oil (50%), soy oil (30%), and medium-chain triglycerides (20%)
Carbohydrate	44	Corn syrup solids and sucrose

Source: Reprinted with permission of Ross Laboratories, Columbus, Ohio, © 1988.

Nutrition needs are based on the recommended dietary allowances for age or the estimation of a basal metabolic rate, with adjustments made on the basis of the child's medical status and activity level (see Tables 10-2 and 10-3). Parenteral solutions used in infants, children older than six years, and adults differ in their amino acid, multivitamin, and mineral composition (Tables 10-6, 10-7A, and 10-7B). Growing children often require greater amounts of essential fatty acids, particularly when they have low adipose

Table 10-6 Comparison of Amino Acid Solutions (per 100 ml of a 1% solution)

	Standard Formula Aminosyn	Infant Formula Aminosyn-PF		Standard Formula Aminosyn	Infant Formula Aminosyn-PF
Nitrogen	157 mg	152 mg	Alanine	128 mg	70 mg
Isoleucine	72 mg	76 mg	Arginine	98 mg	123 mg
Leucine	94 mg	120 mg	Histidine	30 mg	31 mg
Lysine	72 mg	68 mg	Proline	86 mg	81 mg
Methionine	40 mg	18 mg	Serine	42 mg	50 mg
Phenylalanine	44 mg	43 mg	Tyrosine	4 mg	4 mg
Threonine	52 mg	51 mg	Glycine	128 mg	39 mg
Tryptophan	16 mg	18 mg	Glutamic acid	0	82 mg
Valine	80 mg	67 mg	Aspartic acid	0	53 mg
			Taurine	0	7 mg

Source: Abbott Laboratories, Chicago, 1987.

Table 10-7A Intravenous Multiple Vitamins

Ingredient	Amt./24 hours Under 12 Years	Amt./24 hours Over 12 Years
Vitamin A	0.7 mg	1.0 mg
Vitamin B_1	1.2 mg	3.0 mg
Vitamin B_2	1.4 mg	3.6 mg
Vitamin B_6	1.0 mg	4.0 mg
Vitamin B_{12}	1.0 μg	5.0 μg
Vitamin C	80 mg	100 mg
Vitamin D	10 μg	5.0 μg
Vitamin E	7 mg	10.0 mg
Vitamin K_1	200 μg	—
Biotin	20 μg	60 μg
Dexpanthenol	5.0 mg	15.0 mg
Folic Acid	140 μg	400 μg
Niacinamide	17.0 mg	40 mg

Source: Data based on an article in *Journal of Parenteral and Enteral Nutrition*, Vol. 3, No. 4, p. 260, American Society of Parenteral and Enteral Nutrition, July/August 1979. For further information see *Guidelines for Multivitamin Preparations for Parenteral Use*, American Medical Association, 1975.

stores.[21] Children can usually tolerate up to 3 to 4 grams of lipid per kilogram of body weight. Parenteral lipid formulations contribute minimally to the osmotic load while providing an excellent source of calories.

MONITORING AND ONGOING INTERVENTIONS

Infants and children receiving nutrition support should be monitored on a regular basis (Exhibits 10-6 and 10-7). Those receiving enteral nutrition

Table 10-7B Suggested Daily Intravenous Intake of Essential Trace Elements for Pediatric Patients

Component	Amount, μg/kg
Zinc	300*
	100†
Copper	20
Chromium	0.14–0.2
Manganese	2–10

*Premature infants (weight 1500 g) up to 3 kg body weight.
†Full-term infants and children up to 5 years old; thereafter, the recommendations for adults apply, up to 4 mg/day.

Source: Reprinted from *Journal of the American Medical Association*, Vol. 241, p. 2051, with permission of American Medical Association. Copyright 1979, American Medical Association.

Exhibit 10-6 Pediatric Intake Worksheet

PEDIATRIC INTAKE WORKSHEET

Patient's Name: _____

Age: _____ Height/length: _____ cm Weight: _____ kg

Date: _____

		Intake				Total			
			no. of				Protein	Fat	
		ml/hr	hrs	ml/day	ml/kg		(g/kg)	(g/kg)	Kcal/kg
Parenteral:									
_____ % dextrose									
_____ % amino acids									
_____ % Intralipid/Liposyn									

Total:

Enteral:
Tube feeding recipe
    Product: _____
    Additives: _____
          _____
          _____

Total:

Oral (24-hour recall):

Total:

Other:

Total intake:
    _____ ml/kg   _____ kcal/kg
    _____ Protein (g/kg)   _____ % Fat
    _____ % Enteral   _____ % Parenteral
             _____ % Oral

_____ R.D.

support should be seen by the nutrition team responsible for initiating their therapy within one month of discharge from the hospital. Children who live a long distance from the hospital may be seen at a local health care center, provided that close communication is established between the nutrition team and local health care providers.

The initial visit gives the patient and family an opportunity to discuss the progress of or problems with home therapy and provides the nutrition support team an opportunity to assess how well the patient and family have been able to implement and maintain the home care plan. Beyond

Exhibit 10-7 Parenteral/Enteral Patient Monitoring Record

Name:		Date of Birth:			Diagnosis:				
	Date:								
Anthropometric Measures and Laboratory Indexes	Weight*								
	Height*								
	Head Circumference*								
	Blood urea nitrogen*/ creatinine*								
	Glucose								
	Total protein*								
	Albumin*								
	Sodium, potassium,* chloride*								
	Magnesium								
	Calcium phosphate								
	Alkaline phosphatase*								
	Zinc/Copper								
	Total bilirubin								
	SGPT/SGOT								
	Triglycerides								
	Bone age								
Input — Enteral	Formula*								
	ml/kg*								
	kcal/kg*								
	Protein (gm/kg)*								
Input — Parenteral	% amino acids								
	% dextrose								
	% lipids								
	ml/kg								
	kcal/kg								
	Protein (g/kg)								
Input — Total	ml/kg*								
	kcal/kg*								
	Protein (g/kg)*								
Output — Stool	Number*								
Output — Urine	S/A*								
Comments									

* Parameters recommended when on enteral feedings.

Abbreviations: S/A, sugar/acetone; SGOT, serum glutamate oxaloacetate transaminase; SGPT, serum glutamate pyruvate transaminase.

the initial follow-up visit, the level of monitoring must be individualized. Factors influencing the frequency and extent of monitoring include the patient's age, nutrition status, and medical condition, as well as the family's competence. During periods of rapid growth, such as infancy and puberty, frequent adjustments to the nutrition prescription may be required. Growth should be compared to the reference standards for age (Exhibit 10-8), and the feeding regimen should be modified if growth is inadequate or weight gain is too rapid.

Therapy directed toward demonstrating and teaching normal feeding skills should be included for children. Oral motor stimulation programs are particularly important for children younger than four years who have never acquired feeding skills. The nutritionist should ensure that an oral-motor stimulation program is in place when beginning nutrition support, even when the prospect of feeding by mouth is not imminent. Occupational therapists, physical therapists, and speech pathologists are most commonly involved in such programs and should be contacted. Children who do not learn to associate the oral stimulation experienced during feeding with a feeling of fullness and satiety will require a great deal of oral motor and behavioral intervention while learning to eat.

Children who receive TPN are at risk for metabolic abnormalities, infections, nutrition deficiencies, and liver disease. Examples include increased serum phosphorus, bilirubin, and liver enzyme levels and decreased concentrations of serum magnesium, selenium, and biotin.[22,23] Thus these patients should be seen by the nutrition support team weekly for the first month after discharge, biweekly for the second month, and then less frequently unless complications arise.[24] Recommendations for patient monitoring include

- anthropometric measurements (each visit),
- assessment of the patient's transition to enteral feedings (each visit),
- biochemical indexes (e.g., serum electrolytes, calcium, and magnesium) (each visit),
- complete blood cell count (each visit),
- liver function studies (every three months),
- evaluation for deficiencies in trace metals: zinc, copper, selenium (yearly), and
- bone age (every 6 to 12 months).[25]

WEANING FROM NUTRITION SUPPORT

Just as it is important for the nutritionist to recognize patients who will benefit from nutrition support, it is equally important to recognize when

Exhibit 10-8 Reference Standards for Growth

Growth Velocity

Age	*Weight increase* *(grams/day)*
0-3 months	25-35
3-6 months	15-21
6-12 months	10-13
1-6 years	5-8
7-10 years	5-11

Catch-Up Growth

Growth suppression can occur as a result of undernutrition or illness. During the recovery phase, a child can grow at a rate greater than that expected for age. As the more rapid growth proceeds, the child "catches up" to his or her growth curve.

Source: Adapted from *American Journal of Clinical Nutrition*, Vol. 35, pp. 1169–1175, with permission of American Society for Clinical Nutrition, Inc., © 1982.

patients can be weaned from support. Candidates for weaning include

- developmentally delayed children who, despite this deficit, are beginning to show readiness for oral feedings,
- children who have achieved adequate nutrition status and are able to maintain this with oral intake, and
- children with chronic, quiescent diseases (e.g., Crohn's disease or cancer) with adequate nutrition status and the ability to take food by mouth

Certain information should be acquired before a weaning program is begun, including growth parameters, medical status, oral-motor skills, records of the patient's current food and beverage intake, and records of the patient's current enteral or parenteral solutions. Regardless of the initial medical problem, most children will need an organized program to help them maintain their nutrition status by mouth. The program should include behavioral intervention and, if necessary, an oral-motor stimulation program developed by qualified professionals.

The nutritionist's role in assisting the transition of a patient from enteral or parenteral nutrition support to oral intake includes monitoring nutrition status and intake and providing ongoing education to the family. Expectations of nutrient needs and growth rate should be discussed with the family. Children who receive all their nutrition requirements by means of enteral or parenteral support are unlikely to want to eat on their own, as intake in children is closely dictated by activity and growth requirements. When needs are being met, the expectation that the child will eat for "fun" is unfounded. Children who have had negative experiences with eating and drinking (e.g., choking) because of oral-motor abnormalities, or those who have never associated appetite and eating, will require more than a simple decrease in their nutrition support to stimulate their interest in eating. Detailed programs that incorporate a consistent, firm approach to reintroduce feedings will be necessary.[26,27]

FINANCIAL CONSIDERATIONS

Financial limitations can interfere with the successful implementation of nutrition support in the home. If an insurance policy does not cover expenses incurred for nutrition support, a letter should be written to the company by the physician or person responsible for the home nutrition program stating the importance of nutrition intervention. Other organizations offer financial support, including the Crippled Children's Services and the March of Dimes. WIC (Women, Infants and Children's supplemental food program) and Medicaid are available to cover the cost of formula for qualifying patients. In some states, legislation has been passed to cover nutrition supplements for persons with inflammatory bowel disease. Families with children with cystic fibrosis can seek income tax deductions if food items are itemized. Obtaining financial reimbursement for nutrition support can be time consuming and discouraging, but it is often critical to the success of the nutrition support plan.

CONCLUSION

Nutrition support is an essential component of the medical care for many children. The goal of nutrition support in the pediatric population is to promote normal growth and acquisition of feeding skills. Appropriate attention to the child's medical, social, and psychologic needs is critical to the design and successful implementation of a nutrition support plan. The role of the nutritionist is not only as a care provider, but also as a liaison among the patient, family, and other persons involved in the patient's care.

NOTES

1. Michael K. Georgieff et al., "Effect of Neonatal Caloric Deprivation on Head Growth and 1-Year Developmental Status in Preterm Infants," *Journal of Pediatrics* 107 (1985): 581–87.
2. Harry L. Greene et al., "Continuous Nocturnal Intragastric Feeding for Management of Type I Glycogen Storage Disease," *New England Journal of Medicine* 294 (1976): 423–25.

3. A. Roberto Frisancho, "New Norms of Upper Limb and Fat and Muscle Areas for Assessment of Nutritional Status," *American Journal of Clinical Nutrition* 34 (1981): 2540–45.

4. W. Allan Walker and Kristy M. Hendricks, *Manual of Pediatric Nutrition* (Philadelphia, Pa.: W.B. Saunders Co., 1985), 77.

5. Harry L. Greene, Donald R. McCabe, and Gerald B. Merenstein, "Protracted Diarrhea and Malnutrition in Infancy: Changes in Intestinal Morpohology and Disaccharidase Activities during Treatment with Total Intravenous Nutrition or Oral Elemental Diets," *Journal of Pediatrics* 87 (1975): 695–704.

6. Geraldine V. Padilla and Marcia M. Grant, "Psychosocial Aspects of Artificial Feeding," *Cancer* 55 (1985): 301–304.

7. Mary C. Moore and Harry L. Greene, "Tube Feeding of Infants and Children," *Pediatric Clinics of North America* 32 (1985): 401–417.

8. Connie L. Breach and Leila G. Saldanha, "Tube Feeding Complications, Part I: Gastrointestinal," *Nutrition Support Services* 8 (1988): 15–19.

9. Marvin E. Ament, Jorge Vargas, and William Berquist, "Parenteral Nutrition of the Pediatric Patient at Home," *Clinical Nutrition* 6 (1987): 17–27.

10. David E. Larson et al., "Percutaneous Endoscopic Gastrostomy: Indications, Success, Complications, and Mortality in 314 Consecutive Patients," *Gastroenterology* 93 (1987): 48–52.

11. Stuart Berezin et al., "Gastroesophageal Reflux Secondary to Gastrostomy Tube Placement," *American Journal of Diseases of Children* 140 (1986): 699–701.

12. Michael Gauderer et al., "Feeding Gastrostomy Button: Experience and Recommendations," *Journal of Pediatric Surgery* 23 (1988): 24–28.

13. George Ferry, Maija Selby, and Timothy Pietro, "Clinical Response to Short-Term Nasogastric Feeding in Infants with Gastroesophageal Reflux and Growth Failure," *Journal of Pediatric Gastroenterology and Nutrition* 2 (1983): 57–61.

14. Ament, Vargas, and Berquist, "Parenteral Nutrition of the Pediatric Patient at Home," 17–27.

15. Ellen Dwyer, Susan Baker, and Denise Richardson, "Home Parenteral Nutrition," in *Pediatric Nutrition Theory and Practice,* ed. Richard Grand, James Stuphen, and William Deitz (Woburn, Mass.: Butterworth, 1987), 763–69.

16. Christine Kennedy-Caldwell and Michael Caldwell, "Pediatric Enteral Nutrition," in *Enteral and Tube Feeding,* ed. John Rombeau and Michael Caldwell (Philadelphia, Pa.: W.B. Saunders Co., 1974).

17. National Research Council, Food and Nutrition Board, *Recommended Dietary Allowances,* 9th ed. (Washington, D.C.: National Academy of Sciences, 1980).

18. Samuel Fomon, *Infant Nutrition* (Philadelphia Pa.: W.B. Saunders Co., 1974).

19. American Academy of Pediatrics, Committee on Nutrition, "Vitamin and Mineral Supplement Needs in Normal Children in the United States," *Pediatrics* 66 (1980): 1015–21.

20. Fomon, *Infant Nutrition.*

21. John A. Kerner, *Manual of Pediatric Parenteral Nutrition* (New York: John Wiley & Sons, 1983).

22. Ament, Vargas, and Berquist, "Parenteral Nutrition of the Pediatric Patient at Home," 17–27.

23. Dwyer, Baker, and Richardson, "Home Parenteral Nutrition," 763–69.

24. Ibid.

25. Ament, Vargas, and Berquist, "Parenteral Nutrition of the Pediatric Patient at Home," 17–27.

26. Benjamin L. Handen, Fredrick Mandell, and Dennis C. Russo, "Feeding Induction in Children Who Refuse to Eat," *American Journal of Diseases of Children* 140 (1986): 52–54.

27. James A. Blackman and Christy L.A. Nelson, "Rapid Introduction of Oral Feedings to Tube-Fed Patients," *Developmental and Behavioral Pediatrics*, 8 (1987): 63–67.

BIBLIOGRAPHY

American Academy of Pediatrics, Committee on Nutrition. "Commentary on Breast Feeding and Infant Formulas, Including Proposed Standards for Formulas." *Pediatrics* 57 (1976): 278.

Bentler, Mildred, and Maria Stanish. "Nutrition Support of the Pediatric Patient with AIDS." *Journal of the American Dietetic Association* 87 (1987): 488–91.

Bougle, D., M. Iselin, A. Kahyat, and J.F. Duhamel. "Nutritional Treatment of Congenital Heart Disease." *Archives of Disease in Childhood* 61 (1986): 799–801.

Brady, Mary Sue, Karyl A. Richard, Joseph F. Fitzgerald, and James A. Lemons. "Specialized Formulas and Feedings for Infants with Malabsorption or Formula Intolerance." *Journal of the American Dietetic Association* 86 (1986): 191–200.

Chernoff, Ronnie. "Nutrition Support: Formulas and Delivery of Enteral Feeding." *Journal of the American Dietetic Association* 79 (1981): 430–32.

Crocker, K.S., S.S.H. Krey, and W.P. Steffee. "Performance Evaluation of a New Nasogastric Feeding Tube." *Journal of Parenteral and Enteral Nutrition* 5 (1981): 80–83.

Moore, Mary C., Harry L. Greene, William D. Donald, and G. Dewey Dunn. "Enteral-Tube Feeding as an Adjunct Therapy in Malnourished Patients with Cystic Fibrosis: A Clinical Study and Literature Review." *American Journal of Clinical Nutrition* 44 (1986): 33–41.

Motil, Kathleen J. "Aggressive Nutritional Therapy in Growth Retardation." *Clinical Nutrition* 4 (1985): 75–84.

O'Loughlin, Edward, David Forbes, Howard Parsons, Scott Brent, David Cooper, and Grant Gall. "Nutritional Rehabilitation of Malnourished Patients with Cystic Fibrosis." *American Journal of Clinical Nutrition* 43 (1986): 732–37.

"Panel Report on Nutritional Support of Pediatric Patients." *American Journal of Clinical Nutrition* 34 (1981): 1223–34.

Chapter 11

Nutrition Support in Alternative Care Settings

Margaret D. Simko and Kathleen S. Babich

Home health care is a "megatrend,"[1] but it is not always possible to provide total quality health care in the home. Alternative care options, as well as additional support systems, are available that can be incorporated with home care to provide efficient and satisfactory care. A variety of nutrition care options exist for patients to obtain food supplies, meals, and psychosocial support in the community.

NURSING HOMES

Although nursing homes have received some negative publicity, being referred to as "warehouses" of the aged and infirm,[2] they are an available option for provision of nutrition support. When considering a nursing home as a potential provider, questions raised include

- What should the nursing home provide in nutrition support?
- How can this be obtained?

Nutrition Assessment

A comprehensive nutrition assessment, including physical and biochemical data and a diet history, is the first step in determining patient needs for nutrition care and support. A nutrition care plan is then developed to meet the nutrition needs of the patient. A monitoring plan also is established for tracking patient progress toward nutrition care goals.

Food To Meet Nutrition and Other Needs

Meals in the nursing home should be nutritionally adequate, properly and attractively prepared, and palatable. Food should be served at appropriate temperatures and in a pleasant environment. Portion sizes should be adjusted to meet nutrient needs; overly large servings can dull appetite and motivation to eat. Individual needs for consistency, food preferences, and allergies, as well as therapeutic modifications, should be incorporated into the patient's meal plan. The dietitian should review, write, or assist in writing menus that not only meet the recommended dietary allowances, but also are high in nutrient density and reflect patient preferences.[3]

Menu Development

Patient satisfaction is improved with a selective menu that allows individual choice of foods and meals. Waste reduction is an added benefit. Such menus, however, are labor intensive and increase costs. A balance of selective menus on alternate days or for certain meals can improve food acceptance, make mealtime more interesting for the patient, and contain costs. A residents council composed of staff and patient members is helpful in providing more acceptable menus.[4] Menus should incorporate familiar foods, ethnic meal patterns, and foods that are easy to grasp and eat.

Mealtime is a social experience, and residents should be encouraged to eat in the dining room unless they are too ill or too disabled. Communal eating can lead to improved food intake, increased independence, and self-care.

Meeting Residents' Needs for Nutrition Support

Nutrition Education

The registered dietitian is responsible for discussing patient nutrition needs with the resident and family and providing a rationale for any diet restrictions or modifications. Other members of the health care team can reinforce this information and encourage the patient at meals and snack times. Patients need encouragement to change eating habits; undesirable habits should be discouraged and favorable habits encouraged. Efforts should be made to direct them toward consumption of a nutritionally adequate diet, tailored to their individual needs.

Monitoring Food Consumption

Food may be nutritious, but if it is not consumed, patients may not obtain an adequate diet. Results of a study of 21 women in a long-term care facility showed that during a seven-day period only one third of the women consumed 100 percent of the recommended dietary allowances; 40 percent did not meet the allowances for thiamin and niacin.[5]

Monitoring energy and nutrient intake is critical, and mealtime is the best observation period. A checklist can be used by the nursing staff to quantify intake. An intake form can be used to monitor trays, which have been marked in advance (e.g., by different colored tray mats), so that precise amounts of food eaten as meals, nourishments, and snacks can be determined.[6]

Complaints about food are a cue for improved meal service. Negative comments about food by residents are a way of lashing out at their confinement. Suggestions about food should be viewed seriously and used to evaluate and improve food service. Audits can be done to answer several questions:

- Is food attractively served?
- Is hot food hot and cold food cold?
- Are items missing from the tray?
- Are quantities of food left on plates, and uneaten?

Waste studies and frequent reviews of meal trays are good monitors for these potential problems. Findings may reveal portions are too large or certain foods are unpopular or prepared poorly.

Experimenting with new recipes that incorporate ethnic foods or regional favorites may improve acceptance and intake. New recipes should be evaluated for quantities consumed and resident reactions.

Foods from Others

Many patients enjoy receiving and eating familiar, specially prepared foods, but a number of potential problems exist with this practice. The long-term care facility is ultimately responsible for ensuring that all foods the resident consumes are safe to eat and prepared, stored, and served according to specific sanitation and temperature guidelines. Potential problems associated with food that is brought in from outside the facility center around unsafe preparation or storage. Often, food remains unrefrigerated for lengthy periods during transport to the facility or is left at room temperature for extended periods in the resident's room. Certain foods may be contraindicated if the resident is on a restricted diet. Snack gifts of low nutrient density foods eaten before mealtime may dull the appetite and interfere with intake of nutritionally adequate meals provided by the institution.

All facilities have policies regarding food from the outside. Restricted permission of allowing residents food gifts can be a great satisfaction and comfort; however, careful monitoring is required.

Food as the Focus of Activities

Mealtime is important in long-term care facilities. It is an event anticipated by residents, and they often plan their days' activities around meals.
Food may serve as therapy by making it the focus of stimulating activities.

Food Demonstrations

Because food has such significance, food demonstrations are well received by many residents. Demonstrations can be used as an educational
medium to introduce residents to new menu items, the importance of an
adequate diet, or a particular diet modification (e.g., high calorie, high
protein). They can also be used to prepare favorite home-cooked or ethnic
foods that may stimulate appetites. Residents can provide recipes and get
involved in the demonstration process. These experiences often serve as
a psychologic boost to the resident and may help alleviate anorexia related
to depression.

Suggestions for successful food demonstrations include[7]

- Use a quick cooking, simple dish because of the limited attention span
  of some residents.
- Use a hot plate, electric fry pan, wok, or other portable equipment.
  Baked products can be finished in the kitchen.
- Be well organized and have equipment assembled ahead of time.
- Prepare a brief nutrition lesson on the food or opt to talk about food
  and memories.
- Prepare enough so that each participant can taste a small amount.
- Add the dish to the menu if it is well received.
- Distribute the recipe. Even though residents will not be able to prepare
  the dish independently, they will enjoy having the recipe.

Favorite Foods from the Past

Residents often enjoy recalling foods of their childhood, ethnic foods,
and those of their regional background. Variations of such foods, carried
over to menu planning, help promote improved intake. Memories of food
and its association, perhaps with happy times, family occasions and holidays, can be psychologically uplifting.

Nursing homes are an alternative when home nutrition support is not
possible. Nutritionally adequate meals, enhanced by attention to physiologic and psychologic needs and coupled with capitalization on the significance of food, can provide maximum nutrition support.

HOSPICES

Types of Hospices, Goals, and Economics

> Hospice is a holistic health care concept and regards dying and death as an integral part of the life cycle. . . . The goal of hospice is to maintain the highest quality of life possible during the terminal illness and allow dying persons to live in dignity and be as comfortable as possible until they die.[8]

There are four types of hospices: home care-based facilities, hospital-based units, hospital-based teams, and free-standing facilities. Although the free standing hospice is housed in a building, some patients may remain at home while receiving the support of the hospice staff.[9]

Many major medical insurance companies now offer specific benefits for hospice expenses. Hospices also receive Medicare funds.

Meeting the Nutrition Support Needs of the Hospice Patient

Role of the Dietitian

The role of the dietitian in hospice care is to provide expertise in nutrition evaluation and care and meal planning. The greatest concern in this setting, however, is with the comforts that can be gained through food. With hospice care there is a shift from nutrition intervention to food integration into the psychologic and physiologic needs of the patient.

Nutrition histories are valuable tools in the development of the nutrition care plan. Patient requests, small and large, should be elicited to make meals acceptable.

The role of food and nutrition deals not only with nourishment of the body, but also with that of the soul.[10] Food provides one of the last social functions for the hospice patient. There is psychologic comfort in the eating ritual. Mealtime also provides patients with control over the environment and the ability to choose what they eat. Mealtime can be family time and may be accompanied by music and conversation.

Nutrition objectives for the hospice patient include adequate hydration, electrolyte balance, calorie intake to maximize patient energy levels, and food intake patterns to promote comfort.[11] Between-meal feedings and oral supplements help achieve these objectives. Food preferences and tolerances, meal preparation, and service are critical to maximize consumption of food. Success in nutrition support cannot be measured by the amount of food consumed or weight gained but by whether the eating experience is the highest quality possible.

Nutrition Problems

Flexibility is important in providing nutrition care to hospice patients. If the patient cannot eat, sometimes sips of fluid can suffice. Common nutrition problems that may arise include changes in taste perception, anorexia, diarrhea, early satiety, food aversions, food/nutrient-drug interactions, and progressive dysphagia.[12]

Enhancing Intake[13]

Food service personnel need special training to work with hospice patients. Charts, pictures, and serving utensils can be used as aids to emphasize the need for small portions. Smaller plates may be used. Personnel should be taught to be empathetic for the patients, as well as to be patient in dealing with food desires. Bread, butter, and desserts should be saved for between-meal snacks. Eye appeal is important, and even pureed foods should be served in an attractive manner. Meal hours can be adjusted and food made available to patients at all times so the patient, not the hospice, has control over appetite. It is important to remember that meals can be served anywhere at any time. Softer textured foods may be necessary. Families can help incorporate favorite foods into patient menus.

The advent of food processors has made pureed foods a delicacy, and many recipes are now available. Cooked eggs can be added to pureed vegetables, pureed meats can be glazed to add color and calories, and tofu can be used to create pâtés and mousses. Creativity and innovation are the keys in preparing foods with a texture and consistency that can be tolerated by the terminally ill patient and yet retain eye appeal and maximum nourishment. The dining experience can be a creative and successful venture for the patient and his or her family.

Hospice is an important alternative care option for the terminally ill. Understanding, humane, and specialized care can be provided through this health care system.[14]

COMMUNITY NUTRITION SUPPORT SERVICES

For the patient receiving oral nutrition support at home, community meal services provide important benefits, assistance in meal procurement, and, in some circumstances, a social setting for meals. The latter is particularly important for elderly persons. Increased psychosocial interactions may be the stimulus needed to boost energy and nutrient intake. The dietitian needs to consider the patient's psychosocial, financial, and physical assistance needs when planning a home nutrition support program.

Congregate Meals

Two federally funded programs provide food and nutrition services for elderly persons. Operating through Title III of the Older Americans Act they are referred to as congregate meals and home-delivered meals programs.[15] These programs serve nutritionally adequate meals and reduce the isolation of old people.

Congregate meals are potentially valuable sites for nutrition education. Successful programs tend to use social and recreational activities in teaching that involves the participants.[16]

The impact of feeding programs for elderly persons needs to be evaluated in terms of nutrient intake. Results of a study of senior citizens, of which 43 percent regularly attended a Title III–funded nutrition center, reported that calcium, vitamin A and ascorbic acid intake were higher for participants.[17] In a study of congregate meal participants in North Carolina, improved nutrition, greater food acceptance, and better compliance with prescribed diets were benefits of the program.[18]

Day Care for Disabled and Ill

Adult day care centers may fill the gap for persons who require assistance with meals and basic daily living tasks, but who are able to sleep at home. Some hospitals, nursing homes, and private companies have established daytime programs. Attempts are being made to provide Medicare coverage for daytime health care, which includes nutrition. These centers are held to the same standard of nutrition adequacy of meals and sanitation as that required for nursing homes. Patients receiving oral nutrition support may be well managed in such a setting.

Home-Delivered Meals

Federally supported home-delivered meals, commonly referred to as meals-on-wheels, are also funded under Title III of the Older Americans Act.[19] This program is targeted to the frail elderly person with limited mobility. It provides at least one meal a day, which contributes a minimum of one third of the recommended dietary allowances of all nutrients for people older than 60 years. Although these meals provide adequate nutrition, they do not furnish the social contact of congregate meals.

Models for Support

Congregate meal programs often supply meals for homebound persons, but they vary locally in their service and delivery. Some programs add a cold dinner such as a sandwich, milk, and fruit. Others include dry cereal, milk, juice, and bread to provide breakfast in addition to supper. For many homebound persons, these meals allow them to remain at home rather than in a long-term care facility.

In Massachusetts, luncheon clubs of five or six members meet together one or more days a week and share a lunch in the home of one of the members. Bulk meals are delivered to the home of the hostess by the city's meals-on-wheels system.[20] Such programs provide psychologic as well as nutrition support.

Provision of home-delivered meals to meet religious restrictions or ethnic preferences can present a problem. In central Maryland, the meals-on-wheels program has been able to incorporate meals that follow Jewish dietary laws and provide a hot meal at lunch and a cold dairy meal for supper. Reduced sodium and low-concentrated sweets meals for persons with diabetes mellitus are also available.[21]

Another model of home-delivered meals provides meals seven days a week, so that food is available on weekends for people at risk. Frozen meals are convenient for those needing priority service, such as persons recovering from surgery, underweight senior citizens, and those requiring nutrition supplements.[22]

Other Nutrition Options

Catering businesses and food service programs in hospitals and restaurants are among the facilities that provide home-delivered meals. One restaurant in Chicago offers delivery of meals, and clients can order by telephone. It advertises this service on television.

In New York City, "Citymeals on Wheels" provides weekend meals to homebound elderly persons who receive home-delivered meals five times per week, but not on weekends.[23] This program was developed by restaurant critic Gael Greene and others, and supporters now include leaders in the city's restaurant community. To ensure that the needy are reached, Greene suggests that businesses, restaurants, corporations, and individuals adopt specific elderly persons and make certain that they have food.

Finding Community Resources for Nutrition Support

Elderly persons may be timid about seeking out resources. Although there is no exact method for locating these resources, the first step is to check with the local Office for the Aging for information on government-funded and other programs. Churches and synagogues may know of such programs, or operate their own. Some affiliated programs are supported by federal funds, others by the congregation. Other avenues include the Salvation Army, local newspapers, and community social service offices. Friends and acquaintances should not be overlooked. Networking or word of mouth often reveals important information. The goal is to assist persons to be able to take care of themselves.

Exhibit 11-1 provides a community resource list for ambulatory ill and elderly persons to assist them to obtain nutrition and other health services. In each community there are local and state social service agencies and

Exhibit 11-1 Community Resource List

Social Service Organizations
AIDS Family Services
Alcoholism Information and Treatment Centers
Alzheimer's Disease and Related Disorders Foundation
American Cancer Society
American Heart Association
American Hemophilia Foundation
American Lung Association
American Red Cross
Catholic Family Services
Cystic Fibrosis Foundation
Department of Health
Easter Seal Society for Crippled Children and Adults
Family Services Association
Foundation for the Blind
Hand-in-Hand Recreation and Work Programs for the Retarded
Jewish Family Services
Leukemia Society of America
March of Dimes
Mental Health Association
National Multiple Sclerosis Society
National Parkinson's Disease Institute
Office of the Aging
Protestant Family Services
Retarded Children's Association

Professional Organization
Extension Home Economists
State Dietetic Association
State Hospital Association
State Nurses Association

professional organizations that may assist in obtaining nutrition care and other health services for the ambulatory ill.

Use of Community Resources

Resources vary depending on the socioeconomic profile and age of the person. Although this chapter focuses on elderly persons at different economic levels, the indigent person in need of nutrition support outside the hospital also merits consideration. Soup kitchens and food pantries supply meals and packaged foods to the poor.[24] Food banks purchase food at the lowest price and make it available at the lowest cost possible. Some communities provide shopping assistance and transportation for ambulatory homebound persons.

Cooperative and Independent Living

People who live alone can organize and pool their resources for nutrition care. Cooperative shopping and dividing larger packages of food with a companion saves energy and money. Small clubs can be formed in which members take turns preparing a meal. Potluck meals minimize food preparation and provide socialization. Useful ideas and simple recipes for the disabled can be found in *Mealtime Manual for People with Disabilities and the Aging* (available from Campbell Soup Company, Box (MM) 56, Camden, New Jersey 08101).

Progressive living arrangements, known as "life care" or continuing care communities, are a new form of housing for elderly persons. They combine independent living with support services. Meals, linens, cleaning, shopping, and nursing and skilled nursing care are provided when needed. Although there are many financial arrangements and models for life care communities, for all there is usually a one-time entrance fee plus a monthly charge for maintenance and charges for specific services. Caution is recommended in entering into progressive living arrangements as a number of these facilities have gone out of business and clients have lost money in the arrangement.[25]

SUMMARY

Many options are available for obtaining nutrition support in alternative care settings. Networking into the community may reveal innovative alternatives that provide nutritious meals and help maintain independence.

NOTES

1. G. Strand, *Megatrend: Home Health Care* (Salem, Oreg.: Truitt Brothers, 1987), 241–42.

2. C.H. Percy, *Growing Old in the Country of the Young* (New York: McGraw-Hill Book Co., 1974).

3. K. Jernigan, *Nutrition in Long-Term Care Facilities* (Chicago, Ill.: The American Dietetic Association, 1987), 4–5.

4. Lorraine E. Matthews, "Developing a Menu To Meet Residents Needs," *Journal of Nutrition for the Elderly* 5 (Fall 1985): 79–82.

5. Simindokhi Parvizi and Mavis C. Nymon, "A Dietary Study of Elderly Nursing Home Residents in Fargo, North Dakota," *Journal of Nutrition for the Elderly* 2 (Winter 1982): 15–30.

6. Ruth E. Kocher, "Nutrition Care for the Long-Term Patient," in *Nutrition Assessment: A Comprehensive Guide for Planning Intervention*, eds. M.D. Simko, C. Cowell, and J.A. Gilbride (Rockville, Md.: Aspen Publishers, 1984), 223–35.

7. Laura Lefkowitz, "Food Demonstration as a Social Activity in a Nursing Home," *Journal of Nutrition for the Elderly* 2 (Winter 1982): 31–33.

8. Michele Fairchild and Randy Breslin, *Hospice Care* (Chicago, Ill.: The American Dietetic Association, 1987), 1. (Audio cassette)

9. Ibid., 2–4.

10. Ibid., 11.

11. Ibid., 17.

12. Ibid., 19.

13. "Position of the American Dietetic Association: Issues in Feeding the Terminally Ill Adult," *Journal of the American Dietetic Association* 87 (1987): 78–85.

14. Standards of care for hospice patients have been developed by the National Hospice Organization (NHO). For information write for the *NHO Standards Document*, National Hospice Organization, 1901 N. Fort Myer Drive, Suite 402, Arlington, Virginia 22209.

15. Alan Balsam and Maureen Duffy, "Elderly Luncheon Clubs: Bridging the Gap between Congregate and Home Delivered Meals," *Journal of Nutrition for the Elderly* 2 (Summer 1983): 31–34.

16. Helen Smiciklas-Wright, "Nutrition Education and the Elderly," *Journal of Nutrition for the Elderly* 1 (Summer 1981): 3–15.

17. J.P. McNaughton and L.T. Kilgore, "Impact of Title III Funded Feeding Program on Nutrient Intake and Blood Profiles of Elderly in Mississippi," *Journal of Nutrition for the Elderly* 5 (Winter 1985/1986): 35–37.

18. Marie T. Famelli, Georgia Kannon, and Jennifer McDuffie, "An Assessment of the Nutrition Education Needs of Congregate Meal Participants," *Journal of Nutrition Education* 19 (1987): 131–37.

19. Balsam and Duffy, "Elderly Luncheon Clubs: Bridging the Gap between Congregate and Home Delivered Meals," 31.

20. Ibid.

21. Eileen B. McCeney, "Meals on Wheels for Kosher Clients in Central Maryland," *Journal of Nutrition for the Elderly* 5 (Fall 1985): 61–64.

22. Alan L. Balsam and Gary Osteraas, "Developing a Continuum of Community Nutrition Services: Massachusetts Elderly Nutrition Programs," *Journal of Nutrition for the Elderly* 6 (Summer 1987): 51–67.

23. Gael Greene, "Citymeals-on-Wheels," *Journal of Nutrition for the Elderly* 2 (Summer 1983): 27–30.

24. M. Allen, "Channel One: An Integrated Program at Work," *Children Today* 15 (1986): 32.

25. Balsam and Osteraas, "Developing a Continuum of Community Nutrition Services: Massachusetts Elderly Nutrition Programs," 56–57.

Chapter 12

Establishing Standards
of Care

Karen Mueller Buzby

All members of the home care team share the important responsibility of ensuring the safety, quality, and cost effectiveness of specialized nutrition support in the outpatient setting. Successful participation in home health care requires a thorough knowledge of the principles of home nutrition support, as well as an understanding of the unique requirements for the provision of quality care in this environment.

Standards are professionally developed statements that indicate the acceptable level of performance for health care.[1] Standards form the basis of a quality assurance program and are necessary to assist practitioners in identifying, monitoring, and evaluating the elements of optimal care unique to the home environment. Societal, professional, personal, and institutional values influence standards of care. Standards are not only necessary to help the health care professional attain the goal of providing quality patient care through internal review mechanisms, but are required by regulatory agencies that perform external reviews to ensure criteria for certification or reimbursement are met. They include state licensing agencies, Medicare (its *Conditions of Participation* regarding federal certification to bill Medicare and Medicaid for services to patients), and accrediting bodies such as the Joint Commission on Accreditation of Healthcare Organizations (the Joint Commission).[2-4] The need to develop standards for home nutrition support also has been stimulated by pressures from the Health Care Financing Administration (HCFA) and third-party payers, as well as by public demand for quality in home care services.[5,6]

Claiming to deliver quality care is not enough. Just as cost containment dominated health care policy making in the past decade, provider accountability for quality care is quickly becoming the focus of the late 1980s and early 1990s. This chapter examines three quality assessment measures:

1. the standards and criteria for home nutrition support,
2. a monitoring system to evaluate care given, and
3. an evaluation system to correct observed deficits in care.

HOME CARE STANDARDS

Standards formulated by recognized groups of experts and published by several organizations are available for use in developing program-specific standards and criteria for home nutrition support (Exhibits 12-1 and 12-2). Standards of care written specifically for patients receiving home nutrition support have been developed by the American Society for Parenteral and Enteral Nutrition (ASPEN).[7] These are minimal acceptable levels of care designed to ensure that malnutrition is identified and treated. These standards, which focus on the organization of home nutrition support, patient selection, the therapeutic plan, implementation, patient monitoring, and termination of therapy, reflect the essential elements of a well-planned home nutrition support program. Because the standards are written in broad, generic terms, they require adaptation by the home health care provider regarding specific diagnostic tests, treatment modalities, and protocols.[8]

ASPEN also has published standards for hospitalized patients, as well as standards of practice for the nutrition support dietitian, nurse, and pharmacist.[9-12] Ensuring continuity of care from the hospital to the home is an important factor. The need for each home nutrition support professional to account for the quality of his or her practice and to collaborate in multidisciplinary evaluations of total patient care also is an important consideration. Therefore it is suggested that the standards for home patients be used in conjunction with these documents.[13]

In 1988 the Joint Commission published the *Standards for the Accreditation of Home Care* to be used for its new home care accreditation program.[14] This is a voluntary accreditation program that encourages commitment on the part of the agency to quality care. The categories of home care providers currently being accredited are listed in Exhibit 12-3.

Exhibit 12-1 Primary Sources for Standards on Nutrition Support*

Standards for Nutrition Support, Home Patients (1985)†
Standards for Nutrition Support, Hospitalized Patients (1987)
Standards of Practice, Nutrition Support Dietitian (1986)
Standards of Practice, Nutrition Support Nurse (1985)
Standards of Practice, Nutrition Support Pharmacist (1987)

*Standards are available from the American Society for Parenteral and Enteral Nutrition, 8605 Cameron St., Silver Spring, Maryland 20901.
†Revised home care standards are scheduled to be published in fall 1988.

Exhibit 12-2 Primary Sources for Standards on Home Care

Accreditation Program for Home Care and Community Health:
Criteria and Standards (1987)
National League for Nursing
10 Columbus Circle
New York, New York 10019

Conditions of Participation; Home Health Agencies (1986)
Code of Federal Regulations Part 42, Ch. IV
Section on Medicare, pp. 196–207

Standards for the Accreditation of Home Care (1988)
Joint Commission on Accreditation of Healthcare Organizations
875 N. Michigan Ave.
Chicago, Illinois 60611

Standards of Home Health Nursing Practice (1986)
American Nurses' Association
2420 Pershing Rd.
Kansas City, Missouri 64108

All aspects of home care are addressed by the Joint Commission's standards. Accountability to the consumer is recognized by standards concerning patient or client rights. The standards address several provisions:

- the right to make decisions regarding the creation and evaluation of care plans,
- the right to refuse treatment or services,
- the right to confidentiality,

Exhibit 12-3 Categories of Home Care Providers Accredited by the Joint Commission on Accreditation of Healthcare Organizations

1. Medicare-certified home health agencies
2. High technology agencies providing home infusion therapy and related pharmaceutical services
3. Private-duty agencies providing home nursing care and support services
4. Personal care and/or support service organizations
5. Durable home medical equipment companies

Source: Copyright 1988 by the Joint Commission on Accreditation of Healthcare Organizations, Chicago. Reprinted with permission.

- grievance mechanisms, and
- a statement of patient/client responsibilities in the care process.[15]

Another key provision of the standards is the recognition that there must be care coordination to ensure continuity of care; that is, services must be coordinated to ensure appropriate referrals to other organizations, to meet the ongoing needs of the patient/client, to ensure care plan implementation, and to avoid duplication of services.[16] Accreditation by the Joint Commission will have a profound and positive effect on the future of home care.

FRAMEWORK FOR STANDARDS OF CARE

Traditionally, three indicators of quality of care standards have been recognized in clinical practice:

1. the structure in which services are delivered,
2. the process of service delivery, and
3. the outcome of the service.[17,18]

Each category of standards has inherent strengths and limitations. Therefore a combination of structure, process, and outcome measures should be used by the home nutrition support program to develop an internal review mechanism.

Structure

The focus of structure standards is on the organization and framework for care, measuring the ability to deliver services rather than the quality of the actual services provided. Structure standards set requirements for organizational form, facilities and equipment, fiscal resources and management, and staff qualifications, ratios and similar index.[19,20]

Structure standards are measurable and easy to state.[21,22] Their use has been justified on the assumption that the capacity to provide good care will result in its provision.[23,24] The use of structure criteria has not always demonstrated favorable outcomes.[25] Structure elements to be addressed in the development of criteria for selecting a home care company are outlined in Exhibit 12-4.

An important structure element in home nutrition support is the qualifications of the personnel involved in care giving. The increasing complexity of home patient care demands that qualified practitioners ensure

Exhibit 12-4 Suggested Structure Elements To Consider when Developing Criteria for Home Care Agency Selection

Staff
  Number
  Credentials
  24-hour availability
  Continuing education/in-service for staff
  Clinical supervision of staff
  Dietitian on staff

Equipment and Supplies
  Type available
  Method and frequency of delivery
  Inventory and rotation of stock in home
  24 hours-a-day, seven days-a-week delivery
  Access within 12 hours of request
  Maintenance capabilities

Services
  Evaluation of home environment before discharge
  Home visit policies (initial and follow-up)
  Instruction materials
  Geographic range serviced
  Feedback referral
  Provision of laboratory services; processing and reporting results
  Ability to dispense medications, parenteral formula
  24-hour nursing call

Financial Policies
  Billing systems
  Verification of insurance
  Medicare, Medicaid, and private insurance
  Price list availability
  Allowance for creative payment plans for clients
  Process of applications for medical assistance

Quality Control
  Implementation of its quality assurance programs
  Maintenance of industry standards for technique in parenteral admixtures

Communications
  Provision of
  • written reports on all home visits
  • written incident reports
  • written confirmation of all verbal orders to primary physician

Source: Author and Joann Davey McCrae

the provision of quality services. Outpatient care is typically managed by a hospital-based, multidisciplinary nutrition support team. The team usually comprises a registered dietitian, registered nurse, and registered pharmacist, along with the physician director.[26] In-home care is usually provided by professionals employed by a home care agency, company, or vendor. The need for documentation of the professionals' qualifications is stated in the ASPEN standards, which identify appropriate education, specialized training and experience requirements for each discipline. Perhaps in the future, certification of practitioners in the specialty of home nutrition support with the establishment of competencies in each discipline will be one way to ensure quality performance.

The home care company or vendor is an organization that supplies equipment and products or provides services to the patient requiring home nutrition support, with direction from the provider physician.[27] Depending on the patient, supplies, equipment, and services required from a home care company may vary considerably.

Because patient needs can range from limited to comprehensive, the ability of the home care company or vendor to deliver the products or services is an important structure element. Each institution should develop criteria for selecting home care companies to ensure that the supplies or services (or both) available are appropriate to patient needs.

Of particular importance to the dietitian is whether or not the home care company has a registered dietitian on its staff. Unfortunately, dietitians are not employed by all home care companies. This factor should be taken into consideration when selecting a company and when delineating the hospital dietitian's role in outpatient care. Many companies have developed standards for their organization and provide this information on request.

The functioning of the "total" home care team is another important structure element. To ensure quality, the roles and responsibilities of the hospital-based team, the home care company, and the patient must be clearly defined.[28] Effective team collaboration, discipline-specific standards of practice, and multidisciplinary team evaluations are essential elements for the provision of home nutrition support.

Process

Process standards focus on the sequence of established activities or procedures followed in the provision of health care. They are in turn compared to accepted norms for "good care."[29,30] Justification for the assessment of process measures is based on the assumption that quality care will result if the proper procedures are followed.[31] The key process elements in home nutrition support are outlined in Exhibit 12-5.

Exhibit 12-5 Key Process Elements in Home Nutrition Support

1. Evaluation of patient eligibility for home nutrition support, guided by pre-established criteria for patient selection
2. Assessment of nutrition status, including determination of nutrient requirements
3. Development of an individualized therapeutic care plan, including objectives, route, and feeding formulations
4. Selection and establishment of access route for home nutrition support
5. Instruction and training of patient or caregiver (or both) in the techniques and procedures of home nutrition support including
   ● preparation and storage of formula
   ● techniques for formula administration
   ● feeding schedules
   ● care of access route and equipment
6. Selection of a vendor source for supplies, equipment, and in-home services
7. Mechanism for patient monitoring, including frequency of team evaluation, follow-up telephone or home visits, and laboratory studies
8. Communication with other organizations or professionals involved with patient care
9. Assessment of patients' readiness for discharge from the home care program, guided by criteria for termination of therapy
10. Prevention and management of complications in the home
11. Documentation in the medical record
12. Evaluation of care provided through quality assurance activities

Source: Adapted from *Nutrition in Clinical Practice*, Vol. 3, No. 5, pp. 202–205, with permission of American Society for Parenteral and Enteral Nutrition, © October 1988.

An advantage of process criteria is that the actual care given is examined. To determine if criteria were followed during patient care and treatment, the medical records of a sample of clients are examined. Questions addressed might include

● Was the nutrition assessment done in accordance with prescribed requirements?
● Was a proper nutrition care plan developed and implemented?

Process criteria have limitations in that documentation of every procedure and activity is required and performance measures, which require definition of technically correct steps and decisions the provider must make, need to be developed. Also, many home nutrition support patients require long-term care, and process standards for long-term care are difficult to validate.[32] Process standards are time consuming to develop and carry out.

Written protocols identify key process criteria. An essential component of the development of process measures is the development and implementation of policies and procedures that define the program's scope and limitations of services. Although this is the responsibility of the physician, input and review by all members of the home care team is essential.[33]

The first step the practitioner should take toward implementing standards of care is to develop practice-oriented policies and procedures for home nutrition support that reflect professional organization standards. All written policies and procedures regarding the scope and provision of home nutrition services should be reviewed and revised periodically to maintain optimal patient care practices.[34]

Review of the medical record is a key factor in evaluating the process of care. Documentation is one of the most important tasks a health care professional performs. It demonstrates accountability and responsibility and is a means of communicating with physicians and other health professionals.[35] In addition, the medical record is a source of statistical data, demonstrates compliance with regulatory guidelines, and supports reimbursement.[36]

Outcome

Outcome standards are directed toward the end result of care. They address whether there is any measurable change (or stabilization) in the patient's health status, knowledge, or behavior as a result of the services provided.[37,38]

Outcome measures are based on clinical, anthropometric, biochemical, and dietary intake data at the time of discharge from the home care program. Changes in client knowledge and behavior can be viewed as intermediate outcome measures, which may be associated with the correction of a nutrition or health problem but not actually measure the end result of care.[39] A sample of desirable outcomes that may be used to measure the quality of nutrition care for home tube-fed patients is shown in Exhibit 12-6.

Outcome measures have their limitations. The further away one gets from evaluating medical outcomes (i.e., the correction of a nutrition or health problem), the more difficult it is to develop valid measures.[40] Also, if a validated and measurable outcome is not achieved, the process of care would need to be examined before any conclusions regarding quality could be made.[41,42] Another factor that impacts on the development and use of outcome criteria is that home nutrition support clients often have chronic conditions with changes in their health status occurring over months or years.[43,44] Like process criteria, outcome criteria are time consuming to develop and carry out and are expensive to institute.

Structure, process, and outcome standards can be used by the team in developing its own internal review mechanism. The currently available standards for home nutrition support focus on structure, policy, and pro-

Exhibit 12-6 Examples of Outcome Measures for Home Tube-Fed Patients

Intermediate Outcomes	
Patient knowledge	Correctly verbalizes tube feeding schedule
	Identifies signs and symptoms of feeding intolerance
Patient skills/behavior	Correctly prepares formula
	Correctly administers formula
	Performs appropriate tube care
	Identifies equipment malfunctions
	Monitors weight
Patient health status	Tube feeding formula tolerated
	Tube site without skin breakdown or evidence of skin abnormalities
	Oral cavity maintained intact without breakdown, irritation or dryness
Discharge Outcomes	
Patient health status	Weight optimal and stable
	Nutrition status maintained at baseline or improved, when possible
	Adequate fluid intake and output without signs of dehydration
	Adequate food intake to maintain weight

cedure. Although standards measuring basic structure and procedure characteristics are important, improved and strengthened standards are needed that focus on patient-worker interaction and quantifiable outcomes of care.[45]

STANDARD SETTING STAGE

Because medical centers, private industry, and individual professionals have developed various programs for the provision of home health care, there are many ways nutrition support can be provided and coordinated. In all cases, however, appropriate standards and criteria for the home nutrition support program need to be developed.

Development of a set of standards and criteria can be a long and arduous process. The first step is the formation of a panel of experts represented by each discipline of the home care team. The panel may choose to use the standards of care developed by an accreditation body or by an acute care facility, or it may decide to develop its own adaptations to the ASPEN standards.

Developing Process and Outcome Criteria

Because standards evaluate performance or behavior, they must be written in measurable and achievable terms.[46] Criteria statements are specific components of standards that are used to measure a professional's performance or changes in a client's status or behavior.[47] They form the basis of a program's internal monitoring system. There are seven steps required in developing process and outcome criteria (Exhibit 12-7).[48]

Identification of Target Population

The target population is a group of clients who have a specific disease or condition for which the criteria are developed. Representatives from each discipline of the nutrition support team are the ideal group to identify the target population and use the decision-making process to reach a consensus.[49] Initially, the group may focus on the major health problems of the clients served by the nutrition support team. Factors to consider during the selection of the target population include the frequency with which the health problem occurs, as well as whether the nutrition support can significantly alter the health of the client by correcting or preventing further disability and whether experts and practitioners in the field of nutrition support agree on the method of nutrition management.[50,51]

Identification of Population Variables

Population variables define the specific characteristics of the target group including medical diagnosis, nutrition status, age range, adult versus child, or other limiting factors. These help limit the sample size selected during a quality assurance review.

Draft and Refinement of Criteria

Group process is also effective for writing criteria.[52] The goal of developing criteria is not to list every possible process or outcome of patient

Exhibit 12-7 Steps required To Develop Process and Outcome Criteria

---

1. Select the target population
2. Identify variables used to describe the target population
3. Draft and refine criteria specifying the critical time, expected level of performance, and exceptions
4. Identify scientific references that support the criteria
5. Identify the information sources used during the monitoring process to collect data on the criteria
6. Review and accept criteria (by the program's practitioners)
7. Perform a field test to validate the criteria and accept or modify the criteria on the basis of the results

Source: © 1983, The American Dietetic Association. *Guide to Quality Assurance in Ambulatory Nutrition Care.* Used by permission.

care, but to select the key elements of home nutrition support. Program goals and objectives and policies and procedures can serve as references for the essential elements of care.

Process criteria visualize the health care professional carrying out a procedure. Outcome criteria visualize a change in the client's health status, knowledge, or behavior as a result of care. Both should be written in behavioral terms, either expressing a single action or the result of a single action.[53] The criteria must be reliable (repeatable) and valid (measure what they are intended to measure).[54] In theory, behavioral criteria can be measured or verified (or both). It is difficult, however, to specify those that can be measured with reliable and valid tools.[55] Examples of nutrition assessment criteria that can be measured are anthropometric parameters, such as weight and weight change, height, and growth; and laboratory indexes, such as serum albumin, transferrin, and electrolyte levels.

Criteria should be relevant, understandable, measurable, behavioral, and achievable.[56] When developing outcome criteria it is particularly important to choose outcomes that are realistic and measurable. For example, if the program serves a large population of patients with short-bowel syndrome who are receiving home parenteral nutrition, the medical outcome of discontinuing parenteral nutrition is probably not realistic for most of the patients and is not very easily measured for the others because of the prolonged time required to achieve this goal. A behavioral outcome regarding the patient's ability physically to manage his or her parenteral therapy (formula administration, catheter care), however, is realistic.

Explicit criteria can be developed that state the exact data and methods to be used for verification. For example, a home parenteral nutrition client requiring protein repletion will receive 1.5 grams of amino acids per kilogram of body weight per day from parenteral solutions. To determine whether this criterion has been met, the amount of protein supplied by the parenteral formula would be determined and compared to the client's calculated requirements.

In contrast, more flexible criteria that allow for variations in practice in different health care settings can be developed. These are called implicit or general criteria. An example of such a criterion would be: The client's parenteral formula provides adequate protein to meet the goals of therapy. Written protocols must be developed that specify how the evaluators will consistently determine whether the implicit criteria are met.

The criteria also specify the time frame during which the process or outcome should be achieved. For example, the critical time for performing a baseline comprehensive nutrition assessment is before discharge from the hospital or during the client's initial visit. The time frames established should be consistent with current clinical practices.

For each criterion, the expected level of performance should be speci-fied.[57] The desirable level is 100 percent, but this level of performance may not be a realistic expectation. A standard of 100 percent can be established for process criteria because the home program has sufficient control over this area. One hundred percent realization of particular client outcomes, however, cannot be assured.

Establishing realistic percentages requires a data base or an educated guess, made on the basis of clinical experience. Therefore the percentage should indicate the desired practice level, with the goal of working toward increasing performance. When observed performance level fails to reach what is expected, a commitment to improve should follow.

Exceptions should be designated when there are anticipated circum-stances beyond the control of the practitioner or the client that prevent achievement of the outcome or process.[58]

Identification of Supportive Reference

Each criterion should be referenced to substantiate its scientific basis or efficacy and safety (or both).

Verification

Verification is the process of identifying the data sources used to deter-mine if the criteria are met. Examples of data sources include patient records, health care team care plans, or data collected for other purposes such as statistical reports or special surveys. Data should be readily avail-able, and data collection should be an efficient process. If the criteria cannot be measured, given available resources, it should not be used. The devel-opment of sophisticated criteria that cannot be evaluated is purely an academic exercise.

Ratification

The practitioner affected by the quality assessment has the opportunity to contribute to the development of the criteria during the ratification process. Prepared criteria can be distributed to the practitioners for com-ments. This process promotes awareness of the problem and fosters com-mitment to its solution.

Validation

A field test is used to validate formally the criteria. Like a quality as-sessment audit, the field test involves a review of client records and other identified data sources. During this process, however, criteria, not patient care, is judged. On the basis of results of the field test the criteria are revised to produce quality indicators that are more reliable and valid.[59]

IMPLEMENTING A MONITORING AND EVALUATION SYSTEM

Monitoring and evaluation are the final steps in the process of establishing an internal review mechanism. If the data collection capabilities of the program have been addressed properly during criteria development, designing the monitoring system will be easy.

Although monitoring will vary according to each program's capabilities and resources, it should be ongoing and performed on a regular basis. The monitoring mechanism instituted will vary, depending on the target population specified and the number of criteria to be evaluated.

If the monitoring system is developed solely on retrospective chart review, the quality of the record, not the quality of patient care, may be addressed.[60] Prospective methods of data collection can be employed to overcome this drawback. Direct observation of the practitioner-client interaction may be used to assess the process of care. Also mail or telephone surveys, personal interviews, or observations of actual or simulated behavior of the patients may be used to collect data. For example, the patient's ability to administer formula can be evaluated during recertification in home parenteral and enteral nutrition procedures.

Identification of problems or deficiencies in care takes place during the evaluation step. How improvements will be accomplished also are addressed. Actions taken to improve care may include counseling, in-service education, changes in staffing, patient education, development of new or revised policies and procedures, or development of new forms for the medical record.[61] Actions taken to correct identified deficiencies should be positive and not punitive in nature.[62]

SUMMARY

The use of standards and the development of criteria provide a structure to evaluate the quality of care delivered in a home nutrition support program. To demonstrate accountability to the consumers of the service, practitioners are encouraged to take a proactive stance and institute internal review mechanisms that are based on realistic and measurable criteria. As more programs participate in this process, the data generated will contribute to the body of knowledge regarding the appropriate, adequate, and efficient use of nutrition support services. These data can be used to resolve the conceptual and operational uncertainties and problems of home care quality assessment.

NOTES

1. Farah M. Walters, *A Quality Assurance Procedure Manual for Dietitians* (Chicago, Ill.: The American Dietetic Association, 1986).

2. Health and Public Policy Committee, American College of Physicians, "Home Health Care," *Annals of Internal Medicine* 105 (1986): 454–60.

3. Mary Jane Koren, "Home Care—Who Cares?" *New England Journal of Medicine* 314 (1986): 917–20.

4. Joint Commission on Accreditation of Healthcare Organizations, *Standards for the Accreditation of Home Care* (Chicago, Ill., 1988).

5. "Washington Reviews," *Nutrition in Clinical Practice* 21 (1987): 223–24.

6. Charles P. Sabatino, "The 'Black Box' of Home Care Quality," in *Outcome Measures in Home Care, Volume II Service,* eds. Lynn T. Rinke and Alexis A. Wilson (New York: National League for Nursing, 1987) 33–41.

7. American Society for Parenteral and Enteral Nutrition, *Standards for Nutrition Support Home Patients* (Silver Spring, Md., 1985).

8. Ibid.

9. American Society for Parenteral and Enteral Nutrition, "Standards for Nutrition Support Hospitalized Patients," *Nutrition in Clinical Practice* 3 (1988): 28–31.

10. American Society for Parenteral and Enteral Nutrition, "Standards of Practice, Nutrition Support Dietitian," *Nutrition in Clinical Practice* 1 (1986): 216–20.

11. American Society for Parenteral and Enteral Nutrition, *Standards of Practice, Nutrition Support Nurse* (Silver Spring, Md., 1985).

12. American Society for Parenteral and Enteral Nutrition, "Standards of Practice, Nutrition Support Pharmacist," *Nutrition in Clinical Practice* 2 (1987): 166–69.

13. American Society for Parenteral and Enteral Nutrition, *Standards for Nutrition Support Home Patients* (Silver Spring, Md., 1985).

14. Joint Commission on Accreditation of Healthcare Organizations, *Standards for the Accreditation of Home Care* (Chicago, Ill., 1988).

15. Ibid.

16. Ibid.

17. Sabatino, "The 'Black Box' of Home Care Quality," 33–41.

18. Mildred Kaufman, *Guide to Quality Assurance in Ambulatory Nutrition Care* (Chicago, Ill.: The American Dietetic Association, 1983).

19. Sabatino, "The 'Black Box' of Home Care Quality," 33–41.

20. Kaufman, *Guide to Quality Assurance in Ambulatory Nutrition Care.*

21. Sabatino, "The 'Black Box' of Home Care Quality," 33–41.

22. Kaufman, *Guide to Quality Assurance in Ambulatory Nutrition Care.*

23. Sabatino, "The 'Black Box' of Home Care Quality," 33–41.

24. Amy Marie Haddad, "Quality Assurance Issues," in *High Tech Home Care: A Practical Guide,* ed. Amy Marie Haddad (Rockville, Md.: Aspen Publishers, 1987), 148–68.

25. Sabatino, "The 'Black Box' of Home Care Quailty," 33–41.

26. American Society for Parenteral and Enteral Nutrition, *Standards for Nutrition Support Home Patients.*

27. Ibid.

28. Ibid.

29. Sabatino, "The 'Black Box' of Home Care Quality," 33–41.

30. Kaufman, *Guide to Quality Assurance in Ambulatory Nutrition Care.*

31. Sabatino, "The 'Black Box' of Home Care Quality," 33–41.

32. Ibid.

33. American Society for Parenteral and Enteral Nutrition, *Standards for Nutrition Support Home Patients.*

34. Ibid.

35. Florida Association of Home Health Agencies, "Quality Assurance Program" in *Outcome Measures in Home Care, Volume II Service,* eds. Lynn T. Rinke and Alexis A. Wilson (New York: National League for Nursing, 1987) 139–47.

36. Ibid.

37. Sabatino, "The 'Black Box' of Home Care Quality," 33–41.

38. Kaufman, *Guide to Quality Assurance in Ambulatory Nutrition Care.*

39. Ibid.

40. Sabatino, "The 'Black Box' of Home Care Quality," 33–41.

41. Ibid.

42. Kaufman, *Guide to Quality Assurance in Ambulatory Nutrition Care.*

43. Sabatino, "The 'Black Box' of Home Care Quality," 33–41.

44. Kaufman, *Guide to Quality Assurance in Ambulatory Nutrition Care.*

45. Sabatino, "The 'Black Box' of Home Care Quality," 33–41.

46. Haddad, "Quality Assurance Issues," 148–68.

47. Ibid.

48. Kaufman, *Guide to Quality Assurance in Ambulatory Nutrition Care.*

49. Haddad, "Quality Assurance Issues," 148–68.

50. Walters, *A Quality Assurance Procedure Manual for Dietitians.*

51. Kaufman, *Guide to Quality Assurance in Ambulatory Nutrition Care.*

52. Ibid.

53. Ibid.

54. Ibid.

55. Ibid.

56. Ibid.

57. Ibid.

58. Ibid.

59. Ibid.

60. Haddad, "Quality Assurance Issues," 148–68.

61. Florida Association of Home Health Agencies, "Quality Assurance Program," 139–47.

62. Ibid.

Chapter 13

Cost Effectiveness/ Cost Benefit of Nutrition Services

Julie O'Sullivan-Maillet and Judith A. Gilbride

The 1980s have been a period of cost containment. As medical technology has expanded the ability to sustain life, questions of costs versus ethics of health care have escalated. The desire for quality health care services for patients remains, but the issue of cost effectiveness and cost benefit of these services has surfaced.

The amount of monies spent in health care is finite, thus the value of services must be examined to determine which services are essential and which are nonessential. The essential nature of the service is determined by the cost effectiveness or cost benefit (or both) of the service.

This chapter identifies the components to consider in planning cost effectiveness/cost benefit studies in home care and discusses some current studies and the potential studies needed in the area. Health care practitioners must substantiate nutrition services in all aspects of health care.

PROCESS OF JUSTIFYING COSTS

Cost justifications can be either process or outcome oriented. Process orientation deals with the how tos; that is, how to make the service better, more effective, more efficient, more accessible, and so forth. Outcome orientation deals with the whys and whats: why the service is needed, what the endpoint of the service will be. Whatever the orientation, the justification involves a five-part process:

1. identification of the problem to be considered;
2. identification of the possible alternatives or solutions;
3. assessment of the current environment;
4. development of a plan, which includes the appropriate type of cost analysis; and
5. evaluation of the results and costs.

Another important component is identifying the audience that the cost analysis addresses; is it administrators? peers? insurance carriers? clients? or society? The target audience should help direct the analysis.

Problem Identification

The first step in cost analysis is identification of the problem. The problem needs to be narrowly and clearly defined. The broad issue needs to be identified first, and then the specific problem can be addressed.

Consider the cost effectiveness of home care as an example. This issue is too broad and could be narrowed into a number of questions, such as:

- When is home care an appropriate alternative for hospital care?
- What cuts in the current home care system are reasonable without quality of patient care being compromised?
- Do patient outcomes vary or do costs vary by home care companies?

Each of these questions could be refined further. The first question can be addressed better by dividing it into two separate questions: (1) Will the availability of home care result in earlier discharge from the hospital? or (2) will the availability of home care reduce hospital admissions? The second question is a relatively good one, but is the concern about quality or quantity of care, or both? The considerations raised in the third question are good, but they are two separate issues; that is, (1) how do the costs of one company compare to those of the other in terms of the extent of services and staff qualifications? and (2) what are the endpoints when home care is discontinued or nonreimbursable? These problems can be defined further before considering the possible alternatives.

Possible Alternatives

The alternatives identify the potential solutions to the problem or the possible scenarios as a result of the problem. All possible alternatives should be identified, even if they are improbable. Later review may disregard certain alternatives. Of course, cost analysis makes the assumption that there are alternatives. If there are no alternatives or comparisons, cost analysis is not necessary. Cost analysis is done to improve the results or outcomes. If the analysis has no usefulness, it should not be done.

What are some alternatives to the previously posed questions?

1. Concerning the question of early discharge (subdivision of question no. 1):

- Would early discharge from the hospital increase the number of patients receiving home care?
- How many days of home care in relation to days of hospitalization would the patient have?
- Would home care reduce readmissions and save dollars?

2. Concerning question no. 2:

- What is the effect of cost containment on quality of patient care?
- What is the difference in terms of cost and quality for paid home nursing care versus that for care provided by family members?
- Does care by a family member result in lost salary to that person?
- Can services be cut in terms of personnel, materials, labor, or services without losing the integrity of the care provided?

3. Concerning the subdivision of question no. 3:

- Are patient outcomes better with one home care system than another?
- Does company A or company B have better mortality or morbidity rates? Are these data available?
- Are patient adjustments easier or patient attitudes better with one company than another?
- Is the care comprehensive, including nutrition assessment and monitoring?

Assessment of Environment

Exhibit 13-1 lists some of the descriptors of the patient environment to aid in evaluation of care provided. Thorough analysis of the facts will assist in identifying the efficiency of present systems. The standards of care and the descriptors of the services provided give base line data for process-oriented outcomes.

A successful process is a means to obtain the desired end; an effective outcome is when the patient benefits. Exhibit 13-2 identifies potential patient outcomes or benefits. Nutrition care and nutrition services by dietitians must substantiate this positive effect on the patient. How does nutrition affect morbidity and mortality, maintain nutrition status or minimize deterioration, improve the quality of life or increase patient satisfaction?

Exhibit 13-1 Descriptors of Environment

Who is the patient population?
How many patients are there?
How much family support is available?
What type of nutrition support do the patients receive?
What is the average length of care provided by your organization?
What is the reason for termination of care?
How many new patients are added monthly?
How often are the patients assessed nutritionally?
How often does the form of nutrition support for a patient change?
How often are the patients monitored or followed up?
What are the methods of follow-up?
How many minutes or hours does it take to do the average initial visit?
How long does the average follow-up visit take?
What are your standards of care for initial visits, follow-up care, and so forth?
How much time is spent in patient education? patient care?
Who prepares, delivers, or administers the feedings?

One goal of cost containment is to ensure the best patient outcome without extraneous or nonessential services. Analysis of the environment is to know the result of care; that is, how many patients develop infections, lose weight, get readmitted, or change home care companies? Even further, what subjective and objective criteria give indications of patient complications or deterioration in health and nutrition status?

Exhibit 13-2 Potential Benefits of Home Nutrition Care

TO CLIENTS
Medical:
    Decreased health care costs
    Prolonged survival
    Reduced complications
    Improved weight status
    Improved muscle function

Psychosocial:
    Increased feeling of well-being
    Reduced anxiety
    Reduced dependency on home care
    Continued family interaction

TO SOCIETY
Decreased health expenditures
Family involvement
Return to employment and productivity

Plan Development

Once the problem has been identified and its potential solutions and an assessment of the current environment have been completed, a systematic plan should be devised to increase efficiency or demonstrate a positive patient outcome. If necessary, the original problem should be considered and refined or revised. The appropriate type of cost analysis will be determined by the financial and social objectives of the plan and what needs to be accomplished. Cost analysis can provide information for evaluating the results, whether they are process or outcome oriented.

Methods of Cost Analysis

Cost analysis can be approached with the use of four different methods: cost effectiveness, cost benefit, cost utility, and cost feasibility. Each has different strengths and weaknesses and is the appropriate method in specific situations.[1]

Before a study is designed, two decisions must be made: (1) whether a cost analysis should be conducted and (2) what type of analysis should be done. Cost analysis may not be necessary if there are no alternatives, if there is not sufficient time available to do the analysis, or if conducting the study will not change the current level or type of care. The question is: What will occur as a result of a better alternative? If the gains are limited, only a small amount should be invested in the analysis. Conversely, if the potential gain is great, a large investment in the analysis should be worthwhile.

Cost-effectiveness, cost-benefit, and cost-utility analyses all assist in weighing alternatives to determine the lowest cost for a specific outcome or the best outcome for a specific cost. Cost feasibility differs from these methods because it only looks at the costs of an alternative to determine whether it can be considered. If the cost of the project, level of care, or procedure exceeds the budget available, there is no reason to proceed further. Cost feasibility thus provides an analysis of whether the project is worth considering, but it cannot be used to determine which alternative to select when more than one alternative fits within the budget.

Cost-benefit analysis evaluates alternatives regarding costs and benefits, with each measured in monetary terms. With this method each alternative is assessed by a comparison of cost versus benefit, expressed either by the ratio of dollars spent to dollars saved or by the net savings if the benefits are greater than the costs. For an alternative to be considered, its benefits need to exceed its costs and it needs to be demonstrated that the desired alternative would have the highest ratio of benefits to costs. Cost benefit has an advantage of allowing a cost comparison of different outcomes, because the outcomes are assigned a monetary value. This approach presents the hurdle of assigning a price/value to the outcome.

Two difficulties arise with this approach. The first centers on how to assess patient outcomes. What is the monetary value, for example, of a patient's feeling of well-being or improved blood glucose control? Cost benefit should be considered only when benefits can be converted to dollars and cents. When the benefits cannot be determined monetarily, a cost-effectiveness or cost-utility analysis should be used. The second difficulty is the availability of expertise in assigning monetary values. If the expertise in economics is not available, cost effectiveness is more feasible than cost benefit.

Cost effectiveness evaluates alternatives on the basis of their costs compared to some group of outcomes. For this method the outcomes must be expressed in measurable terms; for example, lives saved, days of productivity, complications prevented. Costs are expressed in monetary units, usually in dollars spent. As a prerequisite to the cost-effectiveness analysis, the alternatives must have similar goals that can be compared and can incorporate similar methods of evaluating outcomes.

Cost-effectiveness data are useful to determine the least cost for a given outcome or the greatest effectiveness per given cost. This method might also be useful to compare two or more types of treatments or educational methods; for example, the cost of two enteral products that result in the same outcome or the number of patients educated by individual or small group instruction within a given time span. An estimation of the effectiveness of each treatment/method is needed, along with cost per approach. The end result is a cost-effectiveness ratio. The best ratio is not necessarily the highest or lowest cost or effectiveness but, rather, the best cost for the level of effectiveness desired for the problem or situation. This type of analysis examines alternatives well when comparing the cost to achieve one goal. Nevertheless, cost-effectiveness analysis cannot compare cost-effectiveness ratios with different goals.

Cost-utility analysis evaluates alternatives by comparing costs and the estimated value of the outcome. It allows for subjective assessment of the relative value of the outcome and a subjective estimate of the probability of the outcome. The analysis is based on judgments and intuitive guesses.

The advantage of the method is a reduced need for data, in comparison to the cost-benefit analysis, and the ability to look at various outcomes, which cannot be accomplished with the cost-effectiveness method. The disadvantage is that the results cannot be replicated easily because they are based on the opinions of the person making the analysis. Another evaluator with the same information might come up with very different results. As in cost-benefit analysis, there is a need for expertise in setting values for benefits and probabilities, but in cost utility, the amount of expertise needed is less. The decision to use cost benefit versus cost utility is often made on the basis of time constraints. Cost benefit requires more time, data, and analysis, but it is also more reliable.

Determining Costs

In any cost analysis an evaluation of cost is essential. Any nutrition intervention has an outcome and a cost. Because of the finite amount of resources available for any outcome, every cost has two parts: (1) the actual cost in dollars and cents and (2) the cost of what is sacrificed by the allocation of the resources in the given way. For example, the cost of assessing all patients is a given number of dollars resulting from hours spent. Within the given amount of dollars, the cost of assessing all patients may only allow a limited amount of time to educate patients.

Levin[2] describes an ingredient method to determine costs, which requires that each intervention be described in terms of the resources required to produce the outcome. The intervention is the process itself. If there is a basic standard of care required for the outcome, independent of the alternatives, this base need not be considered. Only the incremental costs for each alternative needs to be considered. Obviously this means that to do cost analysis one must have familiarity with the basic costs plus the costs of all alternatives.

Detailed knowledge of all alternatives is needed. There are several parts of the cost analysis that need to be considered, which are defined as follows:

1. *Personnel:* all human resources, including care providers and their supervisors, paraprofessionals, secretarial support, custodial support, and volunteers, as well as the time provided by each in dollars to conduct the intervention
2. *Physical space:* any classroom space, training or storage areas, and requirements for heating, cooling, or lighting
3. *Equipment:* any and all furniture, audiovisual equipment, computers or data processing equipment, office equipment, enteral and parenteral pumps
4. *Materials:* books, intravenous tubing, total parenteral nutrition (TPN) solutions, enteral formulas, medications
5. *Miscellaneous:* liability insurance, continuing education, travel, depreciation, record keeping
6. *Costs incurred by others:* indirect costs to the client such as transportation to obtain supplies or visit health care providers

These costs and services should be spelled out in as much detail as possible to allow for the most precise estimation of the cost of the intervention. The costs considered should be similar in all comparisons. The higher the cost of any one category the more precisely it should be examined to determine its effect on the cost of the intervention.

Assigning a price to each ingredient is generally done through the current market value for each ingredient. When there is no market price, the price should be estimated. A determination of the market value includes assigning direct, indirect, and intangible costs (Exhibit 13-3). Direct costs are the actual expenditures used in the provision of services, such as equipment, supplies, and hours of professional time. Indirect costs are expenditures incurred in addition to direct costs; for example, time and salary lost from work by clients and increased use of foods and supplements. Intangible costs are the values placed on other "costs" to the patient; that is, psychologic dependency on others, loss of mobility, and any discomfort from the mode of feeding.

Exhibit 13-3 Potential Costs Associated with Home Care

Direct Costs
Professional fees, including

- initial assessment and care plans
- dressings changes and insertion costs
- monitoring—laboratory indexes, tolerance, feedings
- education of client and families
- treatment of complications

Supplies and solutions, including

- hardware—tubes, filters, pumps, bags
- solutions—parenteral, enteral

Indirect Costs
    Administrative fees
    Depreciation on equipment
    Storage of supplies
    Physical space
    Maintenance and utilities
Intangible Costs
    Discomfort
    Immobility
    Psychologic feelings of dependency
    Lost time from other activities
    Impact on family

Exhibit 13-4 addresses analysis of all costs, including the cost to society as a whole. Now, it can be determined who will incur each cost—the home care company, the insurance carrier, the hospital, the patient, or a volunteer organization. In this way the costs for the different groups can be compared. In valuing the analysis from one vantage point, it is important to consider total costs and benefits to limit misunderstanding of the true costs of the intervention.

Once costs are known and the pointers in Exhibit 13-4 are considered, outcomes need to be assessed in terms of benefit, effectiveness, or utility. In the cost-benefit analysis a dollar amount must be attributed to the benefits. This might be appropriate in determining the effect of home stay versus hospital stay, the use of one level of personnel over another, or the use of one procedure over another on the basis of number of complications or number of days absent from work.

The benefit side of the cost-benefit analysis also considers direct, indirect, and intangible rewards. A direct benefit is any outcome directly attributable to the provision of services or nutrition intervention. In home care, direct benefits include weight gain, prolonged survival, and improved quality of life. An indirect benefit could be the saving of a nutritionist's time or the prevention of complications. Intangible benefits could be improved functional status and subjective well-being, both of which are difficult to quantify.

Cost effectiveness removes the monetary requirement and thus is often more readily applied to the care of human beings and quality of life measurements. The measures of effectiveness may be improvement in laboratory data, reduction in number of incidents of diarrhea, or any measure currently in use to evaluate outcome. Thus measures of effectiveness might include evaluation of knowledge or behavior, estimates of physical strength or well-being, or estimates of patient satisfaction. For each outcome, the question arises whether it is a valid method of assessing patient outcome. For example, does serum albumin concentration really explain anything about patient outcome? Is weight change a valid indicator of successful intervention? These questions are beyond the constraints of this chapter. What must be remembered, however, is that no expenditure or resource is justifiable if the program is ineffective and does not have a positive outcome.

For quick evaluation, cost utility might be useful, but it should not be generalized and will not contribute to the pool of data on cost effectiveness of home care and its services. Results should be evaluated fully after the problem is clearly defined, the methods are determined, and the study has been conducted. What alternative looks the best? What are the accomplishments made from the change? Are dollars being saved? Is the system made more cost efficient? Are patient outcomes improved or maintained? Will there be greater savings over time?

Exhibit 13-4 Checklist for Evaluating Cost Analysis Reports

(1) *What is the decision framework?* That is, what is the specific context in which decisions must be made, and on what basis? What are the criteria that should guide the decision?

(2) *Which alternatives are evaluated?* Are these the relevant alternatives, and are there others that ought to be considered?

(3) *How are costs estimated?* Are the ingredients or resource requirements for each alternative set out carefully? Is the method for costing these ingredients appropriate? Are all of the ingredients included in the costing exercise, or does it include only those that are paid for by the sponsor?

(4) *Are the costs evaluated according to who pays them?* If relevant, is the analysis extended to a distribution of cost burdens among constituencies?

(5) *Are costs presented in an appropriate mode, given the nature of the decision context?* Is the cost analysis differentiated for different levels of scale of the alternatives? Is the appropriate cost concept used (e.g., total, average, or marginal cost) in the comparison? Are costs discounted appropriately for their distribution over the time horizon?

(6) *Is the criterion of effectiveness appropriate to the analysis?* To what degree does it omit important outcomes of the alternative that should be taken into consideration? To the degree that there are multiple outcomes, how are they taken into account? Are they weighted appropriately in ascertaining the overall effectiveness of alternatives?

(7) *Are there different distributional effects of the alternatives across populations?* Do the alternatives provide different results for different groups? For example, do some populations benefit more from one type of program while others benefit more from another type? To what degree are these differences accounted for in the analysis, and how are they considered in the evaluation of effectiveness?

(8) *Does the analysis of results meet the overall standards for assessing effectiveness?* Are the experimental or quasi-experimental design and its implementation and methodology sufficient to place high reliability on the estimated effectiveness of alternatives?

(9) *Are the cost-effectiveness comparisons appropriate?* Given all of the previous criteria, are the results used correctly to rank alternatives? What errors or omissions are evident? If these were corrected in the analysis, would the rankings change? Are the differences in cost-effectiveness values among alternatives large enough that you would have confidence in using them as a basis for decisions? How robust are they with respect to different assumptions about the ingredient requirements, imputation of costs to ingredients, choice of discount rates, measure of effectiveness, and weighing of different dimensions of effectiveness?

(10) *How generalizable are the results to other settings?* To what degree are the results likely to have wider generalizability than just the specific decision-context that is considered? For example, could they be applied to alternatives for similar populations and similar objectives in other organizational settings? Is it possible to make cost-estimate adjustments that would enable such generalizability?

Source: Reprinted from H. Levin, *Cost Effectiveness: A Primer,* pp. 138–140, copyright 1985 by Sage Publications, Inc. Reprinted by permission of Sage Publications, Inc.

For measures of cost analysis in the interpretation of the results, consider that

- all methods are based on estimates,
- all considerations cannot be used in any evaluation,
- small differences in any method may not be significant, and
- the magnitude of the difference is important to consider

When evaluating any cost analysis study, it should be determined whether all factors have been analyzed sufficiently and if all the alternatives have been considered. Then the results should be interpreted and whether they can be generalized to other situations determined. Exhibit 13-5 summarizes which costing method can be used to compare two sets of total costs of a service or intervention with the potential results or final objectives.

STUDIES ON COST EFFECTIVENESS

Government studies on health costs have concentrated on whether a program is worth its cost. The goal of a cost-benefit analysis is to maximize

Exhibit 13-5 Quick Method To Select Type of Analysis on the Basis of Variables Being Studied

Type of Analysis	Total Cost 1	Total Cost 2	Result 1 ($)	Result 2 ($)
Cost Feasibility*	X	X	Not evaluated	
Cost Benefit†	X	X	X	X
	X		X	X
	X	X	X	
Cost Effectiveness‡	X	X	X	not possible
Cost Utility∮	X estimated X		X	estimated X

X indicates need for the variable.

*Can compare only costs.
†Can compare the total costs of two items to one result, one cost to two different results, or two or more costs and results.
‡Can compare only costs for one result.
∮Similar to cost benefit, but based on more estimates and cannot be generalized.

social welfare. Welfare economics has at least two dimensions: economic efficiency and distributional justice. The social objective of cost benefit represents consensus of ethical judgments for the good of society. Financial objectives provide a means of monitoring the performance of a decision maker and can substantiate the value of funding approved by legislators and administrators. Does home care really save more money than hospital care? A savings of 30 percent to 60 percent has been estimated, on the basis of government reimbursement schedules.[3] Nevertheless, there is a need for health care providers to conduct cost-benefit and cost-effectiveness studies.

Cost-effectiveness studies in nutrition support have been limited, and none have been done in the home care arena. Two areas can help the nutrition professional to design studies: the nutrition support literature and costing procedures in dietetics.

In a monograph published in 1979 the dietetics literature was reviewed extensively and an economic model for the costs and benefits of nutrition care was presented.[4] Close scrutiny of the literature showed insufficient documentation on effectiveness of nutrition services. Since its publication, no clear-cut methodology has emerged because of differences in organizational structures and the interpretation of nutrition outcomes. The authors of the monograph were unable to locate research studies that validated the American Dietetic Association model. There are few models in the literature that evaluate the costs and benefits of nutrition intervention strategies. Those that are reported have been done with small sample sizes and have methodologic errors common to clinically based studies.

The studies that are beginning to appear concentrate on savings from the decreased length of hospital stay as a result of aggressive nutrition support. Cost effectiveness seems to be the method of choice by researchers in studying these costs. New studies indicate some difficulties in understanding "true costs."[5] From a societal perspective, the correct cost is the opportunity or "value of resources" cost. Home care, like hospitalization, shows variations in how to identify charges (what the patient or third party was asked to pay) versus actual costs of care. This does not preclude the importance of initiating cost-effective techniques in comparing various alternatives. Examples of possible comparisons that can be done to look at cost effectiveness in home care are shown in Exhibit 13-6. Studies are needed to identify the costs of nutrition services related to home care and to examine the long-term follow-up of nutrition support and its impact on the nutrition services. Two publications that can assist with the calculations of the costs and outcomes of nutrition intervention are those by Twomey and Patching[6] and Splett and Caldwell.[7]

Some investigations have compared the costs of nutrition protocols for enteral and parenteral feedings on the basis of different products, handling,

Exhibit 13-6 Areas of Potential Study in Cost Analysis of Home Care

---

Topic: Type of Feeding Modality
  Cost Feasibility: Cost of product A versus that of product B
  Cost Benefit: Does product A or product B decrease complication and hospital readmission?
  Cost Effectiveness: Does product A or Product B decrease abdominal discomfort and diarrhea?

Topic: Provider of Home Care Services
  Cost Feasibility: Cost of self-operation of home care versus contracting of services
  Cost Benefit: Which provider has the lowest complication rate?
  Cost Effectiveness: Which provider's services result in the lowest client dependency on home care?

Topic: Method of Feeding
  Cost Feasibility: What is the cost of feeding specially prepared whole foods, as well as for the training in preparation, versus that with use of routine enteral feedings?
  Cost Benefit: Are persons receiving whole foods, in comparison with those receiving tube feedings, more likely to reenter the job market?
  Cost Effectiveness: Does the use of whole foods improve family interaction?

---

delivery, and monitoring. Even in a controlled environment (e.g., a nutrition support unit in a hospital), it has been difficult to ascertain the value of enteral and parenteral nutrition for selected patient groups.[8] Particularly for parenteral feedings, there are indirect costs and the benefits of TPN are not well-substantiated except in preoperative usage.[9] Results of the studies have shown that it is necessary to specify how costs are distinguished from charges and to be explicit on how the costs are derived.

In comparing the amounts charged for parenteral nutrition, charges for enteral feeding seem quite modest. One home care agency estimates a tenfold increase in parenteral costs over enteral costs. Findings also show that the use of TPN in patients whose complication rate is not considerably reduced can be very expensive.[10,11]

As discussed earlier Levin[12] provides a checklist for evaluating cost analysis reports that are being published (see Exhibit 13-4). The listing may also help the novice establish the pertinent points in designing a cost analysis for home nutrition services and evaluating studies done on the cost and results of home care. A costing work sheet, which incorporates the parts of the cost analysis (discussed earlier) is shown in Exhibit 13-7.

The use of home nutrition products is expected to escalate in the next decade. The objectives for health care providers are to be aware of the costs involved in home care and to utilize health care monies in the most effective way possible. These objectives necessitate that providers keep abreast of the cost analysis studies that are done and contribute to the

Exhibit 13-7 Costing Work Sheet

Factors in Expense	Total Cost	Cost to Home Care Company	Cost to Government Agencies	Cost to Insurance Carriers	Cost to Family and Client
Personnel					
Professional time					
Paraprofessional time					
Office Space and Equipment					
Client					
Materials and Equipment					
Pumps					
Tubes					
Solutions					
Medications					
Other					
Administrative fees					
Liability insurance					
Education costs					
Travel					
Depreciation					
Total Costs					

expansion of knowledge in this area. The ultimate goal is to maximize the benefit/effectiveness of home care regarding both the individual client and society.

NOTES

1. Harry L. Levin, *Cost-Effectiveness: A Primer* (Beverly Hills, Calif.: Sage Publications, 1985).

2. Ibid.

3. Ibid.

4. Marion Mason, ed., *Costs and Benefits of Nutritional Care Phase I* (Chicago, Ill.: The American Dietetic Association, 1979).

5. G.F. Anderson and E.P. Steinberg, "DRG's and Specialized Nutrition Support. Prospective Payment and Nutritional Support: The Need for Reform." *JPEN. Journal of Parenteral and Enteral Nutrition* 10 (1986): 3.

6. Patrick L. Twomey and Steven C. Patching, "Cost-Effectiveness of Nutritional Support." *JPEN. Journal of Parenteral and Enteral Nutrition* 9 (1985): 3.

7. Patricia Splett and Mariel Caldwell, *Costing Nutrition Services: A Workbook* (Chicago, Ill.: U.S. Department of Health and Human Services, 1985).

8. Ross Laboratories, *Benefits of Nutrition Services: A Costing and Marketing Approach* (Columbus, Ohio: 1988).

9. Allan S. Detsky and Khursheed N. Jeejeebhoy, "Cost-Effectiveness of Preoperative Parenteral Nutrition in Patients Undergoing Major Gastrontestinal Surgery." *JPEN. Journal of Parenteral and Enteral Nutrition* 8 (1984): 63.

10. John M. Eisenberg et al., "Measuring the Economic Impact of Perioperative Total Parenteral Nutrition: Principles and Design." *American Journal of Clinical Nutrition* 47 (1988): 382.

11. Jay M. Mirtallo et al., "Cost-Effective Nutrition Support." *Nutrition in Clinical Practice* 2 (1987): 142.

12. Levin, *Cost-Effectiveness: A Primer.*

BIBLIOGRAPHY

Anderson, G.F., and E.P. Steinberg. "DRG's and Specialized Nutrition Support. Prospective Payment and Nutritional Support: The Need for Reform." *JPEN. Journal of Parenteral and Enteral Nutrition* 10 (1986): 3–8.

Brakebill, Janet I, Ronald A. Robb, Marianne F. Ivey, Dale B. Christensen, Jeffry H. Young, and Belding H. Scribner. "Pharmacy Department Costs and Patient Charges Associated with a Home Parenteral Program." *American Journal of Hospital Pharmacy* 40 (1983): 260–63.

Conklin, Martha T. "Cost-Effectiveness of Nutritional Intervention." In *Nutrition Assessment: A Comprehensive Guide for Planning Intervention*, edited by M. Simko, C. Cowell, and J.A. Gilbride. Rockville, Md.: Aspen Publishers, 1984, 259–310.

Detsky, Allan S., and Khursheed N. Jeejeebhoy. "Cost-Effectiveness of Preoperative Parenteral Nutrition in Patients Undergoing Major Gastrointestinal Surgery." *Journal of Parenteral and Enteral Nutrition* 8 (1984): 632–37.

Disbrow, Doris, and Karen Bertram. *Cost Benefit Cost Effectiveness Analysis.* Modesto, Calif.: Bertram Nutrition Associates, 1984.

Eisenberg, John M., Henry Glick, Alan L. Hillman, Jonathan Baron, Steven A. Finkler, John C. Hershey, Risa Lavizzo-Mourey, and Gordon P. Buzby. "Measuring the Economic Impact of Perioperative Total Parenteral Nutrition: Principles and Design." *American Journal of Clinical Nutrition* 47 (1988): 382–91.

Levin, Harry L. *Cost-Effectiveness: A Primer.* Beverly Hills, Calif.: Sage Publications, 1985.

Mason, Marion, ed. *Costs and Benefits of Nutritional Care Phase I.* Chicago, Ill.: The American Dietetic Association, 1979.

Mirtallo, Jay M., Carla L. Powell, Sheila M. Campbell, Philip J. Schneider, and Kenneth Kudsk. "Cost-Effective Nutrition Support." *Nutrition in Clinical Practice* 2 (1987): 142–51.

Ross Laboratories. *Benefits of Nutrition Services: A Costing and Marketing Approach.* Columbus, Ohio, 1984.

Ross Laboratories. *Financing Hospital-Based Nutrition Services.* Columbus, Ohio, 1984.

Splett, Patricia, and Mariel Caldwell. *Costing Nutrition Services: A Workbook.* Chicago, Ill. U.S. Department of Health and Human Services, 1985.

Sugman, Robert, and Alan Williams. *The Principles of Practical Cost-Benefit Analysis*. New York: Oxford University Press, 1978.

Twomey, Patrick L., and Steven C. Patching. "Cost-Effectiveness of Nutritional Support." *Journal of Parenteral and Enteral Nutrition* 9 (1985): 3–10.

Warner, Kenneth E., and B.R. Luce. *Cost-Benefit and Cost-Effectiveness Analysis in Health Care: Principles, Practice and Potential*. Ann Arbor, Mich.: Health Administration Press, 1982.

Chapter 14

Establishing Team Relationships

Ann Winborn

INTRODUCTION

Nutrition support teams evolved as the technology of nutrition support expanded. The need for specialized skills to manage the patient on nutrition support became apparent. It was not possible or safe for one person or one discipline to plan and monitor nutrition support. A multidisciplinary approach developed to meet the broad spectrum of patient care needs.

As the technology permitted, nutrition support moved into the home setting. This created the need for support teams with a different focus. Although the technology used by both hospital-based and home care teams is similar, different skills are required to apply the technique in the home.

Nutrition support teams have taken on many different structures to provide the required specialized skills. Several disciplines may be represented as members of the support team include physicians, dietitians, nurses, pharmacists, social workers, occupational therapists, physical therapists, dietetic technicians, and pharmacy technicians. Although the particular members of a team, as well as their roles or functions, may vary from team to team, there are common features of all multidisciplinary health care teams and common barriers to effective collaboration.

Many different disciplines have come together to work on a nutrition support team. The hospital-based and home care teams come together to work toward an effective discharge plan for a home nutrition support patient. This collaboration is an example of both intrateam and interteam processes in action.

THE TEAM PROCESS

Multidisciplinary health teams bring together members, all of whom are proficient in their own skills and possess knowledge relating to their own

218

discipline. They are able to make their own individual assessments and decisions. Teamwork is the process whereby persons share their expertise and perspectives to define problems and formulate treatment plans. Decisions and plans are team products that are not discipline specific.[1] Brill's comprehensive definition of teamwork can be applied to many settings.

> Teamwork is that work which is done by a group of people who possess individual decisions, who hold a common purpose and who meet together to communicate, share and consolidate knowledge from which plans are made, future decisions are influenced and actions are determined.[2]

Accepting the concept of teamwork can be a difficult process for some members. Working as a team often is a new experience. Health care professionals have little or no training in interdisciplinary team practice and many tend to have a single discipline approach. As team members work together the benefits of multidisciplinary teamwork become apparent. A person can gain much professional satisfaction from working in the kind of encouraging and supportive environment that a team can provide. While members bring their own disciplinary expertise to a team, any disciplinary "blinders" are removed as they learn what other professionals know and do. All members soon function as teacher-learners, sharing their points of view and learning from others' perspectives.[3] A professional's need for individual recognition can now be satisfied within the team setting as the team works toward becoming a cohesive unit.

HEALTH TEAM STRUCTURES

Although the particular structure that a team chooses depends on a variety of factors, such as availability of personnel, physical surroundings, institutional philosophy, team goals, and patient population, there are several basic types of team organizations. Horwitz[4] has described two types: the "leader-centered" team and the "fraternally oriented team."

The leader-centered team is organized around a central figure who makes the decisions and directs the members in their daily activities. The team's stability is strongly linked to the leader continuing in his or her role. An example of this type of team in a health care setting might be one in which the team members are employed by a physician to assist him or her in the management of his or her private patients. The physician utilizes the expertise of the members to facilitate decision making.

The fraternally oriented team functions on the basis of the common decision of team members who are equal in status. It works on a more informal basis with a more flexible structure. Communication tends to be verbal rather than written. Health teams who function on a referral basis work under this type of organizational style. Members make their independent assessments and meet together to formulate a comprehensive management plan. Individual members may change, but the common purpose of the team remains intact within the institution.

Both types of teams may be seen in practice, and each has appropriate application in particular settings. Nutrition support teams may at times function under both styles. In the health care setting the physician is ultimately responsible for the patient and may have to make decisions independent from the team in crisis situations. In determining patient care goals and discharge plans the team may work more in the fraternally oriented style.

STRATEGIES FOR SUCCESSFUL TEAM PRACTICE

Team collaboration requires a great deal of effort on the part of all members. It is a process that evolves over time. The major stumbling blocks to successful team practice tend to occur in three areas: team leadership, role definitions and functions, and communication.[5]

Team Leadership

The team leadership role can be discussed on two levels: the leadership role in patient care and the leadership role in administration of the team.

As discussed earlier, one particular team structure has the physician as the leader of patient care. This may or may not be the selected structure of a hospital-based nutrition support team but, understandably, there are circumstances such as in a crisis situation in which one member of the team must take over the leadership and make a decision without team participation. This may apply to the physician more often, but any team member may need to act quickly after assessing a problem and act without benefit of the team's input.

Responding to the initial consultation may be another area in which one team member assumes a leadership role. It is often difficult for a team to meet each time a new patient is referred. One member may be delegated to make the initial assessment and plan. Well-functioning team members, who have worked together for a period, have learned from each other. The experiences and knowledge they have shared has evolved into a common philosophy, one on which the members will agree in the majority of cases. It is almost as though one member, in essence, can speak for the whole team. At some point the team will meet to fine tune the management plan.

These two areas—crisis intervention and consultation—make up a very small part of the total functions of the team. A well-functioning team spends the majority of its time sharing information and responsibilities to work toward the attainment of a common goal. If these areas and other potential areas of individual leadership are not well defined, understood, and agreed on by all members, however, conflict can arise, and the team's efforts can be segmented and less effective.

In home care the physician is not usually in a position to function as team leader. Physicians in home care agencies may be employed solely in an advisory capacity. It is therefore necessary for home care teams to decide if and how a leader is to be designated. Because team members in home care may not be able to meet as often as members of a hospital-based team, it may be advisable for one person to assume a leadership role for a particular patient's care. This person might be responsible for gathering input from the other team members and then coordinating a care plan for the patient. This position might be termed case manager, and the team member assuming this role may change from patient to patient. Again, if this aspect of team care is not clearly delineated, the potential for conflict is great and effective patient care will suffer.

An administrative leader may be beneficial for both hospital-based and home teams. This position may be more appropriately termed team coordinator. Teams may require someone to focus on administrative issues such as budgets, individual team member coverage, supply acquisition and pricing, and productivity statistics. In the current era of prospective reimbursement strategies, a team member with the responsibility of guiding and coordinating the team in a cost-effective manner may be necessary to document continually the team's viability. This position, however, should not be confused with or extend into that of patient care leadership. These two functions need to remain distinctly separate but work in harmony to maximize patient care and maintain the team's presence.

Role Definition

A major hurdle for health care teams—and nutrition support teams are no exception—is to decide who is going to do what. The potential for role overlap among the disciplines exists, necessitating team discussion and decision making about the responsibilities of each member.

Health professionals are not usually trained in a multidisciplinary setting, and they have little exposure to the manner in which disciplines can complement one another. There is a tendency to view one's own discipline as the superior or the most relevant one. This leads to disputes over turf and authority, which can prevent effective patient care.[6] Team members must learn to appreciate and depend on each other's expertise. Establishing role delineations for new teams may be a difficult task, but with time it will become apparent that one team member or one discipline cannot possibly provide all the care that is required for a nutrition support patient.

Although those involved in nutrition support strive for a multidisciplinary approach, Faulkner[7] reminds all involved that it is vital to maintain disciplinary integrity. Each discipline is represented on the team to contribute its own special expertise. The existing potential for role overlap in nutrition support teams can add to the potential for "role yearning" or role identification with a professional of a perceived higher or more significant status. Much cross-training takes place among the disciplines, but no one person can expect to perform another's job with the same degree of skill. When a team member tries to duplicate another's role in an attempt to gain greater satisfaction or recognition, he or she diminishes the maximum contribution of that discipline. He or she also stifles his or her ability to provide the unique expertise that brought that person to the team originally.

Communication

Effective communication is the key to successful team practice. The two stumbling blocks mentioned earlier can only be avoided or at least minimized by communication. Communication is also essential to patient diagnosis, development of a plan of care, and each member's expected role in that care plan. Conflicts may arise in many areas if team members are not able to communicate their needs and expectations.[8]

Team dynamics occur more easily when members can meet face to face. This is an additional problem for nutrition support teams working in the home as all team members may not be accessible at the same time. Alternatives to face-to-face problem solving are necessary.[9]

Written communication, although less than optimal, can be useful if the communication is not urgent. Written reports work well in updating team members who have been absent or in communicating long-range goals. Although the telephone has always been the first choice for communicating more immediate concerns, the computer terminal is now serving some of the functions once reserved for the telephone. Team members are able to send messages from one work station to another. As one example, while team members are making patient rounds they can send messages to the pharmacy alerting its personnel to potential problems or order changes, possibly avoiding the preparation of an incorrect solution. Computer links can also be established among physicians' offices, laboratories, and home care agencies, allowing for patient clinical data to flow in a timely manner.

Teleconferencing could be a great advantage for teams during discharge planning. The home care agency, in-hospital team, and patient and family could communicate simultaneously without the need for a common location. This could reduce the number of telephone calls necessary in establishing a home nutrition support regimen.

Increasing technology may make it easier to communicate, but team members must recognize the need to initiate communication. Teams need to be structured such that communication is encouraged to avoid conflicts and the breakdown of team practice.

DETERMINING TEAM FUNCTIONS

Basic to team functioning is multidirectional communication linkages among all members; a division of labor, based on function rather than status; and shared responsibility for final decisions.[10]

Traditionally the nurse manages most of the discharge preparation for a patient. Also, until recently, because of a lack of other disciplines working in home care the nurse, possibly with the help of a social worker, has had to assume a wide range of functions including counseling, advocacy, physical therapy, and nutrition services.[11] Now that patients are leaving the hospital with more intensive requirements for home care, other health care members, especially dietitians, are becoming integrally involved in the discharge planning and the home management of patients. As the provision of home care services increases, the need for multidisciplinary involvement is increasing as well.

The discharge needs of a nutrition support patient are oriented toward outcome goals. There are basic functions that need to be performed in preparing a nutrition support patient for discharge and in managing the therapy in the home. These functions can be performed by various team disciplines.

The level of intervention required ranges from relatively uninvolved to quite complex, depending on the type of therapy and nature of the case. The nutrition support dietitian can play an important role in any of these basic functions, solely or in conjunction with other team members.

The basic tasks that need to be accomplished by the team are discharge needs assessment, nutrition support training, making the referral and bridging the hospital/home gap, home monitoring, and follow-up communication and coordination.

Discharge Needs Assessment

The discharge arrangements and needs for the home nutrition support patient are dependent on the patient, his or her primary care provider, the support systems within the home and region where he or she resides, and his or her nutrition goals.

The dietitian is responsible for determining the patient's nutrition needs. The dietitian also needs to communicate closely with the patient's physician, the staff nurse, and the social worker to gain as much other information as possible about the patient. This may be even more true for the dietitian working independent of a support team. Considering the patient's fluid requirements, life style, availability of equipment, and financial abilities, in addition to nutrition requirements, the dietitian can formulate a nutrition prescription for the patient. This may entail a change in products, nutrient concentrations and volumes, and routes of administration. Before undertaking a change, the dietitian needs to communicate the rationale for the planned change to other team members or the health professionals working with the patient so that all concerned can work toward a common goal.

All team members contribute their own individual knowledge of the patient in determining other essential home needs; that is, level of nursing intervention, other health care equipment, other medication needs, and routes of administration. All these factors go into determining which home care agency or agencies would best serve the patient.

Nutrition Support Training

Once the team has determined the method of administration and schedule of the nutrition solution, patient and family training may begin. It has been customary for the nurse or pharmacist (or both) to train the parenteral nutrition patient regarding catheter care and administration and mixing of solutions. While educating the patient on the nutrition purpose and content of his or her formula the dietitian can provide reinforcement and psychologic support.

The nutrition support dietitian can share much of the responsibility in teaching the patient to administer his or her feeding. The patient's nurse can be a valuable ally in this regard. This dietitian should elicit help in providing training and reinforcement and input regarding the patient's tolerance of the feeding regimen. The nurse has the opportunity to observe the patient over long periods and in different situations. Feedback regarding how well the patient is learning can be helpful in designing the training program. While the training is in progress, it is important for the patient to understand each member's role and to which team member he or she can most appropriately refer questions and concerns.

Making the Referral

If the patient is going to use a home care agency either for nursing support or for supplies, all team members need to decide jointly exactly what the patient's needs will be. The dietitian working without a support team may need to organize the necessary health professionals to elicit their help in determining all the patient's needs. When a complete list of all necessary requirements, including nutrition prescription, other medications, and nursing and psychologic needs, is compiled, a home care agency is selected. It may be wise for one team member to make the initial contact with the home care agency. That team member should remain the primary contact person with the agency for the best communication during the case. This team function may not always need to be performed by the same team member, but this person does need to have a good understanding of all aspects of the care needed and be relatively accessible by telephone during business hours for follow-up discussions.

An extension of the referral process is the contact made between the hospital team members and the home health care team members. It is important for the patient to know that continuity of care will take place. The home care team may want to contact the patient while he or she is still in the hospital. This also gives the hospital-based team and the home care team an opportunity to discuss nutrition and nursing goals for the patient. It is also important for the hospital-based dietitian to communicate not only short-term goals but long-term nutrition goals to the team members that will be in the home, especially if a home health dietitian will not be seeing the patient on a regular basis.

Good communication skills are important during the referral process. The person representing the team has to describe the patient's needs in a highly detailed manner leaving little room for interpretation or ambiguity on the part of the home care agency. This will make for a smooth transition for the patient and his or her caretakers.

Home Monitoring

The health team members who visit a nutrition support patient need specialized assessment and technical skills. Follow-up should include monitoring for compliance with technical procedures and physiologic status, reinforcement and updating of teaching, and psychologic support. Team members should also be available for technical assistance.[12] This enables continuity of care when the patient returns to the hospital for follow-up. For the patient followed in the home, it has been traditional for the nurse to provide monitoring functions, thereby assuming many other disciplinary roles. Until current third-party reimbursement regulations change, the dietitian may not be available to make ongoing home visits. Nevertheless, dietitians, especially those working in home health care or in nursing homes, can be instrumental in educating the nurses on the methods and techniques necessary to manage successfully the nutrition support patient outside the hospital setting. The dietitian also has an opportunity to educate the nurse and the home care agency administration to the benefits of having a registered dietitian in home care and provide criteria as to when a consultation from a registered dietitian would be beneficial.

Follow-up Communication and Coordination of Care

Maintaining communication among the home agencies, attending physicians, nutrition support physicians, and hospital-based nutrition teams can be difficult. It is important to arrange an effective communication linkage so that those responsible for decision making receive the most up-to-date patient information. This linkage should be established before the patient leaves the hospital. Communication needs to be in both verbal and written forms, with written communication being reserved for general progress reports and verbal communication for the more immediate or crisis situations.

It is customary to expect communication from a home care agency. Hospital-based professionals in turn need to remember to communicate to the agencies any interaction they may have had with the home patient. Maintaining good relationships between the disciplines and the teams is vital to the patient's well-being. It is beneficial for team members involved in the follow-up of the patient to establish a personal relationship. It also is important for all involved to know who to talk to about a question or concern regarding the patient and his or her progress.

Good relationships and team support can also contribute directly to the members' improved functioning. Teams can provide shared decision making around troublesome issues such as ethics; teams can help prevent burnout by providing personal emotional support for the members; and shared accountability for outcome can remove the burden of any one profession having to be the health care superstar.[13]

CONCLUSION

The primary member of any health care team is the patient, and the primary goal of any team is the well-being of that patient. In meeting this goal, the team's function may vary from maximum intervention to minimum support. This may be particularly true of a team involved in home nutrition support. A nutrition support patient may need extensive intervention when he or she first arrives home. As time at home increases, the patient becomes more proficient with the procedure and may stabilize so that changes become less frequent. The reverse may be true for the terminally ill patient, who requires more intensive help as time in the home increases. Regardless of the level of intervention, members of a health care team must be prepared to engage in patient advocacy.[14] Through a multidisciplinary team approach the best health care can be provided and a team composed of several disciplines is better able to be effective in informing the patient about health conditions and decision-making rights. Each team member has special knowledge to contribute to the patient's understanding of his or her situation and each can help the patient deal with the interaction of the technology of nutrition support and his or her environment.

NOTES

1. Betty L. Pesznecker and Rolanda Paquin, "Implementing Interdisciplinary Team Practice in Home Care of Geriatric Clients," *Journal of Gerontological Nursing* 8 (1982): 504.
2. Naomi I. Brill, *Teamwork: Working Together in the Human Services* (Philadelphia, Pa.: J.B. Lippincott Co., 1976), 22.
3. Audrey O. Faulkner, "Interdisciplinary Health Care Teams: An Educational Approach to Improvement of Health Care for the Aged," *Gerontology and Geriatrics Education* 5 (1985): 36.
4. John Horwitz, *Team Practice and the Specialist* (Springfield, Ill.: Charles C Thomas, 1970), 23–25.
5. Alex Ducanis and Anne K. Golin, *The Interdisciplinary Health Care Team* (Germantown, Md.: Aspen Publishers, 1979), 179.
6. Faulkner, "Interdisciplinary Health Care Teams: An Educational Approach to Improvement of Health Care for the Aged," 30.
7. Ibid., 36.
8. Ducanis and Golin, *The Interdisciplinary Health Care Team*, 177.
9. Faulkner, "Interdisciplinary Health Care Teams: An Educational Approach to Improvement of Health Care for the Aged," 37.
10. Jane Lowe and Marjatta Herranen, "Understand Teamwork: Another Look at the Concepts," *Social Work in Health Care* 7 (1981): 4.
11. Pesznecker and Paquin, "Implementing Interdisciplinary Team Practice in Home Care of Geriatric Clients," 505.

12. Josephine H. Bender and Walter C. Faubion, "Parenteral Nutrition for the Pediatric Patient," *Home Health Care Nurse* 3 (1985): 37.

13. Faulkner, "Interdisciplinary Health Care Teams: An Educational Approach to Improvement of Health Care for the Aged," 38.

14. Ibid., 36.

BIBLIOGRAPHY

Birge, Kristine, and Douglas Maxwell. "Home Health Care: The Dietitian's Role." *Journal of the American Dietetic Association* 74 (1979): 47–49.

Bradford, Leland. *Group Development*. San Diego: University Associates, 1978.

Martin, James. "The AIDS Home Care and Hospice Program." *American Journal of Hospice Care* 3, no. 4 (1986): 35–37.

Sampson, Edward, and Marya Marthas. *Group Process for the Health Professions*. New York: John Wiley & Sons, 1977.

Suski, Nancy. "The Dietitian Makes Home Visits." *Journal of the American Dietetic Association* 79 (1981): 311–12.

Zimmer, James, Annemarie Groth-Juncker, and Jane McCusker. "A Randomized Controlled Study of a Home Health Care Team." *American Journal of Public Health* 75 (1985): 134–41.

Chapter 15

Ethical Issues of Home Nutrition Support

Dorothy King

INTRODUCTION

Health care policy trends appear to be emphasizing the economic and emotional advantages of home care over hospital-based medical care for an increasing number of medical conditions. During the last 30 years the majority of deaths occurred in institutions. There is now a reverse in attitudes, as well as in reimbursement options, which is encouraging a return to the traditional ritual of a home-based death.

Establishing guidelines for an ethical decision-making process that clearly and systemically distinguish between what can technically be done and what may, must, and should, as well as must not, be medically and nutritionally offered for patients is a highly controversial and timely objective for health care providers and administrators, as well as for lawyers, legislators, and the general public. Public debate of what was previously decision making by physicians has evolved into a body of excellent resources to assist in developing a patient-centered, ethically based process.[1]

The most frequent dilemma in bioethics relates to forgoing or discontinuing life support systems. The most hotly debated area centers on the appropriateness of enteral and parenteral nutrition and hydration support. On one hand, nutrients delivered through tubes, catheters, or needles are perceived as heroic, optional medical treatment analogous to other life-sustaining medical treatment decisions. On the other, nutrition support is viewed as a unique life support system; it is perceived as food, an essential part of humane care, in addition to a highly emotionally charged symbolic act of nurturing, loving, and caring.

There are two major issues that arise from these bioethical conflicts. The first relates to clashes between the health care professional's sense of paternalism and beneficence for the patient and the legal/ethical right for the competent patient to refuse treatment against medical advice. The second relates to an equitable determination of allocation of scarce resources, which includes economic factors as well as equipment, medication, and nutrition decisions. This type of analysis most frequently concentrates on the broader or society-based macrolevel of influences—e.g., Medicare-Medicaid standards that limit access to nutrition support by their reimbursement qualifications. This is a very important aspect of public policy, but it is beyond the scope of this chapter.[2]

According to Benjamin and Curtis, "our tools here are words; fine linguistic distinctions, like fine surgical instruments, make possible more precise analysis of complex questions."[3] The discussion of this controversial subject, like all other debatable topics, requires an operational framework or definition of pertinent terms.

DEFINITIONS

The terms *ethical* and *moral* are used synonymously. *Bioethical* refers to the subdivision of ethics that is applied to medical and health care issues. The term *Legal*, although it often interfaces with *ethics*, is a separate term from the latter.

Normative ethical decision making is the ambiguous, complex concept of principles that indicate the shoulds and oughts of good human conduct; what is obligatory, permissible, or forbidden; and the rationale to validate these principles. Ethical principles of good behavior are culturally influenced by a system of values of persons and the society in which they are members.

Another dimension is that "ethics is relative to particular [social] roles."[4] Professional role responsibility also influences appropriate, bioethical behavior. On the basis of public trust in expert knowledge and skill, the health care professional is bound by a legal doctrine called *fiduciary duty*, which requires the professional "to act primarily for the benefit of another in matters connected with his undertaking."[5] There is an incumbent responsibility to protect patients because of their vulnerability.

Legal or *law* refers to rules of human conduct established and enforced by the government. Legal and ethical goals and issues are not the same. One significant difference is based on the authority to punish those who do not abide by the law. Conduct can be ethical but illegal, or unethical and legal. Ideally what is legal is also ethical. Retribution for an immoral act is usually more subtle than breaking the law. The consequences are of a social or religious nature. Understanding what constitutes illegality is too frequently as difficult as distinguishing what is immorality. Information contained within this chapter should not be construed as legal advice. When in doubt, professional legal advice should be sought.

The term *forgo* is used instead of *withhold* when discussing decisions not to use nutrition support. The decision implied in the latter term is one of denying something that is owed, for instance in financial transactions.

Another area is the concept of death from starvation and dehydration as the culmination of forgoing or withdrawing nutrition support. Just as asphyxiation is not used to describe the cause of death resulting from oxygen deprivation after the removal of a ventilator, it is likewise inappropriate to perceive death by starvation as the consequence of the removal of feeding tubes. The President's Commission for the Study of Ethical Problems in Medicine and Biomedical and Behavioral Research has suggested that it is more suitable to conceptualize death under these circumstances as the result of the underlying disease.[6]

PERSONAL RESPONSIBILITY

Know thyself! To foresee and avoid potential clashes of values, it is advisable to have a clear awareness and understanding of your own personal perceptions and values as they relate to life, health, health care, and death.

- Can you differentiate between your intellectual and your emotional responses?
- Are you comfortable with the topics?
- Have you had experience in actually participating, either in a personal or a professional capacity, in these types of medical decisions?

Articulating personal opinions with collaborating rationale is important to approach the professional stage with a clarity about your own predilections.

Clinical decision making is complex. Occasions arise when two ethical principles clash, such as respect for patient autonomy and performance of professional beneficence.[7] Some health care professionals find it morally reprehensible to attend a patient who decides to forgo nutrition support and is unable or unwilling to consume adequate oral nutriture.[8] In 1986 the American Medical Association's Council on Ethical and Judicial Affairs sought to help clinicians clarify perceptions of ethical limits on mechanical feeding with an official statement that comments that "it is not unethical to discontinue all means of life prolonging medical treatment [which] includes nutrition or hydration."[9] A recent commentary, however, classifies feeding and hydration as supportive care, and suggests that death from starvation or dehydration can be looked on as euthanasia.[10]

PROFESSIONAL RESPONSIBILITY

One moral directive—patient advocacy—is articulated by the American Nurses' Association and succinctly captures the essence of responsibility of all health care professionals: "Safeguard the client and the public when health care and safety are affected by the incompetent, unethical, or illegal practice of any person."[11] The current crisis of professional negligence litigation reflects a serious weakening of public trust in the patient–health care practitioner relationship as much as the quality of medical care. The role of patients is evolving into one of greater participation and power over their medical treatment.

Each health care profession has a general code of ethics that presents general and specific concepts of ethical conduct.[12] Integrity, honesty, and truth telling are common moral values stipulated by professional codes. The joint American Dietetic Association/Commission on Dietetic Registration Code of Ethics (see Appendix A, Exhibit A-2 for complete code) "reflects the ethical principles guiding the dietetic profession and outlines commitments and obligations of the dietetic practitioner to self, client, society, and the profession."[13] Exhibit 15-1 illustrates some specific inquiries regarding ethical principles that affect feeding decisions.

Another principle of professional conduct mandates that each patient should be treated with dignity and respect. Unfortunately, economic status can be and usually is a major factor in rationing health care options, such as parenteral nutrition. As in other variables such as diagnosis and prog-

Exhibit 15-1 Ethical inquiries

Is the information presented in the medical chart objective and accurate?
Does the therapeutic privilege legitimize benevolent concealment?[14]
Is it justifiable to misrepresent patient information to health insurance companies to obtain eligibility status for coverage?
What is the practical difference between an error and a lie?
Is there a moral difference between lying for self-protection and lying for protection of patient interests?
Do honorable motives justify deception?
Are white lies acceptable?
What do you do when the patient asks you to lie to other members of the health care team, family, welfare agency, and so forth?
Does confidentiality of patient information extend to the possible endangerment of others (e.g., diagnosis of acquired immunodeficiency syndrome withheld from spouse and medical staff)?
Is physician ownership of the home care nutrition support company disclosed to the patient with options for other companies?[15]

nosis, function rather than age per se should be considered the more reasonable aspect of the variable. Difficult ethical issues such as quality and quantity of life expected are also compounding variables in the decision-making process.[16]

An interdisciplinary nutrition support team is the ideal approach to collaboration with the patient on the specific medical and nutrition, as well as social, factors that contribute to an appropriate therapeutic care plan. Some aspects of patient discussions about an impending decision to forgo or withdraw nutrition support may revolve around religious values and therefore may more appropriately need pastoral consultation. The degree of nutrition decision participation of each professional role and the hierarchy of power, as well as legal accountability, also need to be clearly formulated and understood by each member of the team.

INFORMED CONSENT DOCTRINE

An essential prerequisite to ethical professional conduct is a comprehensive knowledge of the legal doctrine of informed consent for approval or refusal of medical treatment or research (or both). The ethical principle that mirrors this concept is termed *self-determination.*

The U.S. Department of Health and Human Services, Ethics Advisory Board, currently provides extensive guidelines and supervision of medical research involving human subjects. Two principles are stressed: informed (knowledgeable) consent is required and no unnecessary harm should occur.[17]

Several criteria are essential to the process of obtaining informed consent for medical treatment or research: decision capacity, adequate information, and voluntariness of decision. The first criterion is that a patient must possess sufficient medical treatment decision-making capacity. "The individual must have sufficiently stable and developed personal values and goals, an ability to communicate and understand information adequately, and an ability to reason and deliberate sufficiently well about the choices."[18]

Patient competence is the same concept as decision capacity but it has been formally adjudicated by a court. "Absent a judicial determination, the law presumes competence in adults."[19] As a practical matter, the capacity or competence issue does not usually arise until the patient disagrees with the medical system, either hospital policy or physician opinion.

The family's role in medical decisions for the competent patient is essentially determined by the patient. The adult patient's legal right to confidentiality dictates that health care information is not supposed to be shared with the family unless the patient so authorizes. Although most patients welcome family participation, the health care professional is legally bound to the patient's preferences. This becomes a more complicated issue when the family is expected to provide some or most of the home care.

Disclosure of pertinent information by the health care professional and understanding by the patient or surrogate decision maker are the second criterion; they are crucial to an ethical and legal process of informed consent. How much information and for which procedures or treatments is this necessary? Who is responsible for the patient education or information delivery? Comprehension potential by the patient is enhanced by avoiding technical medical and nutrition jargon. The potential factors such as the immediate and long-term consequences to the patient and the reversibility of a particular medical decision are central considerations. The Hastings Center emphasizes that

> there is a legitimate moral and legal presumption in favor of preserving life and providing beneficial medical care with the patient's informed consent. Clearly, however, avoiding death should not always be the preeminent goal; not all technologically possible means of prolonging life need be or should be used in every case.[20]

The emphasis is not on providing or not providing medical intervention as much as on respecting the patient's informed choice.

Health care professionals should also be alert to the guidelines recently published by the Hastings Center, which indicate "all invasive procedures for supplying nutrition and hydration—all enteral and parenteral techniques—should be considered procedures that require the patient's or surrogate's consent, and procedures that the patient or surrogate may choose to forgo."[21]

Voluntariness of decision is the third criterion. The patient's choice must be voluntary in accordance with his or her own values and goals. Coercion, fraud, duress, deceit, and unfair manipulation are all unacceptable methods of obtaining consent.[22]

Clinically objective and understandable advice should include the medical and nutrition alternatives and the potential risks and benefits of each option to the individual patient. The family or home care providers will probably have more influence on the patient than personnel in the health care facility. This ideally should be monitored to ensure that appropriate care is being provided and the patient's preferences are not being unduly compromised.

The decision to start or withdraw nutrition support should be an ongoing reassessment process. No legal or ethical distinction should be made between forgoing and withdrawing of nutrition support.[23] Lynn[24] emphasizes the clinical advantage of this posture. It is frequently not possible to predict who will benefit from a certain medical or nutrition intervention. There should be the flexibility of attempting a therapeutic plan and, when proved futile, to be able to discontinue it without legal intervention.

Incompetence

Honoring patients' right to control the integrity of their body becomes much more perplexing when patients are incompetent to authorize their treatment decisions. Some patients are permanently incompetent or decisionally incapacitated (e.g., persons who are in a permanent vegetative state, some severely retarded or psychotic patients, or severely senile patients). Other categories of decisional incapacitation are those who are temporarily (e.g., a comatose patient or adolescent patient) and transiently (e.g., the patient who fluctuates in and out of alertness, the patient in an acute stage of severe depression or suffering from other psychiatric episodes, or the patient with symptoms of disease such as pain) incapacitated.

LEGAL PRECEDENT OR CASE LAW

Three court cases—*In re* Conroy,[25] *Brophy v. New England Sinai Hospital, Inc.*,[26] and *In re* Rodas[27]—have been selected to review the legal and ethical principles in specific cases that adjudicated petitions to withdraw hydration and nutrition support feeding tubes. One case, *In the Matter of Cole*,[28] is included as a provocative lesson that encourages caution and reflection. Thus far, no known cases have addressed withdrawing or withholding of home nutrition support as a result of patient or family request or lack of financial resources. In fact, many home care vendors will service a limited number of partial-pay or no-pay patients.

Claire Conroy was an 84-year-old, formally judged incompetent, nursing home patient with severe organic brain syndrome, necrotic decubitus ulcers, and numerous other medical problems. She was unable to move or speak. Medical experts testified that there was no reasonable chance of mental or medical improvement. Conroy had never married and her only surviving relative, a nephew, was the court-appointed guardian.

The lower court wrote in its opinion that removing the feeding tube would constitute homicide.[29] The patient died, with the tube in place, several days before the New Jersey Supreme Court reversed the lower court decision. The New Jersey court concurred that "analytically, artificial feeding by means of a nasogastric tube or intravenous infusion can be seen as equivalent to artificial breathing by means of a respirator."[30]

The Massachusetts case of Paul Brophy was the first case to question whether nonelderly, nonterminally ill but permanently vegetative patients were legal candidates to withdraw artificial feeding procedures. Brophy, a 46-year-old fireman and emergency medical technician, suffered a sub-arachnoid hemorrhage and never regained consciousness. He was able to breathe entirely on his own. Nutrition was provided through a gastrostomy tube. Brophy's wife, a registered nurse, was his guardian. After two years, Mrs. Brophy, in accordance with the unanimous consensus of the children, the patient's 92-year-old mother, and siblings, petitioned the court for permission to remove the feeding tube. There was extensive consistent evidence presented by the wife that Paul Brophy had been adamant about not wanting to be medically maintained as a "Karen Ann Quinlan."

The hospital's chief physician rebuked the Brophy family decision. Re-calling his experience at the end of World War II of liberating Dachau, the Nazi concentration camp, he described death by starvation as inhu-mane.[31] This case dramatically illustrates the conflict potential when there is a clash of strongly held opposing values by the patient and the physician.

In the fall of 1986, the highest court in the state of Massachusetts granted permission to discontinue the gastrostomy feedings (three and one half years after feedings were begun). The patient was transferred to another facility and died after eight days, with his family in attendance.

On February 10, 1986, Hector Rodas, a businessman with a wife and two young children, suffered brain damage as a result of intravenous po-lydrug use and was paralyzed below the neck. He could move his head, blink, and move his eyes. He also could laugh, cry, and make vocal noises but was unable to speak or swallow. Feeding was accomplished through a gastrostomy stoma. He was not expected to make any significant recovery in his ability to use his hands, arms, legs and feet, or to speak or swallow, but was not terminally ill.

In June 1986, Rodas began communicating (by means of a letter board) to the medical staff that he wanted to die. The next month his lawyer contacted the facility and indicated that his client wanted to discontinue the feeding and hydration procedure. Subsequent to several psychiatric examinations by different psychiatrists, the court ruled that Rodas was competent to reason and comprehend the consequences of his decision. On January 22, 1987, the court granted Rodas permission to withdraw feeding and hydration. The patient died 16 days after this action was in-stituted.

Several points are highlighted to clarify the issues in this case. Rodas's brother and sisters were fighting his decision and the facility feared a lawsuit.[32] The gastrostomy had been inserted without patient authorization or explanation of its impact on his life. The facility did not have a mission statement that forbid withdrawal of tube feeding under these circumstances until after the patient's request.[33]

The final case demonstrates that a person can hold a strong opinion about a theoretic situation such as "pulling the plug" but react very differently when something really happens. The ability of a person to predict what he or she would actually want under real and specific circumstances cannot be accurately anticipated and predicted.

During the spring of 1986, 43-year-old Jacqueline Cole from Baltimore, Maryland, suffered a stroke and went into a coma. After 41 days in a nonresponsive coma, her husband, a Presbyterian minister, asked the physician to withdraw all support systems. Mrs. Cole had periodically repeated to her husband and children that she would not want to survive under the quality of life that her mother's prolonged illness previously had created. This strong feeling was not translated into a formal living will but was repeated to her daughter at the onset of her symptoms.

A neurosurgeon predicted that "chances of any reasonable significant neurologic recovery are probably somewhere within a one in a hundred thousand, one in a million."[34] Death resulting from the immediate removal of aggressive interventions that supply oxygen, hydration, and food would not be painful. The attending physician refused to comply with the family's request and the case was referred to the Baltimore Circuit Court.

The judge denied the petition because "too brief a time has elapsed, this is May 9th and the stroke was March 29th,"[35] and considered the neurosurgeon's medical testimony to be insufficient.

Six days after the court ruling, the patient awoke, smiled and returned her husband's kiss. She is currently living the quality of life that she adamantly, hypothetically rejected.

CONCLUSION

Ethical questions and dilemmas surrounding nutrition support in institutions and in the home will continue to challenge the wisdom of a biblical Solomon. Health care professionals and the public must face these perplexing choices with deliberation and continued public discussion. Among the issues to be considered are

- How should the patient's financial and psychosocial status determine or affect home feeding decisions?
- How should professionals handle the terminally ill patient who cannot take in adequate calories orally or enterally?
- What decisions should be made regarding terminal patients who wish to discontinue home feedings?
- What courses of action are available and advisable for patients who disregard medical advice once at home?

Lynn cautions against the natural proclivity of crusades of laudatory practices taking a careless, incorrect, and thoughtless diversion from the principles promoted by the pioneers. The warning is that "in our society we have a solid history of seeing things that were initially introduced as possibilities for choice or discretion turned into matters of mandatory behavior."[36]

All health care professionals are expected to be patient advocates. Each patient is unique, medically and personally. The subject is so profound that extensive reading, reflecting, and discussing the issues and alternatives with rationale are highly recommended as a means to provide the wisdom of an ethical decision-making process that respects the pluralistic values of our society, but sets moral limits. We are to proceed with caution, erring on the side of prolonging life.[37]

NOTES

1. See The Hastings Center, *Guidelines on the Termination of Life-Sustaining Treatment and the Care of the Dying* (Briarcliff Manor, N.Y.: The Hastings Center, 1987), 57–62, 120–26; President's Commission for the Study of Ethical Problems in Medicine and Biomedical and Behavioral Research, *Deciding to Forgo Life-Sustaining Treatment* (Washington, D.C.: Government Printing Office, 1982); Congress of the U.S.: Office of Technology Assessment (OTA), *Life Sustaining Technologies and the Elderly* (Washington, D.C.: Government Printing Office, 1987); Gary Anderson and Valarie Glesnes-Anderson, *Health Care Ethics: A Guide for Decision Makers* (Rockville, Md.: Aspen Publishers, 1987); Ronald Cranford and Edward Doudera, eds., *Institutional Ethics Committees and Health Care Decision Making* (Ann Arbor, Mich.: Health Administration Press, 1984); Edward Doudera and Douglas Peters, eds., *Legal and Ethical Aspects of Treating Critically and Terminally Ill Patients* (Ann Arbor, Mich.: Health Administration Press, 1982); Marshall Kapp et al., *Legal and Ethical Aspects of Health Care for the Elderly* (Ann Arbor, Mich.: Health Administration Press, 1985); Joanne Lynn, ed., *By No Extraordinary Means: The Choice to Forgo Life-Sustaining Food and Water* (Bloomington, Ind.: Indiana University Press, 1986).

2. See Marc D. Hiller, *Medical Ethics and the Law: Implications for Public Policy* (Cambridge, Mass.: Ballinger Publishing Co., 1981); The Hastings Center, *Guidelines on the Termination of Life-Sustaining Treatment and the Care of the Dying*, 119–26; John A. Robertson, *The Rights of the Critically Ill* (New York: Bantam Books, 1983), 146–53.

3. Martin Benjamin and Joy Curtis, *Ethics in Nursing* (New York: Oxford University Press, 1986), 13.

4. Anderson and Glesnes-Anderson, *Health Care Ethics: A Guide for Decision Makers*, 23.

5. Steven H. Gifis, *Law Dictionary* (Woodbury, N.Y.: Barron's Educational Series, 1975), 83.

6. President's Commission, *Deciding to Forgo Life-Sustaining Treatment*, 2.

7. Anderson and Glesnes-Anderson, *Health Care Ethics: A Guide for Decision Makers*, 254.

8. Lynn, *By No Extraordinary Means: The Choice to Forgo Life-Sustaining Food and Water*, 222.

9. Statement from the American Medical Association, Council on Ethical and Judicial Affairs, "Withholding or Withdrawing Life Prolonging Medical Treatment," March 1986; also in "To Feed or Not To Feed? An A.M.A. Panel Rules on the Ethics of Treating the Comatose," *Time Magazine*, March 31, 1986, 60; and Lawrence K. Altman, "A.M.A. Sets Ethics on

Coma Patients: Approves Halting Treatment Including Food and Water," *New York Times*, March 16, 1986, 1.

10. Fred Rosner, "Withdrawing Fluids and Nutrition: An Alternate View," *New York State Journal of Medicine* (November 1987): 591–93.

11. American Nurses' Association, *Code for Nurses, Interpretative Statements*, Kans., 1976; also in Joyce Beebe Thompson and Henry O. Thompson, *Ethics in Nursing* (New York: Macmillan Co., 1981), 11.

12. National Committee of Allied Health, *In the Future of Allied Health Education* (San Francisco, Calif.: Jossey-Bass, 1980).

13. "New Code of Ethics Developed for the Dietetic Profession," *American Dietetic Association Courier* 27, no. 5 (1988) 2.

14. Sissela Bok, *Secrets: On the Ethics of Concealment and Revelation* (New York: Vintage Books, 1983). See also Sissela Bok, *Lying: Moral Choice in Public and Private Life* (New York: Vintage Books, 1978).

15. Robert S. Henler and Susan Miranda, "Home Nutrition Therapy, 1987," *Nutrition Support Services* 7 (1987): 24–25.

16. Dorothy G. King and Julie O'Sullivan-Maillet, "Position of The American Dietetic Association: Issues in Feeding the Terminally Ill Adult," *Journal of the American Dietetic Association* 87 (1987): 78–85. See also Thompson and Thompson, *Ethics in Nursing*, 11; OTA, *Life Sustaining Technologies and the Elderly*; Kapp et al., *Legal and Ethical Aspects of Health Care for the Elderly*; The Hastings Center, *Guidelines on the Termination of Life-Sustaining Treatment and the Care of the Dying*; and President's Commission, *Deciding to Forgo Life-Sustaining Treatment*.

17. Thompson and Thompson, *Ethics in Nursing*, 30. See also Sidney Morgenbesser, "Experimentation and Consent: A Note" in *Philosophical Medical Ethics: Its Nature and Significance*, ed. Stuart F. Spicker and H. Tristran Engelhardt, Jr. (Boston: D. Reidel Publishing Co., 1977), 97–110.

18. President's Commission, *Deciding to Forgo Life-Sustaining Treatment*, 45.

19. The Hastings Center, *Guidelines on the Termination of Life-Sustaining Treatment and the Care of the Dying*, 7.

20. Ibid., iv.

21. Ibid., 61

22. President's Commission, *Deciding to Forgo Life-Sustaining Treatment*, 45. See also Faden, 255–57, 295n, 344–46; and Albert R. Jonsen et al., *Clinical Ethics: A Practical Approach to Ethical Decisions in Clinical Medicine* (New York: Macmillan Publishing Co., 1982), 52–58.

23. President's Commission, *Deciding to Forgo Life-Sustaining Treatment*, 2.

24. Joanne Lynn and James F. Childress, "Must Patients Always Be Given Food and Water" in *By No Extraordinary Means: The Choice to Forgo Life-Sustaining Food and Water*, ed. Joanne Lynn (Bloomington, Ind.: Indiana University Press, 1986), 55–57.

25. *In re* Conroy, 98 N.J. 321, 486 A.2d 1209 (1985).

26. *Brophy v. New England Sinai Hospital, Inc.*, 398 Mass. 417, 497 N.E2d 626 (1986).

27. *In re* Rodas, No. 86PR139 (Colo. Dist. Ct. Mesa County Jan. 22, 1987) (Buss, J.).

28. *In the Matter of Cole*, No. 8611053/CE49265, Baltimore Circuit Ct. (Trans. of Proc 5/9/86).

29. Joseph W. Kukura and Gary R. Anderson, "Withdrawing or Withholding Treatment," in *Health Care Ethics: A Guide for Decision Makers*, ed. Gary Anderson and Valarie Glesnes-Anderson (Rockville, Md.; Aspen Publishers, 1987), 140.

30. Ronald Sullivan, " 'Right to Die' Rule in Terminal Cases Widened in Jersey," *The New York Times*, January 18, 1985, A1.

31. Andrew H. Malcohm, "A New Legal Test of the Right to Die," *The New York Times*, May 27, 1985, 9.

32. Ellen Haddow, "Rodas Gets Death Wish, Begins Starving," *Rocky Mountain News*, January 23, 1987, 6.

33. In re Rodas, 11.

34. In the Matter of Cole, 10.

35. In the Matter of Cole, 49.

36. Lynn, *By No Extraordinary Means: The Choice to Forgo Life-Sustaining Food and Water*, 64.

37. The Hastings Center, *Guidelines on the Termination of Life-Sustaining Treatment and the Care of the Dying*, 9.

Ancillary Information on Home Nutrition Support

Mindy Hermann-Zaidins and Riva Touger-Decker

INTRODUCTION

This appendix has been compiled to provide the reader with additional information on specific subject areas discussed in the text. Efforts were made to include the most recent publications pertaining to the field of nutrition in home care.

The American Dietetic Association (ADA) and the American Society for Parenteral and Enteral Nutrition (ASPEN) periodically issue publications on feeding, nutrition support, and ethics and standards. This appendix features summaries of legislative and public policy statements by the Dietitians in Nutrition Support (formerly Dietitians in Critical Care) Dietetic Practice Group on nutrition in home care and on the prospective payment system (Exhibit A-1). The joint ADA/Commission on Dietetic Registration Code of Ethics (Exhibit A-2), revised as of January 1989 and discussed in Chapter 15, outlines the commitments and obligations of dietetic practitioners. ADA's newly released position paper on home enteral and parenteral nutrition also has been included (Exhibit A-3). ASPEN continually addresses issues regarding the feeding of patients requiring specialized nutrition care. We have included its recently published Standards for Home Nutrition Support (Exhibit A-4).

Sample documents from hospital-based home care programs provide information that the practitioner can adapt to his or her particular setting (Exhibits A-5A and A-5B). Memorial Sloan-Kettering's Home Enteral Form and Training Summary combine all patient and process information used for training and documentation; the second page is used as part of the hospital's quality assurance program. The Home Patient Procedure Manual (Exhibit A-6) outlines the operation of a hospital-supplier contractual agreement for home parenteral feeding. The Crawford Long Hospital Home Care Services Criteria (Exhibit A-7) enumerates performance expectations of suppliers servicing that hospital's patient population. It is an excellent tool developed for the vendor selection process described in Chapter 3.

The Medicare Enteral and Parenteral Screens (Exhibits A-8A and A-8B), discussed in several chapters, are being applied nationwide to determine reimbursement for home nutrition support. The practitioner is encouraged to become familiar with Medicare's payment system to plan appropriate and cost-effective feeding systems.

Sherwood Medical's chart of enteral formulas* allows nutrient-by-nutrient comparison of several enteral products.

The listing of home feeding instruction manuals enables practitioners to order and utilize pre-existing patient teaching materials (Exhibit A-9).

Finally, a description of The Oley Foundation for Home Parenteral and Enteral Nutrition offers information to clinicians regarding patient and professional support services (Exhibit A-10).

Exhibit A-1 American Dietetic Association Timely Statements

The Dietitians in Critical Care Dietetic Practice Group has written papers on "Nutrition Support Services in Home Health Care" and "Impact of Prospective Payment on Critical Care Nutrition." These two papers were approved at the May 1985 Board of Directors meeting; the summaries are issued as timely statements.

"Nutrition Support Services in Home Health Care"

STATEMENT SUMMARY

1. Nutrition Support services for the home patient should be delivered by health care professionals utilized in the hospital setting. One out of 7 hospital nutrition support teams include the physician, registered dietitian, pharmacist and nurse. The nutrition support dietitian has a strong academic background and experience in providing nutrition support.
2. Mandate that Title XVIII (Medicare) and Title XIX (Medicaid) provide coverage and reimbursement for services delivered by a registered dietitian to home nutrition support patients as outlined in paragraph 3 below.
3. Mandate reimbursement for home nutrition support services provided by or under the supervision of a qualified registered dietitian who has specialized knowledge of feeding modalities and nutrition support regimens. Services would include, but not be limited to:
   - initial and periodic assessment of nutritional status;
   - determination of nutritional requirements of patients;
   - determination of the most appropriate parenteral, enteral, or oral support regimens;
   - periodic review of the efficacy of the support modality and/or formula;

*See enclosure. *Source*: Sherwood Medical, St. Louis, Missouri. © 1989 Sherwood Medical.

Exhibit A-1 continued

- interaction with team members in determining transition among feeding regimens;
- monitoring and assisting patients in transition among parenteral, enteral, and oral feedings;
- educating and counseling patients and their families on nutrition therapy regimens;
- supervision of and education resource to other team members providing care to the home patient.
4. Mandate that Medicare coverage of enteral feedings be expanded to include the oral administration of supplemental enteral formulas exceeding $5.00 per day, evaluated for patient need on a quarterly basis.
5. The hospital based registered dietitian working with patients who are potential consumers of home nutrition support should canvass [*sic*] the local home health care agencies and refer patients to the most complete program for safe, efficient, and cost effective nutrition care.
6. The standards of care published by the American Society for Enteral and Parenteral Nutrition should become the minimal industry standards of care for home nutrition support.

"Impact of Prospective Payment on Critical Care Nutrition"

STATEMENT SUMMARY

1. Despite recent advances in health care technologies, up to 50% of hospitalized patients suffer from malnutrition and in many cases its resulting complications.
2. Dietitians in Critical Care, Dietetic Practice Group of the 50,000 membered American Dietetic Association, recognized the need to control the rapidly rising cost of health care. We are, however, concerned about the potential impact of changes in Medicare reimbursement policy from cost-based to prospective payment.
3. The implementation of Medicare Prospective Payment System should in no way compromise the delivery of nutrition support therapies to hospitalized patients by limiting financial or human resources.
4. Consequences of failure to provide appropriate nutrition support therapies in a timely fashion include increased morbidity and mortality and unnecessary financial penalties due to costs associated with delayed convalescence.
5. Dietitians in Critical Care encourages the Prospective Payment Assessment Commission to consider treatment of malnutrition in advising the Secretary of Health and Human Services on the adequacy of [Diagnosis-related groups] DRG[s] payment weights and the preciseness of DRG classifications:
   One hundred and four of the 468 DRGs are classified according to the presence or absence of a complication or comorbidity factor (CC) and the payment per case will vary accordingly. Adequate payment may not be forthcoming because many DRGs that are associated with complications of malnutrition (e.g., 049-Major Head and Neck Procedures and 179-Inflammatory Bowel Disease) are not classified with CCs.
6. Dietitians in Critical Care supports Peer Review Organizations in efforts to ensure that Prospective Payment does not achieve cost containment at the expense of quality nutritional care.
7. Congressional action to provide research funds is crucial for the development of improved nutrition support therapies aimed for speeding patient recovery and decreasing health care costs.

Exhibit A-1 continued

8. As a profession, we can do the following to ensure the delivery of quality nutritional care:
   a. Collaborate with hospital administrators to ensure adequate expenditures for delivery of nutritional care. Mutual goals are to decrease incidence of complications due to malnutrition and decrease length of hospital stay.
   b. Implement admission screening programs to identify patients at risk for complications due to malnutrition. If identified early, patients at risk can receive nutrition support that can prevent complications and speed recovery.
   c. Define and document the type and amount of nutrition services provided to justify the cost effectiveness and the cost benefits of such services.
   d. Develop policies for documenting nutritional CCs using ICD-9-CM codes to ensure accurate assignment of DRG codes for appropriate payment per case. This effort may be coordinated through nutrition committees and medical records departments.

Source: Dietitians in Critical Care Dietetic Practice Group: "Nutrition Support Services in Home Health Care, and Impact of Prospective Payment on Critical Care Nutrition." Copyright the American Dietetic Association. Reprinted by permission from *Journal of the American Dietetic Association,* Vol. 85, 981, 982, 1985.

Exhibit A-2 Joint American Dietetic Association/Commission on Dietetic Registration Code of Ethics

New Code of Ethics Developed for the Dietetic Profession

Preamble

The American Dietetic Association and its credentialing agency, the Commission on Dietetic Registration, believe it is in the best interests of the profession and the public they serve that a Code of Ethics provide guidance to dietetic practitioners in their professional practice and conduct. Dietetic practitioners have voluntarily developed a Code of Ethics to reflect the ethical principles guiding the dietetic profession and to outline commitments and obligations of the dietetic practitioner to self, client, society, and the profession.

The purpose of the Commission on Dietetic Registration is to assist in protecting the nutritional health, safety, and welfare of the public by establishing and enforcing qualifications for dietetic registration and for issuing voluntary credentials to individuals who have attained those qualifications. The Commission has adopted this Code to apply to individuals who hold these credentials.

The Ethics Code applies in its entirety to members of The American Dietetic Association who are Registered Dietitians (RDs) or Dietetic Technicians, Registered (DTRs). Except for sections solely dealing with the credential, the Code applies to all American Dietetic Association members who are not RDs or DTRs. Except for aspects solely dealing with membership, the Code applies to all RDs and DTRs who are not ADA members. All of the aforementioned are referred to in the Code as "dietetic practitioners."

Exhibit A-2 continued

Principles

1. The dietetic practitioner provides professional services with objectivity and with respect for the unique needs and values of individuals.
2. The dietetic practitioner avoids discrimination against other individuals on the basis of race, creed, religion, sex, age, and national origin.
3. The dietetic practitioner fulfills professional commitments in good faith.
4. The dietetic practitioner conducts him/herself with honesty, integrity, and fairness.
5. The dietetic practitioner remains free of conflict of interest while fulfilling the objectives and maintaining the integrity of the dietetic profession.
6. The dietetic practitioner maintains confidentiality of information.
7. The dietetic practitioner practices dietetics based on scientific principles and current information.
8. The dietetic practitioner assumes responsibility and accountability for personal competence in practice.
9. The dietetic practitioner recognizes and exercises professional judgment within the limits of his/her qualifications and seeks counsel or makes referrals as appropriate.
10. The dietetic practitioner provides sufficient information to enable clients to make their own informed decisions.
11. The dietetic practitioner who wishes to inform the public and colleagues of his/her services does so by using factual information. The dietetic practitioner does not advertise in a false or misleading manner.
12. The dietetic practitioner promotes or endorses products in a manner that is neither false nor misleading.
13. The dietetic practitioner permits use of his/her name for the purpose of certifying that dietetic services have been rendered only if he/she has provided or supervised the provision of those services.
14. The dietetic practitioner accurately presents professional qualifications and credentials.
    a. The dietetic practitioner uses "RD" or "registered dietitian" and "DTR" or "dietetic technician, registered" only when registration is current and authorized by the Commission on Dietetic Registration.
    b. The dietetic practitioner provides accurate information and complies with all requirements of the Commission on Dietetic Registration program in which he/she is seeking initial or continued credentials from the Commission on Dietetic Registration.
    c. The dietetic practitioner is subject to disciplinary action for aiding another person in violating any Commission on Dietetic Registration requirements or aiding another person in representing himself/herself as an RD or DTR when he/she is not.
15. The dietetic practitioner presents substantiated information and interprets controversial information without personal bias, recognizing that legitimate differences of opinion exist.
16. The dietetic practitioner makes all reasonable effort to avoid bias in any kind of professional evaluation. The dietetic practitioner provides objective evaluation of candidates for professional association memberships, awards, scholarships, or job advancements.
17. The dietetic practitioner voluntarily withdraws from professional practice under the following circumstances:
    a. The dietetic practitioner has engaged in any substance abuse that could affect his/her practice;

Exhibit A-2 continued

   b. The dietetic practitioner has been adjudged by a court to be mentally incompetent;
   c. The dietetic practitioner has an emotional or mental disability that affects his/her practice in a manner that could harm the client.
18. The dietetic practitioner complies with all applicable laws and regulations concerning the profession. The dietetic practitioner is subject to disciplinary action under the following circumstances:
   a. The dietetic practitioner has been convicted of a crime under the laws of the United States which is a felony or a misdemeanor, an essential element of which is dishonesty and which is related to the practice of the profession.
   b. The dietetic practitioner has been disciplined by a state and at least one of the grounds for the discipline is the same or substantially equivalent to these principles.
   c. The dietetic practitioner has committed an act of misfeasance or malfeasance which is directly related to the practice of the profession as determined by a court of competent jurisdiction, a licensing board, or a governmental body.
19. The dietetic practitioner accepts the obligation to protect society and the profession by upholding the Code of Ethics for the Profession of Dietetics and by reporting alleged violations of the Code through the defined review process of The American Dietetic Association and its credentialing agency, the Commission on Dietetic Registration.

Source: American Dietetic Association, © January 1989.

Exhibit A-3 Position of The American Dietetic Association: Nutrition monitoring of the home parenteral and enteral patient[1]

   More patients are now being discharged from hospitals but kept on parenteral and enteral nutrition support at home. The result is nutritional rehabilitation of many patients and a decrease in health care costs. However, increased use of home parenteral and enteral nutrition support has also brought about increased complications. The need for comprehensive nutritional monitoring by a team of qualified nutrition professionals is imperative.
   , Home parenteral and enteral nutrition has been lifesaving to thousands of patients. However, with increased use of those modalities, many unique side effects associated with home parenteral and enteral support have become apparent. Although the pathophysiology of many of the complications is not fully understood, the majority may be prevented by comprehensive nutritional monitoring of the patient. To provide that

[1]Approved by the House of Delegates on October 2, 1988, as Position Paper No. 88-02, to be in effect until October 1993, unless it is reaffirmed or withdrawn as directed in the position development procedures of the House of Delegates. The American Dietetic Association authorizes republication of this position, *in its entirety,* provided full and proper credit is given.

Exhibit A-3 continued

vital service, professionals familiar with the intricacies of nutrition support must be included as part of the health care team managing the patient.

The position of The American Dietetic Association is that patients on home parenteral and enteral nutrition must be closely monitored by qualified nutrition professionals to assure appropriate nutrition support and minimize complications.

In recent years, rising costs associated with hospitalization have led to an increased emphasis on the use of outpatient therapy in the treatment of many illnesses. Since nutrition support remains a valuable therapeutic modality that can be administered in the home, an ever-increasing demand for home nutrition services has developed (1). However, the availability of adequate support services has not kept pace with the demand.

In 1985, it was estimated that up to 5,000 parenteral and 20,000 enteral patients were receiving home nutrition therapy in the United States. That population included patients of all ages, with increasing representation of both pediatric and geriatric groups (2). Though malignancy and gastrointestinal disease remain the most common diagnoses in those patients, increasing applicability of home parenteral and enteral nutrition in diverse disease states has become evident. The nutrition support allows patients to return to a comfortable home environment, thereby avoiding lengthy institutionalization. In some cases, the nutrition makes a critical contribution to a patient's complete rehabilitation.

According to one published report, home delivery of enteral or parenteral nutritional therapy results in a cost savings of 50% for enteral and 25% for parenteral nutrition, in comparison with identical therapies administered in an inpatient setting (2). However, in order to realize those financial savings, an accurate assessment of the nutritional requirements of the individual is necessary to avoid wastage of nutritional supplies (3–5). In addition, careful monitoring of the patient contributes to the avoidance of potential infectious, mechanical, and metabolic complications and thus the costs associated with recurrent hospitalizations (6–8). Appropriate monitoring includes review of biochemical, electrolyte, and hematological data, performance of nutrition assessments, determination of nutrient requirements, assessment of major organ function, review of diagnostic tests, and periodic physical examinations to determine tolerance to nutrition therapy and prevention of adverse effects.

Although enteral and parenteral nutrition are most often used in the treatment of malnourished patients, overfeeding or inappropriate feeding can be just as detrimental as underfeeding (6–8). Therefore, an individualized nutrition prescription is required for the success of home parenteral or enteral therapy. Such a prescription must be based on caloric, carbohydrate, protein, and fat requirements, as well as on the provision of electrolytes, vitamins, minerals, trace elements, and fluid. Special attention should be focused on the contribution, if any, of absorbed oral intake to the nutrition support regimen to assure adequacy and prevent redundant or excessive delivery of specific nutrients.

Complications from fatty acid and vitamin deficiencies have been reported when long-term parenteral nutrition is used (9,10). Deficiencies of trace elements, such as zinc, molybdenum, chromium, and selenium, have been documented in the parenteral nutrition population (11–17). In addition, the literature describes deficiencies of carnitine, taurine, and choline in certain home parenteral and enteral nutrition patients who are unable to synthesize those nutrients (16–19). Because they are considered nonessential, the nutrients are generally not provided in the nutrition formula. Knowledge of potential deficiencies is critical when one is determining the optimal nutrient prescription.

Exhibit A-3 continued

Once specific nutrient needs have been addressed, appropriate monitoring is essential to assure maintenance of homeostasis. The amount of micronutrient supplementation and the mechanisms for monitoring micronutrient status in home parenteral and enteral nutrition remain controversial (20–24). Repletion of certain substances may be difficult. For example, parenteral supplementation of iron may be associated with anaphylaxis and hapatic toxicity if proper precautions are not employed (25). The providers of home parenteral and enteral nutrition must pay scrupulous attention to detail to avoid complications.

Parenteral nutrition has been implicated in the development of several clinical syndromes. For example, metabolic bone disease has occurred after long-term parenteral feeding. Although the etiology of the syndrome remains unclear, vitamin D content, aluminum contamination of parenteral solutions, hypercalciuria secondary to infusion of protein or cyclic nutrient infusion, and deficiencies or excesses of carbohydrates, proteins, trace elements, and minerals may all play a role (26–29). Liver disease, possibly secondary to excessive caloric supplementation, may also be associated with parenteral nutrition, with hepatobiliary dysfunction and steatosis being the most common clinical manifestations (30,31).

Enteral feeding may also be associated with several complications. Even though diarrhea and dehydration with subsequent electrolyte imbalance are the most frequently reported problems, drug-nutrient interactions resulting in under-medication or inactivation of nutrients may occur when a feeding tube is used as a means of drug as well as nutrient delivery (32–36). In addition, an improperly placed feeding tube may lead to aspiration and subsequent pneumonia (37). Furthermore, even at volumes necessary to meet caloric requirements, enteral formulas may provide minimal levels of nutrients such as carotene and choline while providing excesses of others (e.g., specific vitamins) (19,21,38). All enteral prescriptions must be assessed for nutritional completeness.

Health care professionals with appropriate education and specialized training or experience in the delivery of parenteral and enteral nutrition are necessary to adequately supervise its administration (39,40). Appropriate supervision requires a multidisciplinary approach involving registered nurses, pharmacists, and dietitians who make recommendations to the physicians responsible for the management of the patient. The Position Paper on Home Health Care of the American College of Physicians (41) identifies the dietitian as a qualified provider of nutrition care. In addition, the legislative and public policy statement on nutrition support services in home health care (6), the congressional briefing testimony of The American Dietetic Association (7), and the Standards for Home Nutrition Support proposed by the American Society for Parenteral and Enteral Nutrition (42) all consider a nutrition support dietitian to be an integral part of the health care team involved in home parenteral and enteral delivery.

Nutrition support dietitians are educated in indications, applications, and monitoring of specialized nutrition support. Dietitians' expertise includes assessment of dietary histories, calculation of enteral and parenteral intake, determination of macronutrient and micronutrient requirements, formulation and implementation of nutrition care plans, performance of serial nutrition assessments, review of laboratory indexes and other nutrition-related diagnostic data, monitoring for therapeutic effects and signs of intolerance, and education of the patient and/or caregiver. Furthermore, dietitians are instrumental in coordinating the transition from parenteral and enteral therapy to an oral diet, resulting in nutritional rehabilitation and significant cost savings. The total estimated national cost of persons on parenteral and enteral nutrition in the

Exhibit A-3 continued

United States in non-hospital settings in 1986 was $680 million (43). Documentation of the ability to ingest and absorb adequate nutrients by the oral or enteral route is cost-effective since it allows for termination of specialized nutrition support.

As the demand for home-based nutrition support continues to grow, it is imperative that qualified health care professionals be employed to supervise its administration. Each member of the health care team should be utilized for his/her expertise. In that light, dietitians should assume an increasingly active role in the management of the patient on home parenteral or enteral nutrition support. This can only be facilitated by recognition of the need for third-party private insurers, Medicare, and Medicaid to reimburse dietitians and all members of the multidisciplinary team for their unique services. Greater use of outpatient nutrition support should be encouraged only when it can be appropriately monitored.

References

1. Compher, C.W., Coliazzo, T.M., and Rieke, S.: Changes in nutrition support services between 1984 and 1986. Submitted for publication, J Am Diet Assoc.
2. Howard, L., Heaphey, L.L., and Timchalk, M.: A review of the current national status of home parenteral and enteral nutrition from the provider and consumer perspective. JPEN 10:416, 1986.
3. O'Brien, D.D., Hodges, R.E., Day, A.T., Waxman, K.S., and Rebello, T.: Recommendations of nutrition support team promote cost containment. JPEN 10:300, 1986.
4. Detsky, A.S., McLaughlin, J.R., Abrams, H.B., Whittaker, J.S., Whitwell, J., L'Abbe, K., and Jeejeebhoy, K.N.: A cost-utility analysis of the home parenteral nutrition program at Toronto General Hospital: 1970–1982. JPEN 10:49, 1986.
5. Traeger, S.M., Williams, G.B., Milliren, G., Young, D.S., Fisher, M., and Haug, M.T.: Total parenteral nutrition by a nutrition support team: Improved quality of care. JPEN 10:408, 1986.
6. Dietitians in Nutrition Support Dietetic Practice Group: Nutrition support services in home health care. Timely Statement. J Am Diet Assoc 85:981, 1985.
7. American Dietetic Association: Congressional Briefing on the Cost Effectiveness of Nutrition Support. Washington, DC, January 23, 1986.
8. Klein, G.L., and Rivera, D.: Adverse metabolic consequences of total parenteral nutrition. Cancer 55:305, 1985.
9. Holman, R.T., Johnson, S.B., and Hatch, T.F.: A case of human linolenic acid deficiency involving neurological abnormalities. Am J Clin Nutr 35:617, 1982.
10. Mock, D.M., Baswell, D.L., Baker, H., Holman, R.T., and Sweetman, L.: Biotin deficiency complicating parenteral alimentation: Diagnosis, metabolic repercussions, and treatment. J Pediatr 106:762, 1985.
11. Brown, M.R., Cohen, H.J., Lyons, J.M., Curtis, T.W., Thunberg, B., Cochran, W.J., and Klish, W.J.: Proximal muscle weakness and selenium deficiency associated with long-term parenteral nutrition. Am J Clin Nutr 43:549, 1986.
12. Fleming, C.R., Lie, J.T., McCall, J.T., O'Brien, J.F., Baillie, E.E., and Thistle, J.L.: Selenium deficiency and fatal cardiomyopathy in a patient on home parenteral nutrition. Gastroenterology 83:689, 1982.
13. Brown, R.O., Forloines-Lynn, S., Cross, R.E., and Heizer, W.D.: Chromium deficiency after long-term total parenteral nutrition. Dig Dis Sci 31:661, 1986.

Exhibit A-3 continued

14. Oleske, J.M., Westphal, M.L., Shore, S., Gorden, D., Bogden, J.D., and Nahmias, A.: Zinc therapy of depressed cellular immunity in acrodermatitis enteropathica: Its correction. Am J Dis Child 133:915, 1979.
15. Abumrad, N.N., Schneider, A.J., Steele, D.R., and Rogers, L.S.: Acquired molybdenum deficiency. Clin Res 27:774A, 1981.
16. Worthley, L.I., Fishlock, R.C., and Snoswell, A.M.: Carnitine balance and effects of intravenous L-carnitine in two patients receiving long term parenteral nutrition. JPEN 8:717, 1984.
17. Bowyer, B.A., Miles, J.M., Haymond, M.W., and Fleming, C.R.: L-Carnitine therapy in home parenteral nutrition patients with abnormal liver tests and low plasma carnitine concentrations. Gastroenterology 94:434, 1988.
18. Geggel, H.S., Ament, M.E., Heckenlively, J.R., Martin, D.A., and Kopple, J.D.: Nutritional requirements for taurine in patients receiving long-term parenteral nutrition. N Engl J Med 312:142, 1985.
19. Chawla, R.K., Berry, C.J., Kutner, M.H., and Rudman, D.: Plasma concentrations of transsulfuration pathway products during nasoenteral and intravenous hyperalimentation of malnourished patients. Am J Clin Nutr 42:577, 1985.
20. Shils, M.E., Baker, H., and Frank, O.: Blood vitamin levels of long-term adult home total parenteral nutrition patients: The efficacy of the AMA-FDA parenteral multivitamin formulation. JPEN 9:179, 1985.
21. Berner, Y., Morse, R., Frank, O., Baker, H., and Shike, M.: Vitamin plasma levels in long-term enteral feedng patients. Clin Res 36:754A, 1988.
22. Gleghorn, E.E., Eisenberg, L.D., Hack, S., Parton, P., and Merritt, R.J.: Observations of vitamin A toxicity in three patients with renal failure receiving parenteral alimentation. Am J Clin Nutr 44:107, 1986.
23. Howard, L.: Assessment of vitamin status in patients undergoing acute nutritional repletion, JPEN 11:217, 1987.
24. Davis, A.T., Franz, F.P., Courtnay, D.A., Ullrey, D.E., Scholten, D.J., and Dean, R.E.: Plasma vitamin and mineral status in home parenteral nutrition patients. JPEN 11:480, 1987.
25. Nortan, J.A., Peters, M.L., Wesley, R., Maker, M.M., and Brennan, M.F.: Iron supplementation of total parenteral nutrition: A prospective study. JPEN 7:457, 1983.
26. Klein, G.L., Alfrey, A.C., Miller, N.L., Sherrard, D.J., Hazlet, T.K., Ament, M.E., and Coburn, J.W.: Aluminum loading during total parenteral nutrition. Am J Clin Nutr 35:1425, 1982.
27. Bengoa, J.M., Sitrin, M.D., Wood, R.J., and Rosenberg, I.H.: Amino acid-induced hypercalciuria in patients on total parenteral nutrition. Am J Clin Nutr 38:264, 1983.
28. Shike, M., Shils, M.E., Heller, A., Alcock, N., Vigorita, V., Brockman, R., Holick, M.F., Lane, J., and Flombaum, C.: Bone disease in prolonged parenteral nutrition: Osteopenia without mineralization defect. Am J Clin Nutr 44:89, 1986.
29. Wood, R.J., Bengoa, J.M., Sitrin, M.D., and Rosenberg, I.H.: Calciuretic effect of cyclic versus continuous total parenteral nutrition. Am J Clin Nutr 41:614, 1985.
30. Baker, A.L., and Rosenberg, I.H.: Hepatic complications of total parenteral nutrition. Am J Med 82:489, 1987.
31. Bowyer, B.A., Fleming, C.R., Ludwig, J., Petz, J., and McGill, D.B.: Does long-term home parenteral nutrition in adult patients cause chronic liver disease? JPEN 9:11, 1985.

Exhibit A-3 continued

32. White, K.C., and Harkavy, K.L.: Hypertonic formula resulting from added oral medications. Am J Dis Child 136:931, 1982.
33. Vanlandingham, S., Simpson, S., Daniel, P., and Newmark, S.R.: Metabolic abnormalities in patients supported with enteral tube feeding. JPEN 5:322, 1981.
34. Cataldi-Betcher, E.L., Seltzer, M.H., Slocum, B.A., and Jones, K.W.: Complications occurring during enteral nutrition support: A prospective study. JPEN 7:546, 1983.
35. Cutie, A.J., Altman, E., and Lenkel, L.: Compatibility of enteral products with commonly employed drug additives. JPEN 7:186, 1983.
36. Bauer, L.A.: Interference of oral phenytoin absorption by continuous nasogastric feedings. Neurology 32:570, 1982.
37. Olivares, L., Segovia, A., and Revuelta, R.: Tube feeding and lethal aspiration in neurological patients: A review of 720 autopsy cases. Stroke 5:654, 1974.
38. Bowen, P.E., Mobarhan, S., Henderson, C., Stacewicz-Sapuntzakis, M., Friedman, H., and Kaiser, H.: Hypocarotenemia in patients fed enterally with commercial liquid diet. JPEN 12:484, 1988.
39. Koren, M.J.: Home care—Who cares? N Engl J Med 314:917, 1986.
40. ASPEN Board of Directors: Guidelines for use of home total parenteral nutrition. JPEN 11:342, 1987.
41. Health and Public Policy Committee, American College of Physicians: Position Paper on Home Health Care, Ann Intern Med 105:454, 1986.
42. American Society for Parenteral and Enteral Nutrition: Standards for Home Nutrition Support. Nutr Clin Prac 3:202, 1988.
43. Oasis. Home Nutritional Support Patient Registry. Annual Report—1985 Data. Oley Foundation, Albany, NY, and ASPEN, Silver Spring, MD, 1987.

- *ADA Position adopted by the HOD on October 2, 1988.*
- *Recognition is given to the following for their contributions:*
  -Organization units:
  Dietitian in Nutrition Support
  Association Position Committee
  -Authors: JoAnn Davey McCrae, MS, RD, CNSD; Lucinda Lysen, RD, RN; Laurie Mello, RD, CNSD; Regina O'Shea, MS, RD; Nancy Hall, MMSc, RD, CNSD
- *Reviewers: Evelyn B. Enrione, PhD, RD; Janice Glascock, PharmD; Mitchell Kaminsky, Jr., MD; Diann Martin, RN, MS; Eva Shronts, MMSc, RD, CNSD; Susan Wiegert, RD*
  Consultant Dietitians in Health Care Facilities

Source: Copyright the American Dietetic Association. Reprinted by permission from *Journal of the American Dietetic Association*, Vol. 89:263, 1989.

Exhibit A-4 Standards for Home Nutrition Support

STANDARDS FOR HOME NUTRITION SUPPORT

American Society for Parenteral and Enteral Nutrition

INTRODUCTION

A.S.P.E.N. is a professional society whose members are health care professionals—physicians, nurses, dietitians, pharmacists, and nutritionists—dedicated to optimum nutrition support of patients during hospitalization and rehabilitation.

A.S.P.E.N.'s diverse professional membership emphasizes the basic importance of good nutrition to good medical practice and the multidisciplinary team approach to sound nutrition.

These Standards have been developed, reviewed, and approved by the following A.S.P.E.N. groups: Standards Committee, Executive Committee, and Board of Directors.

These Standards of Practice for Home Nutrition Support should be used in conjunction with the following A.S.P.E.N. publications:

Definitions of Terms Used in A.S.P.E.N. Guidelines and Standards
Standards for Nutrition Support, Hospitalized Patients
Standards of Practice, Nutrition Support Dietitian
Standards of Practice, Nutrition Support Pharmacist
Standards of Practice, Nutrition Support Nursing
Standards of Practice, Nutrition Support Physician

A.S.P.E.N. has developed these standards to promote the health and welfare of those patients in need of enteral and parenteral nutrition. The standards represent a consensus of A.S.P.E.N.'s members as to that minimal level of practice necessary to assure safe and effective enteral and parenteral nutrition care. A.S.P.E.N. disclaims any liability to any health care provider, patient, or other persons affected by these standards.

ORGANIZATION STANDARDS

Standard 1. Providers of specialized home nutrition support services shall be clearly defined.

1. The provider of specialized home nutrition support is the physician who is primarily responsible for the patient's nutrition care. He should be assisted by a registered nurse, a registered dietitian, and a registered pharmacist, each having appropriate education, specialized training, and experience in the discipline of specialized nutrition support.
2. Specialized home nutrition support services shall be initiated and coordinated by the provider.
3. There shall be a clear understanding among the provider, the vendor, and the patient, specifying responsibilities of each, including: the manner in which services shall be coordinated and evaluated; the role of the provider, the vendor, and the patient in the establishment and monitoring of patient care; and the mechanisms and responsibility for payment for services, equipment, and products.

Standard 2. The providers of specialized home nutrition support services shall be guided by written policies and procedures.

1. There shall be written policies and procedures concerning the scope and provision of specialized home nutrition support services.

Exhibit A-4 continued

2. These written policies and procedures shall be developed by the provider, in conjunction with the medical/surgical, dietetics, nursing, pharmacy, and other staff as appropriate.
3. These shall be reviewed annually and revised as appropriate to reflect optimal standards of care.
4. Written policies and procedures shall include but not be limited to the following:
    4.1 The roles, responsibilities, and 24-hour availability of provider care.
    4.2 Defined criteria for patient eligibility and selection, including: medical suitability; rehabilitative potential; social and economic factors; and educational, psychological, and emotional factors pertinent to the patient and others who are significantly included in this care.
    4.3 A mechanism for patient monitoring (e.g., frequency of follow-up contact, laboratory studies, and physical examination).
    4.4 Availability of consultative medical services and services of other professionals (such as psychologists and social workers) and nonprofessionals (such as patient support groups) as appropriate.
    4.5 Reimbursement mechanisms for services, equipment, and supplies.
    4.6 Acquisition of enteral or intravenous nutrients, equipment, and supplies for home delivery.
    4.7 Education materials for patient and family training and use at home.
    4.8 Preparation and/or storage of enteral formulas or intravenous nutrient solutions in the home, and techniques for the administration of enteral formulas or intravenous nutrient solutions, feeding schedules, care of feeding tubes for patients receiving enteral formulas, and care of catheters and tubing for patients receiving intravenous nutrition.
    4.9 Prevention and management of complications in the home, and emergency consultation with professional staff.
    4.10 Mechanism for quality assurance.

Standard 3. Specialized home nutrition support services shall be documented.
1. Medical records shall be maintained for every patient receiving specialized home nutrition support services and shall include:
    1.1 Designation of physician having primary responsibility for patient's home nutrition care.
    1.2 All pertinent patient diagnoses and prognoses, including long and short term objectives of treatment.
    1.3 Initial and follow-up physical examinations.
    1.4 Scope and results of training and retraining.
    1.5 Plan of care, including types and frequency of services to be provided, functional limitations of the patient, activities permitted, psychosocial needs of the patient, suitability and provision of home nutrition services, and name of other individual(s) who will assist in the care of the patient if required.
    1.6 Composition, rate, and mode of administration of feeding formulation and all medications.
    1.7 Signed and dated progress notes for each home visit, clinic visit, and telephone contact, such progress notes to report response to therapeutic regimen including results of serial monitoring, complications, and revisions in the therapeutic regimen.
    1.8 A summary statement at termination of nutrition therapy, which includes results of therapy, complications, outcome, and disposition of patient.

Exhibit A-4 continued

Standard 4. The specialized home nutrition support regimen shall be reviewed and evaluated regularly to determine overall effectiveness and safety.
1. Evaluation of patient's need for and response to specialized home nutrition support shall be the responsibility of the providers.
2. The review and evaluation shall be performed and documented at least every 90 days.
3. Deficiencies found in the review should be corrected by modifying services, protocols, procedures, and educational programs.

PATIENT SELECTION STANDARD

Standard 5. Indications and contraindications for specialized home nutrition support shall be clearly defined.
1. The patient shall be carefully evaluated prior to selection for specialized home nutrition support.
   1.1 A candidate for specialized home nutrition support is that patient who is unable to meet nutrient requirements by oral enteral nutrition.
   1.2 The patient's clinical status and quality of life must be such that treatment at home would be appropriate.
   1.3 Specialized nutrition support being given at home should be designed to achieve the nutrition objectives.
   1.4 The patient's home environment should be appropriate for the safe use of home nutrition support.
2. An evaluation of the nutrient needs of the patient shall be performed prior to the initiation of specialized nutrition support.
   2.1 Nutrition requirements will take into account the special disease state, the patient's nutrition status and growth requirements, and the duration of anticipated intake.
   2.2 The type and amount of the nutrition needed by the patient shall be determined.

STANDARD THERAPEUTIC PLAN

Standard 6. The objective(s) of specialized nutrition support shall be determined and documented.
1. The required characteristics of the objectives of home nutrition support should address the short and long term needs of the home patient.
   1.1 Short term needs might include resolution of disease progression, wound healing, progression to enteral support, and recovery from nutrition depletion.
   1.2 Long term needs include maintenance of normal nutrition and rehabilitation to physical and social independence.
   1.3 The objectives should be developed prior to the institution of nutrition support.

Standard 7. The route(s) selected to provide specialized nutrition support shall be appropriate to meet assessed nutrient requirements and achieve therapeutic goals and objectives.
1. The safest, most cost-effective route which meets the patient's needs should be utilized.

Exhibit A-4 continued

2. It should be recognized that as the patient's therapy progresses the optimal mode of feeding may change and may, at times, utilize both enteral and parenteral feedings.

Standard 8. The selected feeding formulations shall be appropriate to the disease process and compatible with the access route and shall meet nutrient needs.
1. The formulation selection and modification should be under the direction of the provider and should be based on knowledge of the patient and his/her specific clinical disease processes, as well as available products and their costs.
2. The patient should be given a prescription copy of the feeding formulation and other medications.

IMPLEMENTATION STANDARDS

Standard 9. The access route(s) shall be appropriate for home use.
1. The type of device used should be placed, recommended, or approved by the provider and documented in the patient's medical records.
2. Access should be placed, or be directly supervised, by a physician or other specially trained health care professional who is proficient in such placement.
3. Selected patients or responsible others who have been trained may insert enteral feeding tubes.
4. Standard techniques or protocols should be established for gaining access.
5. The access selected must be appropriate for the type of therapy to be delivered and should be as simple as possible for home care and use, offer appropriate durability for the duration of therapy, and minimize the potential for occurrence of complications.

Standard 10. The patient and/or responsible other shall receive education and demonstrate competence in feeding formulation preparation and administration.
1. The patient should be educated in the following areas: knowledge of appropriate formulation components, determination of proper dosages, aseptic (parenteral) or clean (enteral) technique, manipulation and maintenance of equipment, and infusion method.
2. The patient receiving enteral nutrition must be instructed in clean techniques of feeding formulation preparation, storage, and infusion.
3. Closed containers should be used for feeding formulation storage and administration.
4. Enteral formulations should not be left hanging for longer than 12 hours, but hanging time may be more limited for specific products.
5. Admixed parenteral formulations should not be left at room temperature for longer than 24 hours.
6. The patient receiving parenteral nutrition should be taught to check the integrity of the feeding formulation containers and to inspect for abnormalities in appearance, proper storage of the feeding formulations, and filtering techniques, if used.
7. For cyclic enteral and parenteral infusion methods, specific instruction should be given.
8. Control of the infusion rate to maintain an accurate flow rate requires an infusion control device which the patient or responsible other must be taught to use.

Exhibit A-4 continued

Standard 11. The patient and/or responsible other shall receive education and demonstrate competence in access route care.

1. The patient receiving parenteral infusions must be trained in aseptic technique of dressing care, connecting and disconnecting the intravenous tubing to the catheter, and post-infusion flushing to prevent catheter occlusion.
2. The enterally fed patient must be trained in clean techniques for handling the tube, maintaining the access site, and flushing the tube to maintain patency.

Standard 12. The patient and/or responsible other shall receive education and demonstrate competence in the recognition and appropriate response to complications in equipment maintenance and malfunctions.

1. The patient must be taught to recognize and respond to potential complications. However, the provider is still responsible for the care of the home enteral and parenteral nutrition patient and must provide 24-hour availability to advise and/or intervene if potentially serious complications arise.
2. Common important clinical complications include sepsis, glucose intolerance, fluid and electrolyte imbalance, catheter or tube occlusion, and breakage and equipment malfunction.

Standard 13. Educational material shall be provided to the patient or responsible others.

Standard 14. Patient education shall include periodic reassessment and retraining as needed.

PATIENT MONITORING STANDARD

Standard 15. The patient shall be monitored for therapeutic efficacy, adverse effects, and clinical changes that may influence specialized nutrition support.

1. Protocols shall be developed for periodic review of the patient's clinical and biochemical status.
2. Routine monitoring should include: nutrient intake; review of current medications; signs of intolerance to therapy; weight changes; biochemical, hematologic, and other pertinent data, including clinical signs of nutrient deficiencies and excesses; adjustment of therapy; changes in lifestyle; psychosocial problems; and changes in the home environment.
3. Assessment of the patient's major organ functions should be made periodically.

TERMINATION OF THERAPY STANDARDS

Standard 16. The patient shall demonstrate the ability to ingest and absorb adequate nutrients by the enteral route prior to discontinuing parenteral and enteral nutrition.

1. Parenteral nutrition should not be discontinued by the provider or vendor until estimated nutrient requirements are tolerated by the gastrointestinal tract.
2. Parenteral nutrient formulations should be decreased over time while enteral feedings are increased.
3. Documentation of ingestion and absorption of adequate nutrients via the gastrointestinal tract should be made in the medical records.

Exhibit A-4 continued

Standard 17. Specialized nutrition support shall be discontinued when complications so indicate.

1. Complications which are uncontrollable and/or life-threatening require immediate assessment of the patient by the provider physician and, if necessary, immediate discontinuation of the specialized nutrition support therapy.
2. Treating emergent life-threatening conditions takes precedence over the delivery of specialized nutrition support.
3. Specialized nutrition support should be reinstituted following the correction of such complications as indicated.

Standard 18. Specialized nutrition support shall be terminated when the patient no longer benefits from the therapy.

1. When, in the course of a patient's disease, the proposed objectives can no longer be met, the decision to discontinue specialized nutrition support must be made according to accepted community standards of medical care and in compliance with applicable law.

Source: Reprinted from *Nutrition in Clinical Practice,* Vol. 3, No. 5, pp. 202–205, with permission of American Society for Parenteral and Enteral Nutrition, © October 1988.

Exhibit A-5A Memorial Sloan-Kettering Home Enteral Form

DATE _____

NAME _____ TELEPHONE: HOME _____ WORK _____

ADDRESS _____ CHART # _____

SEX _____ AGE _____ HEIGHT _____ WEIGHT _____ USUAL WEIGHT _____

DIAGNOSIS _____

DISCHARGE MEDS _____ KARNOFSKY INDEX _____

REASON FOR TUBE FEEDING (TF) _____ WEIGHT, START TF _____ DATE _____

M.D. _____ TELEPHONE EXT. ___ ROOM # ___ TEAM ___ NONTEAM ___

CARE PLAN

TUBE TYPE/SIZE _____ DRESSING TYPE/CARE _____

DELIVERY METHOD: BOLUS/GRAVITY/PUMP   PUMP TYPE _____

GOAL KCAL/VOLUME _____ USE OF TUBE: FEEDING/FLUID/MEDS

D/C DATE _____ FORMULA _____ RATE _____ VOLUME _____

Exhibit A-5A continued

PATIENT FOLLOW-UP

DATE	WEIGHT	RATE	KCAL	COMMENTS

DATES OF HOSPITALIZATION _____

SUMMARY OF CARE

END DATE _____ REASON FOR STOPPING TF _____

Source: Courtesy of Memorial Sloan-Kettering Cancer Center, Nutrition Support Service, New York, New York.

Exhibit A-5B Training Summary

PATIENT _____

MEMORIAL SLOAN-KETTERING CANCER CENTER

LIAISON _____

PRIMARY CAREGIVER: PATIENT/FAMILY/NURSING/OTHER _____

CAREGIVER NAME _____ RELATIONSHIP _____

AVAILABILITY _____

LANGUAGE SPOKEN BY: PATIENT _____ PRIMARY CAREGIVER _____

	DATE COMPLETED	COMMENTS
TUBE INSERTION BY PATIENT/FAMILY		
TUBE CARE/FLUSHING		
FORMULA PREPARATION AND HANDLING		
FEEDING RATE/SCHEDULE		
PUMP OPERATION/ALARMS		
GRAVITY/BOLUS TECHNIQUES		
MONITORING: WEIGHT, STOOL, URINE, FLUID STATUS		

Exhibit A-5B continued

INTERVENTIONS REVIEWED FOR THE FOLLOWING COMPLICATIONS:
PUMP FAILURE ___   TUBE BLOCKAGE ___   TUBE DISPLACEMENT ___
DIARRHEA ___   CONSTIPATION ___   ABDOMINAL DISTENTION ___
NAUSEA ___   VOMITING ___   ASPIRATION ___
FEVER ___   INFECTION ___   OTHER _____

QUALITY CONTROL SUMMARY

	DATE	INITIALS
INSTRUCTION ENTERED INTO HOME FEEDING LOG		
HOME CARE PROGRAM OFFICE NOTIFIED		
SUPPLY NEEDS CALCULATED AND DOCUMENTED		
WRITTEN INSTRUCTIONS PROVIDED AND REVIEWED		
TELEPHONE FOLLOW-UP PROCEDURE EXPLAINED		
CLINIC FOLLOW-UP EXPLAINED		

Source: Courtesy of Memorial Sloan-Kettering Cancer Center, Nutrition Support Service, New York, New York.

Exhibit A-6 Home Patient Procedure Manual

1. *MANAGEMENT OF HOME TOTAL PARENTERAL NUTRITION (TPN) PATIENTS*
   1.1. *Initial Order for Home TPN*
       1.1.1. Referral source
       1.1.2. Patient assessment
       1.1.3. Data gathering and transmittal to supplier
   1.2. *Explanation of the Homecare Service*
       1.2.1. Discussion with patient and care providers
       1.2.2. Review of educational materials
       1.2.3. Financial issues
   1.3. *Training and Certification*
       1.3.1. Training procedures
       1.3.2. Training certification
   1.4. *Home TPN Prescription*
       1.4.1. Initial prescription
       1.4.2. Communication with supplier
   1.5. *Home TPN Orders and Supply List*
       1.5.1. Communication with supplier
       1.5.2. Supply list for patient

Exhibit A-6 continued

1.6. *Patient Discharge*
    1.6.1. Finalization of date with supplier
    1.6.2. Coordination of other equipment and staffing needs
    1.6.3. Final patient preparation
1.7. *Home Visitation*
    1.7.1. Initial nursing visit
    1.7.2. Home visitation report
1.8. *Outpatient Follow-up*
    1.8.1. Laboratory tests
    1.8.2. Clinic visits
    1.8.3. Telephone follow-up
    1.8.4. Prescription renewal and certification forms
1.9. *Rehospitalizations*
    1.9.1. Notification of team and supplier
    1.9.2. Prescription changes
    1.9.3. Readmission log
1.10. *Termination of Home Parenteral Nutrition*
    1.10.1. Notification of team and supplier
    1.10.2. Supply pick-up

Source: Courtesy of Memorial Sloan-Kettering Cancer Center, Nutrition Support Service, New York, New York.

Exhibit A-7 Crawford Long Hospital's Home Care Services Criteria

1. The Home Care Service will provide written patient education materials related to procedures, operation, and care of equipment and supplies. This material will meet approval of Crawford Long Hospital (CLH) professionals. The Home Care Service will follow CLH protocols when available.
2. The Home Care Service will explain financial arrangements to the patient and/or patient's family prior to patient discharge.
   —If the insurance coverage is less than 100%, explain to the patient the process and timing of billing.
   —Provide the name of the contact person with the Home Care Service to discuss any billing problems.
   —Any problems with the patient and/or patient's family member, the Home Care Service will contact the CLH referring professional.
   —The CLH referring professional will explain the financial status to the "reduced pay" patients.
   —The Home Care Service will accept some reduced pay patients.
3. Follow-up reports will he legible and within 7 days. Reports will be sent to the primary care physician and the CWL Social Services Department.
   A. Initial Report
      —Review of teaching techniques according to CWL protocols and guidelines.
      —Evaluation of patient's competencies.

Exhibit A-7 continued

—Evaluation of patient's clinical status.
—Teaching of any equipment and documentation.
B. Summation of patient problems/evaluation of patient's progress at least once a month.
C. Discharge summary report (termination of service).
4. Any professional service or therapy will have a professional for initial and routine visits for teaching follow-up and evaluation. Supplies and equipment will be delivered at the time of discharge. Initial nursing visits will be made within 24 hours of discharge or sooner if indicated.
5. The Home Care Service will be available and provide service 24 hours/day, including weekends and holidays. A 24-hour telephone number will be given to the patients.
6. The Home Care Service will have documented evidence of qualified personnel and update CLH on changes in staff. This would include credentials and resumes for all professionals involved with patient care. The Home Care Service should also have an ongoing quality assurance program.
7. The Home Care Service will coordinate equipment recommendations with CLH referring professionals.
8. The Home Care Service will define geographical limitations and mechanisms for alternate services.
9. It is the primary responsibility of the Home Care Service personnel who implement a change in therapy or in patient care to coordinate this with other agencies involved and to communicate this change immediately.
   Examples:
   A. Nutritional service personnel making changes in tube feeding, identifying teaching needs or intolerance problem must communicate this to the involved visiting nurse service.
   B. Respiratory service personnel assessing changes in patient's condition, identifying additional needs for patient education, or changes made in the respiratory care plan must communicate this to the involved visiting nurse service.
10. The Home Care Service representative (HCSR) making hospital visits to the patient must follow the procedure outlined below.
    A. Prior to hospital visit, the HCSR must contact the nursing unit coordinator and/or staff nurse to arrange time of visit. Visits should be made during the day shift hours unless otherwise arranged.
    B. Report to Social Services Department to complete the HCSR form. Department hours are 8 A.M. to 5 P.M.
    C. Display proper identification (name badge) during hospital visit.
    D. Present approved HCSR form to the nursing unit coordinator and return the form to Social Services when leaving the hospital.
    E. Communicate all information/needs to staff nurse.
    F. Patient's medical record will be viewed only with the staff nurse present.
11. Documentation in the patient's medical record by the Home Care Service personnel is not permitted. Any teaching and/or equipment demonstrations will be documented by the staff nurse assigned to the patient.

Source: Courtesy of Jeannie Zebrida, M.M.Sc, R.D., Crawford Long Hospital of Emory University, Atlanta, Georgia.

Exhibit A-8A Medicare Screens—TPN

The Medicare screens for total parenteral nutrition (TPN) are based on a standard prescription of two bottles of lipids weekly and a 30-day month. The only reimbursement that varies is that for the solution, which is evaluated by grams of protein administered daily. Medicare covers 80 percent of the screen.

		Screen Per Day			
Category	Screen Per Code	Gm Protein: 10–51	52–73	74–100	>100
Solution		$97.90	$133.00	$172.45	$226.69
Lipids, 10%	60.00/EACH	17.14	17.14	17.14	17.14
Supply Kit	182.98/MONTH	6.09	6.09	6.09	6.09
Administration Kit	600.00/MONTH	20.00	20.00	20.00	20.00
Pump Rental	300.00/MONTH	10.00	10.00	10.00	10.00
Pole Rental	20.00/MONTH	0.66	0.66	0.66	0.66
Total Screen Per Day		$151.79	$186.89	$226.34	$280.58

Exhibit A-8B Medicare Screens—Enteral

The Medicare screens for enteral feeding are based on a standard prescription of 2,000 calories per day, two nasogastric (NG) tubes per month, and a 30-day month. Categories designate formula types: Category I—Intact protein/protein isolate, semisynthetic; Category IB—Blenderized; Category II—Intact protein/protein isolate, calorically dense; Category III—High nitrogen hydrolyzed protein/amino acids; Category IV—Special metabolic needs (renal, hepatic, trauma); Category V—Modulars; and Category VI—Standard hydrolyzed protein/amino acids. Screens have not been set for Category IV and Category V formula; reimbursement is calculated on an individual basis.

		Screen Per Day				
Category:		I	IB	II	III	VI
Formula	Per 2,000 KCAL	$10.20	$24.40	$8.60	$30.00	$21.00
NG Tube with Stylet	16.75/EA	1.11	1.11	1.11	1.11	1.11
Pump Supply Kit*	275.00/MO	9.16	9.16	9.16	9.16	9.16

Exhibit A-8B continued

Pump Rental	92.00/MO	3.06	3.06	3.06	3.06	3.06
Pole Rental	20.00/MO	0.66	0.66	0.66	0.66	0.66
Total Screen Per Day		$24.19	$38.39	$22.59	$43.99	$34.99

*Gravity supply kit = $195.00 per month or $6.50 per day; syringe supply kit = $150.00 per month or $5.00 per day.

Exhibit A-9 Available Instructive Materials on Home Tube Feeding

Ross Laboratories
  Mastering the Technique of Tube Feeding at Home by Gastrostomy or Jejunostomy
  Mastering the Technique of Tube Feeding at Home by Nasogastric, Nasoduodenal,
    or Nasojejunal Tube
The American Dietetic Association
  Home Tube Feeding Instruction Packet (Karen J. Mueller, editor)

Exhibit A-10 The Oley Foundation—Patient and Professional Support Services

The Oley Foundation for Home Parenteral & Enteral Nutrition was established in 1983 to foster home [parenteral and enteral nutrition] (PEN) research and education and to provide a support network for those sustained on home nutritional therapy. Over the years Oley has formed a community composed of everyone involved in home enteral and parenteral nutrition. Because the focus is on a therapy rather than a specific disease, Oley's community encompasses home PEN patients and families dealing wth many different underlying diseases, clinicians from several disciplines, and a variety of home care services and third-party payers.

Oley's services include:
  Publication of the *Lifelineletter*, a bimonthly newsletter describing advances in homePEN technology and providing a forum for patient-to-patient sharing. As part of Oley's education and support network it is provided at no charge to patients/patient families.
  Maintenance of the homePEN national registry. Known as OASIS, this is a cooperative research project undertaken with the American Society for Parenteral and Enteral Nutrition that provides a database for analyzing the outcomes and complications associated with home therapy.

Exhibit A-10 continued

Coordination of a national system of regional volunteers who provide support and education at the local level.

An annual summer conference focused on issues of concern to homePEN patients. The conference is followed by an annual picnic where providers, patients, and others meet and share in an unstructured atmosphere.

Participation in research studies on the delivery, technology, cost effectiveness and psychosocial impact of nutritional support in nonhospital settings.

Educational materials including audio/video tapes, bibliographies, and in-service outlines with special emphasis on psychosocial issues and issues related to tube feedings in nursing homes.

Source: Courtesy of The Oley Foundation for Home Parenteral and Enteral Nutrition, Albany, New York.

Index

development of, 195–199
framework for, 190–195
monitoring and evaluating, 199
sources for, 188–189
Home care teams, 218
communication within, 223–224, 226
functions of, 108, 109, 223–226
process, 218–219
strategies, 220–223
structures of, 219–220
Home environment evaluation, 48, 92–93
Home mix formula, 107
Home monitoring, 97–98, 108–111,
139–140. *See also* Outpatient
follow-up
Home nutrition support
ethical issues of, 229–237
evolution of, v–vii
factors influencing growth in, 1–3
family and, 132
impact of regulatory and
reimbursement issues of, 18–22
under Medicaid program, 13–14
under Medicare program, 7–15
trends in, 26–27
Home patient procedure manual, 37,
259–260
Home total parenteral nutrition (HTPN),
vii
Home-delivered meals, 181–182
Horwitz, John, 219
Hospices, 135, 179–180
Hospital pharmacies, 30
Hospital–based education system, 29
Hospitals
impact of regulatory and
reimbursement issues in, 15–16
Medicaid coverage of nutrition support
in, 14
Medicare coverage of nutrition support
in, 5, 6
Hospital-supplier relationship
contracts and, 36–37
importance of communication in, 34
joint ventures, 36
legal implications of, 38
Hydration, 60

Hypercalcuiria, 114
Hyperemesis gravidarum, 76
Hyperglycemia, 85, 122
Hyperkalemia, 122
Hyperphagia, 86
Hyponatremia, 122
Hypophosphatemia, 122

I

Implantable access devices, 79
In re Conroy, 235
In re Rodas, 235, 236
Incompetence, 235
Indirect calorimetry, 78, 102
Indirect costs, 209
Infant formulas, 158, 160–164
Informed consent doctrine, 233–235
Infusion pumps, 72–73, 82, 157
Insulin, 99
Intangible costs, 209
Intermediaries, 6
Intermittent feedings, 71
Intravenous pole, 82
Iodine, 120
Iron, 81, 120, 160
Iron deficiency, 120, 122

J

Jejunostomy tubes, 69, 70, 155
Joint American Dietetic
Association/Commission of Dietetic
Registration Code of Ethics, 244–246
Joint Commission of Accreditation of
Healthcare Organizations, 187

K

King, Dorothy, 229
Klein, G.L., 113
Koo, Winston W., 113

L

Laflam, Maureen E., 58
Lang, Carol E., 58